Microsoft

KT-415-231

Step by Step

Microsoft®
Windows®XP

Online Training Solutions, Inc.

PUBLISHED BY
Microsoft Press
A Division of Microsoft Corporation
One Microsoft Way
Redmond, Washington 98052-6399

Library of Congress Cataloging-in-Publication Data
Microsoft Windows XP Step by Step / Online Training Solutions, Inc.
       p. cm.
    Includes index.
    ISBN 0-7356-1383-4
    1. Microsoft Windows XP.   2. Operating systems (Computers).   I. Online Training
Solutions (Firm).

    QA76.76.O63 M5241322558   2001
    005.4'4769-dc21   2001044689

Printed and bound in the United States of America.

2 3 4 5 6 7 8 9   QWT   6 5 4 3 2 1

Distributed in Canada by Penguin Books Canada Limited.

A CIP catalogue record for this book is available from the British Library.

Microsoft Press books are available through booksellers and distributors worldwide. For further information about international editions, contact your local Microsoft Corporation office or contact Microsoft Press International directly at fax (425) 706-7329. Visit our Web site at www.microsoft.com/mspress. Send comments to *mspinput@microsoft.com*.

Acquisitions Editor: Kong Cheung
Project Editor: Jenny Moss Benson

Body Part No. X08-04881

Contents

1 Getting Started with Windows XP 1

2 Working Efficiently in Windows XP 16

3 Managing Computer Security 40

10 Solving Problems 248

Quick Reference 283

Glossary 303

Index 323

What's New in Microsoft Windows XP

You'll notice some changes as soon as you start Microsoft Windows XP. The desktop background, **Start** menu, and taskbar have a new look. But the features that are new or greatly improved in this version of Windows go beyond just changes in appearance. Some changes won't be apparent to you until you start using the program.

Windows XP comes in three editions:

■ **Windows XP Professional** is designed for businesses of all sizes, and in some cases may be appropriate for home use, if you have a networked environment within your home. You can upgrade to Windows XP Professional from Microsoft Windows NT Workstation or Microsoft Windows 2000 Professional.

■ **Windows XP Home Edition** is designed for home computers that are not operating within a network domain. (Windows XP Home Edition computers can be included in a network, but not under a domain controller.) Windows XP Home Edition is designed as the upgrade from Microsoft Windows 98 or Microsoft Windows Millennium (Windows Me). Windows XP Home Edition includes great new features that make it easy to work (and play) with the multimedia and Internet capabilities of your computer.

■ **Windows XP 64-Bit Edition** will run only on specific types of computers that support 64-bit computing. These computers are designed for specialized work that requires a lot of memory, such as high-level graphic and multimedia design. This book does not cover the Windows XP 64-Bit Edition.

The exercises in this book cover the features of Windows XP that you are most likely to need and assume that you have **administrative privileges** on your computer. Unless an exercise is specifically for Windows XP Home Edition, screenshots depict the Windows XP Professional user interface.

To help you quickly identify features that are new or greatly enhanced with this version, this book uses the **New for Windows XP** icon in the margin whenever those features are discussed or shown. If you want to learn about only the new features of the program, you can skim through the book, reading the topics that show the **New for Windows XP** icon.

The table on the next page lists the new features that we think you'll be interested in, as well as the chapters in which those features are discussed.

To learn about this new feature	See
Automatic Updates	Chapter 1, page 4
CD Burning	Chapter 4, page 82
Compressed (Zip) Folders	Chapter 5, page 113
Text to Speech: Speech Recognition	Chapter 6, page 148; Chapter 6, page 153
Desktop Cleanup Wizard	Chapter 2, page 37
Fast User Switching for Multiple Users of a Computer	Chapter 1, page 5 Chapter 3, page 57
Fax Service	Chapter 4, page 78
International Options	Chapter 6, page 141
Internet (Online) Photo Ordering	Chapter 9, page 241
Internet Connection Firewall	Chapter 7, page 164
Internet Connection Sharing	Chapter 7, page 164
Internet: New Connection Wizard	Chapter 7, page 158
Media Folders (My Music, My Pictures)	Chapter 5, page 92
MSN Explorer Service	Chapter 9, page 220
My Pictures Screen Saver	Chapter 6, page 133
Printing: Photo Printing Wizard	Chapter 9, page 241
Remote Assistance	Chapter 1, page 4 Chapter 10, page 271
Scanner and Camera Wizard	Chapter 4, page 78
Search Companion Integration	Chapter 1, page 3 Chapter 5, page 122
Start Menu	Chapter 2, page 20
Theme Improvements	Chapter 6, page 128
Visual Styles: Improved Consumer/Professional "Look and Feel"	Chapter 1, page 2
Welcome Screen	Chapter 1, page 10
Windows Media Player 8	Chapter 9, page 226
Windows Movie Maker	Chapter 9, page 228

For additional information on these and other new features, consult the Windows XP Help and Support Center.

For more information about Windows XP, see *www.microsoft.com/windows/*.

Getting Help

Every effort has been made to ensure the accuracy of this book and the contents of its CD-ROM. If you do run into problems, please contact the appropriate source for help and assistance:

Getting Help with This Book and Its CD-ROM

If your question or issue concerns the content of this book or its companion CD-ROM, please first search the online Microsoft Knowledge Base, which provides support information for known errors in or corrections to this book, at the following Web site:

mspress.microsoft.com/support/search.htm

If you do not find your answer at the online Knowledge Base, send your comments or questions to Microsoft Press Technical Support at:

mspinput@microsoft.com

Getting Help with Microsoft Windows XP

If your question is about a Microsoft software product, including Windows XP, and not about the content of this Microsoft Press book, please search the Microsoft Knowledge Base at:

support.microsoft.com/directory/

In the United States, Microsoft software product support issues not covered by the Microsoft Knowledge Base are addressed by Microsoft Product Support Services. The Microsoft software support options available from Microsoft Product Support Services are listed at:

support.microsoft.com/directory/

Outside the United States, for support information specific to your location, please refer to the Worldwide Support menu on the Microsoft Product Support Services Web site for the site specific to your country:

support.microsoft.com/directory/

Using the Book's CD-ROM

The CD-ROM inside the back cover of this book contains all the practice files you'll use as you work through the exercises in this book. By using practice files, you won't waste time creating samples files and folders—instead, you can jump right in and concentrate on learning how to use Microsoft Windows XP.

Important

The CD-ROM for this book does not contain the Windows XP operating system. You should purchase and install that operating system before using this book.

Minimum System Requirements

To use this book, your computer should meet the following requirements:

Computer/Processor
Computer with a Pentium 133-megahertz (MHz) or higher processor

Memory
64 MB of RAM

Hard Disk
Hard disk space requirements will vary depending on configuration; custom installation choices may require more or less hard disk space.

245 MB of available hard disk space with 115 MB on the hard disk where the operating system is installed.

Operating System
Microsoft Windows XP Professional or Microsoft Windows XP Home Edition

Drive
CD-ROM drive
Floppy disk drive

Display
Super VGA (800 × 600) or higher-resolution monitor with 256 colors

Required Peripheral Devices
Microsoft Mouse, Microsoft IntelliMouse, or compatible pointing device

Optional Peripheral Devices

Scanner	Printer	Speakers
Camera	External storage device	Microphone

Optional Applications
Microsoft Office XP

Installing the Practice Files

You need to install the practice files on your hard disk before you use them in the chapters' exercises. Follow these steps to prepare the CD's files for your use:

1 Insert the CD-ROM into the CD-ROM drive of your computer.

A menu screen appears.

Important

If the menu screen does not appear, start Windows Explorer. In the left pane, locate the icon for your CD-ROM and click this icon. In the right pane, double-click the file named *StartCd.exe*.

2 Click **Install Practice Files**.

3 Click **OK** in the initial message box.

4 If you want to install the practice files to a location other than the default folder (*C:\SBS\WindowsXP*), click the **Change Folder** button, select the new drive and path, and then click **OK**.

Important

If you install the practice files to a location other than the default folder, the file location listed in some of the book's exercises will be incorrect.

5 Click the **Continue** button to install the selected practice files.

6 After the practice files have been installed, click **OK**.

Within the installation folder are subfolders for each chapter in the book.

7 Click **Exit**, and then remove the CD-ROM from the CD-ROM drive.

Copying Practice Files

If an exercise instructs you to copy files from the practice folders to your desktop, follow these steps:

1 Click the **Start** button, and then click **My Computer**.

2 In the My Computer window, browse to the folder that contains the practice files for that exercise.

3 Hold down the ⌨Ctrl key, click each of the specified files until you've selected them all, and release the ⌨Ctrl key.

4 Press ⌨Ctrl+C to copy the files to the clipboard.

5 Right-click a blank spot on the taskbar, and click **Show the Desktop**.

6 Press ⌈Ctrl⌉+⌈V⌉ to paste the files to the desktop.

Using the Practice Files

Each chapter's introduction lists the folders where you will find the files that are needed for that chapter. Each topic in the chapter explains how and when to use any practice files. The file or files that you'll need are indicated in the margin at the beginning of the procedure above the CD icon, like this:

FileName

The following table lists the folders that contain each chapter's practice files.

Chapter	Folder Name	Subfolder Name
Chapter 1: Getting Started with Windows XP		
Chapter 2: Working Efficiently in Windows XP	Working	Shortcuts
		Arranging
		Cleaning
Chapter 3: Managing Computer Security	Computer	ProfileHE
Chapter 4: Adding Hardware and Software	Adding	Software
Chapter 5: Working with Files and Folders	Structure	Views
		Information
		Creating
		Organizing
		Searching
Chapter 6: Personalizing Windows XP	Personalizing	Screensaver
		SpeechToText
Chapter 7: Making Connections	Connecting	Sharing
Chapter 8: Communicating with Other People		
Chapter 9: Having Fun with Windows XP	Playing	Playlist
		Photos
Chapter 10: Solving Problems	Solving	Backup

Uninstalling the Practice Files

After you finish working through this book, you should uninstall the practice files.

Tip

If you saved any files outside the *SBS\WindowsXP* folder, they will not be deleted by the following uninstall process; you will have to manually delete them.

1 On the Windows taskbar, click the **Start** button, and then click **Control Panel**.

2 Click the **Add or Remove Programs** icon.

3 Click **Microsoft Windows XP SBS Files**, and then click the **Change/Remove** button.

4 Click **Yes** when the confirmation dialog box appears.

5 Click the **Close** button to close the **Add or Remove Programs** dialog box.

Important

If you need additional help installing or uninstalling the practice files, please see the section "Getting Help" earlier in this book. Microsoft's product support does not provide support for this book or its CD-ROM.

Conventions and Features

You can save time when you use this book by understanding how the *Step by Step* series shows special instructions, keys to press, buttons to click, and so on.

Convention	Meaning
1 **2**	Numbered steps guide you through hands-on exercises in each topic.
●	A round bullet indicates an exercise that has only one step.
(CD icon)	This icon at the beginning of a chapter indicates the list of folders that contain the files that the exercises will use.
FileName (CD icon)	This icon often appears at the beginning of an exercise, preceded by a list of the practice files required to complete the exercise.
new for **Windows**XP	This icon indicates a new or greatly improved feature in this version of Microsoft Windows XP.
Tip	This section provides a helpful hint or shortcut that makes working through a task easier.
Important	This section points out information that you need to know to complete the procedure.
Troubleshooting	This section shows you how to fix a common problem.
start	When a button is referenced in a topic, a picture of the button appears in the margin area.
Alt + Tab	A plus sign (+) between two key names means that you must press those keys at the same time. For example, "Press Alt+Tab" means that you hold down the Alt key while you press Tab.
Boldface type	Program features that you click or press are shown in black boldface type.
Blue boldface type	Terms explained in the glossary are shown in blue boldface type.
Red boldface type	Text that you are supposed to type appears in red boldface type in the procedures.
Italic type	Folder paths, URLs, and emphasized words appear in italic type.

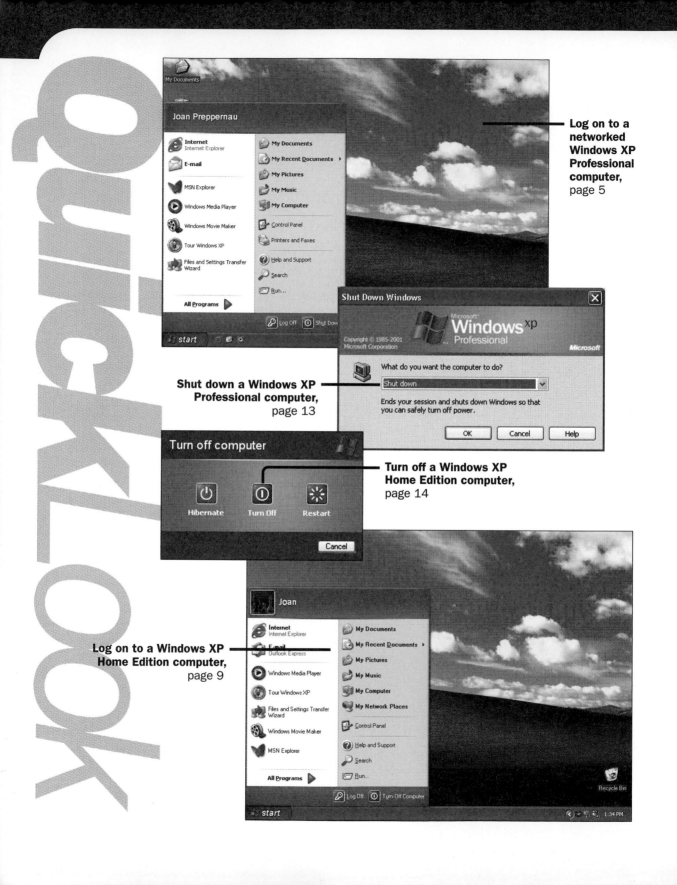

Log on to a networked Windows XP Professional computer, page 5

Shut down a Windows XP Professional computer, page 13

Turn off a Windows XP Home Edition computer, page 14

Log on to a Windows XP Home Edition computer, page 9

Chapter 1
Getting Started with Windows XP

After completing this chapter, you will be able to:

✔ Talk knowledgeably about the Windows XP operating system.

✔ Log on to your computer.

✔ Log off of your computer.

✔ Shut down your computer.

Microsoft Windows XP is the latest in the line of Windows operating systems. Windows XP is the successor to Microsoft Windows 2000 and Microsoft Windows Millennium Edition (Windows Me), and it is the first operating system expressly designed by Microsoft to fill the needs of both business and personal users.

This chapter provides an overview of Windows XP and takes you through the process of logging on to a computer that is running either Windows XP Professional or Windows XP Home Edition. Whether you are new to Windows or familiar with an earlier version, you will find useful information in this chapter. However, many of the features introduced with Windows XP run behind the scenes and are not obvious to the casual observer, or they are used to set up and maintain (administer) a network. We don't cover these features in this book because most people never have to deal with them.

Tip

For an explanation of the different editions of the Windows XP operating system and how they are addressed in this book, please read "What's New in Microsoft Windows XP" at the beginning of this book.

Unlike most of the exercises in this book, some of the exercises in this chapter are specific to Windows XP Home Edition or Windows XP Professional because of differences in the procedures for logging on and off and shutting down your computer. You can work through the exercises that are designated for the version of Windows XP you have installed, and skip the exercises designed for the other version. For all the exercises, we assume Windows XP Professional or Windows XP Home Edition is already installed on your computer, and that you know your user name and password (if you need them).

There are no practice files for this chapter.

Understanding Windows XP Basics

The Windows XP operating system provides an easy way for you to work with your computer without knowing anything about its inner workings. The operating system functions as the brain and nervous system of your computer; it tells your computer what to do and how to do it. The operating system interacts with **software programs** installed on your computer and enables your computer to communicate with other computers and other types of hardware, such as a printer, scanner, modem, or network interface card. A Windows-based operating system, such as Windows XP, also acts as the interface between you and your computer. You tell your computer what to do by means of a graphical **user interface (UI)** that helps you work in an intuitive, visual way, such as choosing commands by clicking graphic representations.

Windows XP is designed to be very reliable and has been visually redesigned to give you a personalized, task-focused computing experience. If you are accustomed to the traditional Windows user interface, you might at first be somewhat surprised by the changes, but the increased capabilities of Windows XP will quickly win you over.

So what exactly can you expect from your new operating system? First and foremost, you can expect a smooth way of carrying out common computer tasks and communicating with your programs. For those of you who are already somewhat familiar with other versions of Windows, here are the Windows XP features that both Professional and Home Edition users are most likely to take advantage of:

Updated user interface

■ The operating system's updated look uses graphics to simplify moving around and completing common tasks.

■ Its task-focused design and dynamic menus display options specifically associated with the task or file you are working on.

Upgrading to Windows XP

You can upgrade your computer's operating system to Windows XP Home Edition from Microsoft Windows 98 or Windows Me. You can upgrade to Windows XP Professional from Microsoft Windows NT Workstation or Windows 2000.

Upgrading to Windows XP should not affect your personal files and settings. However, it is always a good policy to back up important files before upgrading.

Fast User Switching

new for
WindowsXP

■ The Fast User Switching feature makes it easy for multiple users to share a single stand-alone computer without interfering with each other's programs.

Important

Fast User Switching is not available for computers logged on to a network domain.

Redesigned Start menu

new for
WindowsXP

■ The redesigned **Start** menu can be customized by each user so that frequently used files, folders, and programs are grouped together for easy access.

■ The Welcome screen can be personalized and secured with a password for each person who has an account on the computer.

Search Companion

new for
WindowsXP

■ The Search Companion feature identifies what kind of help you need and retrieves search information relevant to your current task.

■ The file management system makes it easy for you to arrange files according to your own needs, and provides optional **thumbnail** images for easy scanning of folder contents.

Album view thumbnail images and photo management

new for
WindowsXP

■ The My Music folder is a place where you can organize and view your music files, and create lists of songs (called **playlists**) to play.

■ The My Pictures folder is a specialized place where you can store and organize photos, view images as thumbnails or a slideshow, publish pictures to the Internet, compress photos so that they are easier to e-mail, order photo prints from the Internet, and optimize print settings to make the best use of high-quality photo paper.

■ The **Scanner and Camera Wizard** makes it easy to scan single or multiple images into one or more image files.

■ The **Web Publishing Wizard** takes you through the process of publishing pictures and other files to the Web so that you can share them with other people.

■ The **Network Setup Wizard** takes you through the key steps of setting up a network, including sharing files, printers, and devices; sharing an Internet connection; and configuring an **Internet Connection Firewall**, which protects your computer from intrusion when you are connected to the Internet.

■ Internet Connection Sharing makes it easy for multiple computers to share a single Internet connection.

■ Microsoft Internet Explorer 6, the Web browser that comes with most configurations of Windows XP, includes new and enhanced features that simplify your daily Internet tasks while helping you to maintain the privacy of your personal information on the Web. (You can choose to install a different browser if you want.)

■ The Help and Support Center combines features such as Search, Index, and Favorites with up-to-the-minute online content, including help from other Windows XP users and online support professionals.

■ The Remote Assistance feature enables you to share control of your desktop with another Windows XP user who can see your screen and control the keyboard and mouse from his or her computer.

■ The Windows Update Web site allows you to easily implement Windows XP improvements, including new device drivers and security updates. With your permission, updates can be automatically **downloaded** in the background while you are connected to the Internet for another reason.

■ Application compatibility improvements enable many programs that don't run on Windows 2000 to run on Windows XP, and you can use the **Program Compatibility Wizard** to run an incompatible program as if it were in an earlier version of Windows.

■ The System Restore feature enables you to restore a Windows XP computer to a previous state without losing personal data or document files.

■ Windows Installer helps you install, configure, track, upgrade, and remove software programs correctly.

■ Multilingual support helps you easily create, read, and edit documents in many languages with the English version of Windows XP Professional.

■ The Windows XP environment adapts to the way you work, enabling you to easily find crucial information and programs.

■ Increased virus protection enables you to block the execution of e-mail attachments, and your system administrator can remotely manage whether certain types of programs are allowed to run on your computer.

■ Troubleshooters available through the Help and Support Center help you or an administrator configure, optimize, and troubleshoot numerous Windows XP Professional functions.

■ ClearType triples the horizontal resolution available for text displayed on a computer screen, making it crisper and easier to read.

■ Up to 4 gigabytes (GB) of RAM and one or two processors can be installed in your computer.

■ Audio and video conferencing have been improved and now include audio and video quality, reduced audio response time, support for new cameras, support for synchronization of video and voice, and support for larger video sizes.

- Hibernate mode saves the computer's memory to the **hard disk** when power is shut down so that when you restore power, all of your applications are reopened exactly as you left them.

- Peer-to-peer networking support allows you to interact with computers running earlier versions of Windows and to share resources such as folders, printers, and peripherals.

- Most of the situations in which you had to restart your computer in Windows NT 4.0, Windows Me, Windows 98, and Microsoft Windows 95 have been eliminated.

Logging On to a Windows XP Professional Computer on a Network Domain

Many computers running Windows XP Professional are connected to a **local area network (LAN)** and are configured as part of a **network domain**. Others might be connected to a LAN but not one that uses a domain, or they might be stand-alone computers. This section applies to the first kind of computer.

The process of starting a computer session is called **logging on**. To log on to a network domain, you must have a valid **user account**, and you must know your **user account name** and **password**. You must also know the **domain name**. You can get all this information from your network administrator.

Tip

Each user account is associated with a **user profile** that describes the way the computer environment looks and operates for that particular user. This information includes such things as the color scheme, desktop background, fonts, shortcuts, and what you can do on the computer.

When Windows XP is installed on a computer, an account is created with the **administrative privileges** required to control that particular computer. Someone—usually a **network administrator**—can use that account to create other accounts on the computer. These accounts are generally for specific people, and they might have more restricted privileges that prevent the account owners from changing some of the settings on the computer.

In this exercise, you will log on to a computer that has Windows XP Professional installed and is part of a network domain.

Activating Windows XP

When you upgrade your computer's operating system from Windows NT Workstation or Windows 2000 Professional to Windows XP Professional, or from Windows 98 or Windows Me to Windows XP Home Edition, or the first time you start a new computer on which Windows XP has been installed by the original equipment manufacturer (OEM), you are prompted to activate your copy of Windows XP.

Windows
Product
Activation

new for
WindowsXP

Windows Product Activation is a security measure instituted by Microsoft to help prevent the distribution and use of unlicensed (or pirated) versions of Windows. **Software piracy** is a multi-billion dollar industry that is harmful to software creators and software users for these reasons:

■ Unlicensed software is ineligible for technical support or product upgrades.

■ Abuse of software licenses can result in financial penalties and legal costs, as well as a bad reputation for you or for your company. Individual company executives can be held criminally and civilly liable for copyright infringements within their organization.

■ Pirated software can contain harmful viruses with the potential to damage individual computers or entire networks.

■ The counterfeit software manufacturing industry stifles the potential growth of the high tech industry and contributes to loss of tax revenue.

For more information on software piracy, see *www.microsoft.com/piracy/*.

The goal of Windows Product Activation is to reduce a form of software piracy known as *casual copying* or *softlifting*, which is when people share software in a way that infringes on the software's **end user license agreement**. Each copy of Windows XP must be activated within 14 days of the first use. You can activate Windows XP over the Internet or by telephone. You don't have to give any personal information about yourself or your computer, although you are given the option of registering to receive information about product updates, new products, events, and special offers.

There is no working folder for this exercise, but you do need to know your user account name, your password, and your domain name.

Important

This exercise assumes that your computer is physically connected to a network and logging on to a domain, rather than dialing in or connecting over the Internet.

Follow these steps:

1 Start your computer.

   After the computer starts, or **boots**, a **Welcome to Windows** screen appears.

2 Hold down both the ⌐Ctrl⌐ and ⌐Alt⌐ keys, and press ⌐Del⌐.

   Windows XP displays a **dialog box** and waits for you to give it the information it needs to proceed. Dialog boxes are the main means of communication between the computer and the computer user in Windows and in Windows-based programs. Each dialog box presents all the possible options associated with an action, and you set the options to indicate how you want the action carried out.

   In this case, the **Log On to Windows** dialog box appears.

Important

When you press ⌐Ctrl⌐+⌐Alt⌐+⌐Del⌐, Windows temporarily halts any other programs that are running on your computer. This precaution ensures that your password remains secure because it prevents programs called **Trojan horses**, which might have been planted on your system by **hackers**, from capturing your user account name and password. The requirement to press ⌐Ctrl⌐+⌐Alt⌐+⌐Del⌐ is turned on by default. A user with administrative privileges can change this requirement, but making this change is definitely not recommended.

3 Enter your user account name in the **User name** box.

4 Enter your password in the **Password** box.

5 If the **Log on to** box is not shown, click **Options** to expand the dialog box. Then click the down arrow to the right of the **Log on to** box, and click the correct domain name in the drop-down list.

Troubleshooting

If your domain is not available in the drop-down list, contact your network administrator.

6 Click **OK** to log on to Windows XP Professional and your network domain.

   The Windows XP Professional desktop appears, as shown on the next page.

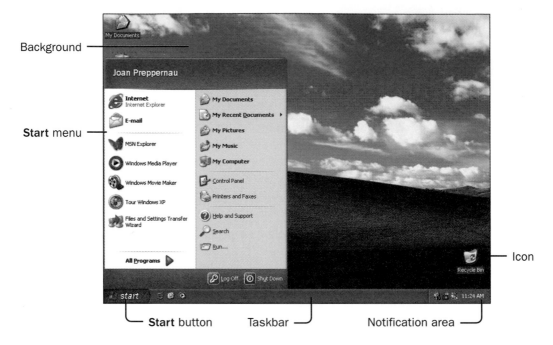

Background —

Start menu —

Icon —

Start button ——— Taskbar —— Notification area ——

Using Your Mouse

For new computer users who are not familiar with the standard Windows mouse actions, we'll briefly summarize them here:

■ **Clicking** an object involves moving the mouse pointer over it and quickly pressing and releasing the primary mouse button once. (By default, the primary mouse button is the left one.)

■ **Double-clicking** an object involves moving the mouse pointer over it and pressing and releasing the primary mouse button twice in rapid succession.

■ **Right-clicking** an object involves moving the mouse pointer over it and clicking the secondary mouse button once. This displays the object's **shortcut menu**, which is a set of actions that can be performed with the object you right-clicked. Choose the action you want by clicking it on the shortcut menu.

■ **Dragging** an object involves moving the mouse pointer over the object, holding down the primary mouse button, moving the mouse until the pointer is in the location where you want the object to appear, and releasing the mouse button. You can also drag to select multiple objects from a list.

If you prefer to click, double-click, and drag with the right mouse button, you can switch the buttons by adjusting the **Mouse** settings in Control Panel. (You can access Control Panel by clicking the **Start** button and then clicking **Control Panel** on the **Start** menu.)

Important

Don't worry if your Windows XP desktop looks different from the ones shown in this and subsequent chapters. The desktop varies, depending on whether Windows XP is installed on a brand new computer or as an upgrade on a computer that has been running a previous version of the Windows operating system. In the latter case, Windows XP will retain many aspects of the previous desktop. Windows XP might also carry over some of the settings made in a previous version, which can alter the look of the screen slightly. These differences affect the way Windows XP looks but do not affect your ability to successfully complete the exercises in this book. If you prefer to have the desktop icons that appeared in previous versions of Windows available, you can right-click the desktop, and click **Properties** on the shortcut menu. Then in the **Display Properties** dialog box, click the **Desktop** tab, click **Customize Desktop**, select the check boxes of the icons you want, and click **OK**.

Logging On to a Windows XP Home Edition Computer

Your computer might be used by only you, or it might be used by several people. If only you use your computer, it needs only one configuration, or **user account**. If other people use your computer, everyone can use the same account, or you can set up a separate user account for each person. Each account is associated with a **user profile** that describes the way the computer environment looks and operates for that particular user. This information includes such things as the color scheme, desktop background, fonts, and shortcuts, and it can vary from profile to profile.

The process of starting a computer session is called **logging on**. If only one user account has been set up, Windows XP automatically logs on using that account when you start the computer. If multiple accounts have been set up, Windows XP prompts you to select your user profile and, if your account has been password-protected, to enter your password.

Tip

By default, Windows XP Home Edition creates two accounts: *All Users* and *Guest*. The All Users account can be used to make certain files or settings available to anyone who logs on to the computer. Users who don't have their own account can log on to the computer using the Guest account. The Guest account can be disabled if you don't want to allow people without accounts to log on to your computer.

Each user has a **user account name** and a **user account picture**. Each user can change his or her own account name and account picture; users with administrative privileges can change any user's account name and picture.

In this exercise, you will log on to a computer that has Windows XP Home Edition installed and that has been configured to include multiple accounts (with or without passwords).

There is no working folder for this exercise.

Follow these steps:

1 Start your computer.

After the computer boots, a logon screen appears.

Welcome
screen

The logon screen displayed by Windows XP Home Edition is called the Welcome screen. This screen displays graphic representations of all the user accounts on the computer. These accounts can be created during setup or later to keep each user's data separate.

Important

If your computer is configured to include only one account, you now see the Windows XP desktop and can skip the remaining steps.

2 Move the mouse pointer over the available user names.

Notice that the selected user name is bright, while the other user names are dimmed.

3 Click your user account name or user account picture.

4 If your account is password-protected, enter your password in the **Type your password** box, and then click the arrow button to continue.

Tip

If you forget your password, click the question-mark button to see any password hint that was specified when your password was set.

While Windows XP is loading your profile, your user account name and user account picture move to the center of the screen, and the other options disappear. When you are logged on to your account, the Windows XP Home Edition desktop appears:

Background ——

Start Menu ——

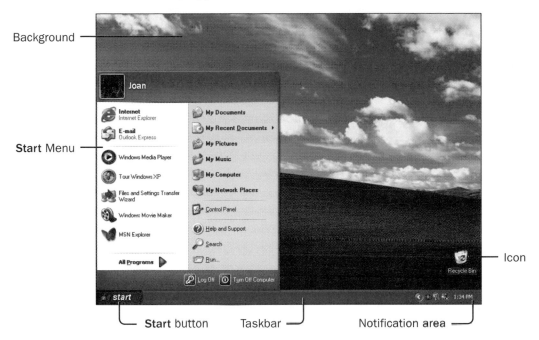

—— Icon

—— **Start** button   Taskbar ——   Notification area ——

Logging On to a Stand-Alone
Windows XP Professional Computer

Windows XP Professional is generally used in a networked environment, but you do not have to be connected to a network domain to run it. For example, you might have Windows XP Professional installed on a laptop computer that you use both at the office and at home; or you might travel with your Windows XP Professional computer, **work offline**, and connect to your network over a remote connection.

When you log on to a Windows XP Professional computer that has been, but is no longer, connected to a network domain, you log on in the ordinary manner, and your user information is validated against information that was stored on the computer the last time you logged on to the domain. If your Windows XP Professional computer is not currently configured to work on a network, the process of logging on is identical to that of Windows XP Home Edition. Valid user accounts are displayed on a central logon screen, and the Fast User Switching option is available and turned on by default.

Logging Off of Windows XP

The process of ending a computer session is called **logging off**. Logging off ends the Windows session for your account but leaves the computer turned on. It is important to log off when you leave for the day, or even when you leave your computer for an extended period of time, to safeguard against other people accessing your personal information. For example, if your account has administrative privileges and you go out to lunch without logging off or otherwise protecting your computer against intrusion, someone could create a local user account with administrative privileges for themselves and later use that account to log on to your computer.

In this exercise, you will log off of your Windows XP user account. Both Windows XP Professional and Windows XP Home Edition users can complete this exercise.

There is no working folder for this exercise.

Follow these steps:

1 If the **Start** menu is not displayed, click the **Start** button.

The **Start** menu is displayed. Your user information appears at the top of the menu. Depending on the programs installed on your computer, the **Start** menu looks something like this:

Tip

Windows XP Home Edition displays the user account name and user account picture at the top of the **Start** menu. Windows XP Professional displays only the user account name.

2 At the bottom of the **Start** menu, click **Log Off**.

The **Log Off Windows** dialog box appears.

Tip

When your current Windows XP configuration includes Fast User Switching, that option is shown in the **Log Off Windows** dialog box.

3 Click **Log Off** to complete the process and display the Welcome screen or logon screen.

4 Enter your password (Professional), or click your user account name (Home Edition) to log back on.

Tip

If bubble notes appear above the notification area while you are working, read them, and then click the X (the **Close** button) in the bubble's top right corner.

Shutting Down a Windows XP Professional Computer

Rather than simply logging off of your computer, you might want to turn it off, or **shut down**, to conserve energy. Shutting down closes all your open applications and files, ends your computing session, and shuts down Windows so that you can safely turn off the computer's power. This process ensures that your data is safely stored and any external connections are appropriately disconnected.

Important

Always shut down Windows XP before turning off your computer; otherwise, you could lose data.

In this exercise, you will shut down your Windows XP Professional computer.

There is no working folder for this exercise.

Follow these steps:

1 Click the **Start** button.

The **Start** menu is displayed. Your user information appears at the top of the menu.

2 At the bottom of the **Start** menu, click **Shut Down**.

The **Shut Down Windows** dialog box appears:

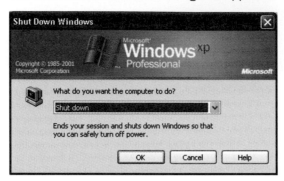

The most recently selected shut-down option is displayed in the option box, and a description of that option appears below the box.

3 Click the down arrow to display the other options, and select each option in turn to display its description.

4 Select **Shut down** as the option, and click **OK** to end your Windows session.

Shutting Down a Windows XP Home Edition Computer

Rather than simply logging off of your computer, you might want to **shut down** or **turn off** the computer completely. Turning off closes all your open applications and files and ends your Windows session, as well as turning off your computer. This process ensures that your data is safely stored and all your external sessions are appropriately disconnected.

Important

Always shut down Windows XP before turning off your computer; otherwise, you could lose data.

In this exercise, you will turn off your Windows XP Home Edition computer.

There is no working folder for this exercise.

Follow these steps:

1 Click the **Start** button.

The **Start** menu is displayed. Your user information appears at the top of the menu.

2 At the bottom of the **Start** menu, click **Turn Off Computer**.

Tip

The **Turn Off Computer** command is also available on the Welcome screen.

This **Turn off computer** dialog box appears:

3   Click **Turn Off** to end your Windows session and turn off your computer.

Other Options

In addition to logging off and shutting down your computer, the Windows XP Professional **Shut Down** dialog box presents these options:

- **Restart** ends your session, shuts down Windows, and then starts Windows again without turning off the computer.

- **Stand by** maintains your session (the programs that are open and any work you are doing in them) and keeps the computer running on low power with your data still in the memory. To return to a session that is on stand by, press [Ctrl]+[Alt]+[Del].

- **Hibernate** saves your session and turns off your computer. The next time you start the computer, your session is restored to the place where you left off.

The Windows XP Home Edition **Turn off computer** screen provides the **Restart** and **Hibernate** options, but not the **Stand by** option.

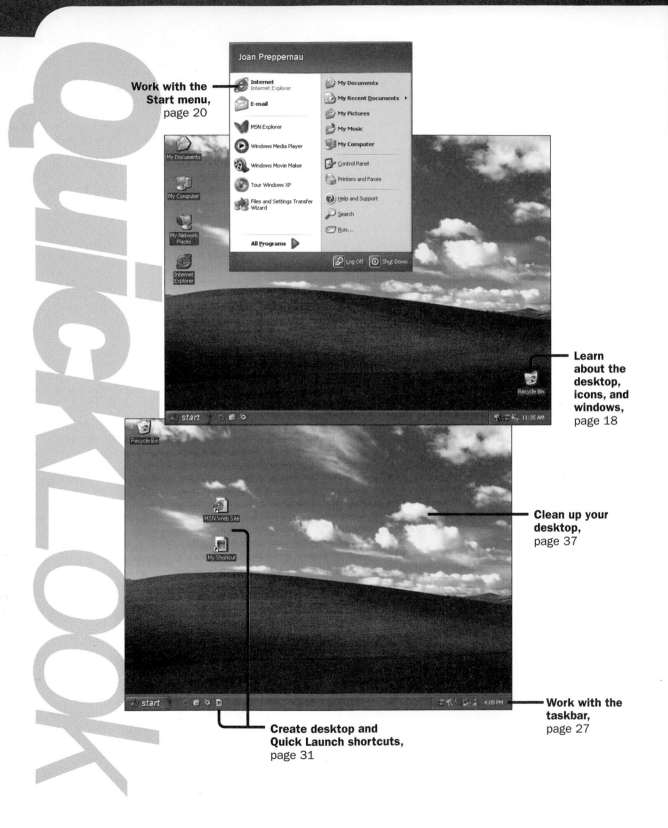

Work with the Start menu, page 20

Joan Preppernau

Internet
Internet Explorer

E-mail

MSN Explorer

Windows Media Player

Windows Movie Maker

Tour Windows XP

Files and Settings Transfer Wizard

All Programs ▶

My Documents

My Recent Documents ▶

My Pictures

My Music

My Computer

Control Panel

Printers and Faxes

Help and Support

Search

Run...

Log Off | Shut Down

Learn about the desktop, icons, and windows, page 18

Clean up your desktop, page 37

Work with the taskbar, page 27

Create desktop and Quick Launch shortcuts, page 31

QuickLook

Chapter 2
Working Efficiently in Windows XP

After completing this chapter, you will be able to:

✔ **Work comfortably in the Windows XP desktop.**

✔ **Work with the Start menu and taskbar.**

✔ **Create and arrange shortcuts on the desktop and Quick Launch toolbar.**

✔ **Clean up your desktop.**

Working in the Microsoft Windows environment is a lot like working in a real-world office environment. You have a **desktop** where all your work tools are displayed, and you have **folders** in which to organize all your **files**. Windows incorporates all these elements into its user interface, which is the means by which you and your computer communicate with each other.

Windows XP presents its tools, commands, and structure through a graphical user interface. Each type of file is represented by a picture and description, and each command is represented by a button. Programs are arranged on a series of menus to make it easy to locate them.

In this chapter, you will explore some of the elements of the Windows user interface and the various ways in which you can look at the information on your computer. You will then see how to tailor some of these elements to suit the way you work.

The practice files for this chapter are located in the *SBS\WindowsXP\Working* folder. (For details about installing the practice files, see "Using the Book's CD-ROM" at the beginning of this book.)

Getting to Know the Windows Desktop

When you start Windows XP, your computer screen looks something like this:

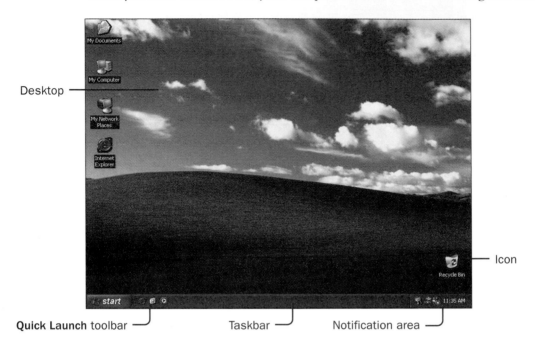

Desktop

Icon

Quick Launch toolbar   Taskbar   Notification area

The most basic element of the Windows user interface is a background screen called the **desktop**. All your other programs are opened over this background screen. The **taskbar** at the bottom of the screen is used by Windows XP to give you information about what's going on with your computer and to provide a way of easily opening and closing programs.

You might have one or more **icons** visible on your desktop, depending on how the programs that are installed on your computer are set up, and on your Windows XP settings. Icons are graphics that provide a simple method of identifying and starting programs from the Windows desktop. When an icon appears on the desktop, you can double-click it to start the associated program.

Below the icon is the name of the element it represents. If the name is too long, it is truncated by an ellipsis (...) when it is not selected, and displayed in full when you click it. Positioning the mouse pointer over an icon usually displays a box, called a **ScreenTip**, containing a few words that tell you something about the program.

Some icons are placed on the Windows desktop when you install the programs they represent. If the icon has an arrow in its bottom left corner, it is a **shortcut**. Shortcuts are links to programs that are stored in another location. If you delete a shortcut, you aren't actually deleting the file, folder, or program to which it points. Many programs create shortcuts when you install them. You can also create your own shortcuts to programs; to specific files, folders, or network locations; or to Web sites. Windows XP assigns graphics to each shortcut based on the type of element it represents, so you can easily locate the one you are looking for.

One of the icons on the desktop is the **Recycle Bin**, which is where Windows temporarily stores files you have deleted. It is also the place where you manage deleted files. You can recover deleted files from the Recycle Bin, or you can empty the Recycle Bin and permanently delete the files to free up space on your hard drive.

When you purchase a new computer, the **original equipment manufacturer (OEM)** might have installed programs and shortcuts for you. If you upgrade to Windows XP from a previous version of Windows, your existing shortcuts will still be available.

In this exercise, you will open, size, and close the Recycle Bin.

There are no practice files for this exercise.

Follow these steps:

1   Log on to Windows, if you have not already done so.

2   Double-click the **Recycle Bin** icon.

The Recycle Bin opens in a **window,** something like this:

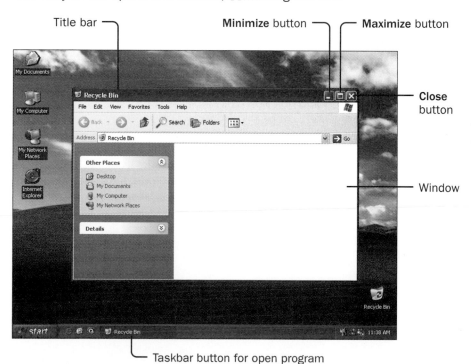

Title bar   **Minimize** button   **Maximize** button

Close button

Window

Taskbar button for open program

The program's title appears in the **title bar** at the top of the window. If the content of the window is too large to fit in the window, a **scroll bar** is displayed down the right side and/or across the bottom of the window. A button representing the program is displayed on the taskbar to indicate that it is open.

Minimize

3 Click the **Minimize** button near the right end of the title bar.

The window is minimized so that it is no longer visible on the desktop. The program is still running and is represented by a button on the taskbar.

4 Click the Recycle Bin's taskbar button to redisplay the window.

Maximize

5 Click the **Maximize** button.

The window expands to fill your entire screen.

Restore Down

6 Click the **Restore Down** button.

The window returns to its original size. The **Restore Down** button is available only when the window is maximized.

Tip

You can manually resize a window by positioning the mouse pointer over the window's frame and, when the pointer changes to a double-headed arrow, dragging the frame to make the window smaller or larger. You cannot manually resize maximized windows; you must first restore the window to its non-maximized state.

Close

7 Click the **Close** button.

Closing the window closes the program and removes the corresponding button from the taskbar.

Working with the Start Menu

The **Start menu** is a list of options that is your central link to all the programs installed on your computer, as well as to all the tasks you can carry out with Windows XP. The first time you start Windows XP, the **Start** menu is displayed until you click something else. Thereafter, you open the **Start** menu by clicking the **Start** button at the left end of the taskbar.

The **Start** menu has been significantly redesigned in Windows XP to provide easier access to your programs. When it first opens, it looks something like this:

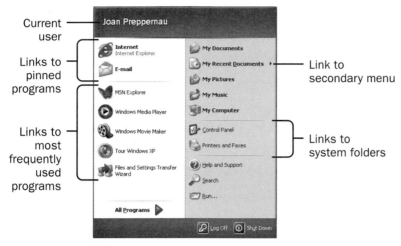

Current user

Links to pinned programs

Links to most frequently used programs

Link to secondary menu

Links to system folders

Tip

If you are accustomed to the previous menu style, which is now called the **Classic** menu, you might find that the change takes a little getting used to. If you are unable to adjust, you have the option of changing back to the Classic version. However, the new menu is designed to increase efficiency, so we recommend that you at least give it a try!

Pinning programs

new for **Windows**XP

You can pin links to your favorite programs to a special area at the top of the left side of the **Start** menu to make the programs easy to find and start. You can rearrange the pinned programs by dragging them into whatever order you want. By default, Microsoft Internet Explorer and Microsoft Outlook Express are pinned to the **Start** menu. If you change your default Web browser or e-mail program, the pinned area is automatically updated to reflect that change.

Below the first horizontal line on the left side of the **Start** menu is a list of links to your most frequently used programs, which includes the last six programs you started. (You can adjust that number if you want.) The first time you start Windows XP, the list displays some of the new programs that are available: MSN Explorer, Windows Media Player, Windows Movie Maker, **File and Settings Transfer Wizard**, and Tour Windows XP. (The tour is somewhat long and sales-oriented, but it does introduce you to new features of Windows XP that you will work with in this book.)

On the right side of the **Start** menu are links to the locations where you are most likely to store the files you create, a link to a directory of other computers on your network, and links to various tools that you will use while running your computer.

The commands you will use to log off of or shut down your computer are located at the bottom of the **Start** menu.

In this exercise, you will first clear the most frequently used programs links from the **Start** menu. Then you will pin links to two programs to the top of the menu, rearrange them, and remove them from the pinned programs area.

There are no practice files for this exercise.

Follow these steps:

1   Log on to Windows, if you have not already done so.

2   Close any open windows so that no buttons appear on the taskbar.

3   Click the **Start** button to open the **Start** menu, and note which programs are currently listed in the most frequently used programs list.

Tip

If your most frequently used programs list is empty, you can still follow along with this exercise so that you will know how to clear the list later.

4   Right-click the **Start** menu, and click **Properties** on the shortcut menu.

The **Taskbar and Start Menu Properties** dialog box appears, like this:

This is where you have the option to change to the Classic **Start** menu.

5 Make sure that **Start menu** is selected, and then click **Customize**.

The **Customize Start Menu** dialog box appears. The default settings are shown here:

6 Click **Clear List** to clear the list of most frequently used programs.

7 Click the **Advanced** tab to display the advanced **Start** menu options:

8 Scroll through the list of options to see what is available, but don't change any of the default settings at this time.

9 Click **OK** to close the **Customize Start Menu** dialog box, and then click **OK** to close the **Taskbar and Start Menu Properties** dialog box.

10 Click the **Start** button to open the **Start** menu.

The most frequently used programs list has been cleared.

11 Point to **All Programs**.

The **All Programs** menu expands with your currently installed programs listed, something like this:

As with other types of menus in Windows XP, the right-pointing arrows indicate that clicking the menu entry, or simply hovering the mouse pointer over it for a few seconds, will open a secondary menu.

12 On the **All Programs** menu, point to **Accessories**.

The secondary **Accessories** menu expands. All the programs on this menu are part of the basic Windows XP installation:

13 On the **Accessories** menu, click **Calculator**.

The Calculator opens, and a **Calculator** button appears on the taskbar.

14 Click the **Start** button to open the **Start** menu.

Calculator now appears in the most frequently used programs area, like this:

Calculator has been added to the most frequently used programs list.

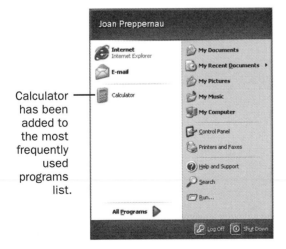

15 Now you'll pin a program to the **Start** menu. Point to **All Programs**, and then point to **Games**.

Tip

You can pin programs to the **Start** menu from the **All Programs** menu or from the most frequently used programs list.

The secondary **Games** menu expands:

All the games on this menu come with Windows XP.

16 On the **Games** menu, right-click **FreeCell**, click **Pin to Start menu** on the shortcut menu, and then move the mouse pointer over the **Start** menu to close the **Games** and **All Programs** menus.

FreeCell is added to the pinned programs area of the **Start** menu:

FreeCell has been pinned to the **Start** menu for easy access.

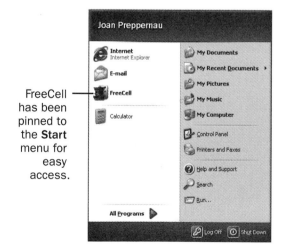

17 On the **Start** menu, right-click **Calculator**, and click **Pin to Start menu** on the shortcut menu.

Calculator is moved from the most frequently used programs area to the pinned programs area.

Tip

When the most frequently used programs area is empty, the horizontal line separating it from the pinned programs area disappears.

18 Drag the Calculator link to the top of the pinned programs list.

While you are dragging the link, a thick black line behind it indicates where it will appear if you release the mouse button.

19 Drag the FreeCell link above the Calculator link.

20 Right-click the Calculator link, and click **Unpin from Start menu** on the shortcut menu.

The Calculator link is moved from the pinned programs area back to the most frequently used programs area. You could have clicked **Remove from This List** to remove it entirely.

21 Right-click the FreeCell link, and click **Unpin from Start menu** on the shortcut menu.

The FreeCell link disappears from the pinned programs area. Because it was never on the most frequently used programs list, it also disappears from the **Start** menu.

22 Click away from the **Start** menu to close it.

Close

❌

23 On Calculator's title bar, click the **Close** button.

Calculator closes, and its button disappears from the taskbar.

Using the Taskbar

The **taskbar** is your link to current information about what is happening on your Windows XP computer. In addition to the **Start** button, the taskbar displays a button for each open program. You click a taskbar button to activate the window of the program it represents. The taskbar buttons are resized depending on the number of programs that are currently open, and they disappear when you close the programs they represent.

Tip

The taskbar does not display buttons for open dialog boxes, message boxes, or warnings.

If you start the same program more than once so that several instances of the program are open at the same time (for example, three instances of Internet Explorer, or two Microsoft Word documents), and the taskbar is becoming crowded, similar windows are grouped onto one button that is labeled with the name of the program. A number following the **program icon** on the button indicates the number of open windows represented by the button. You can click the button to display a pop-up list of the open windows and then click the one you want to activate. This new feature makes it easier to work with your open windows.

Tip

If windows are grouped on a taskbar button, you can close all windows in the group by right-clicking the button and clicking **Close Group** on the shortcut menu.

By default, the taskbar displays one row of buttons and is **docked** at the bottom of the desktop, but you can control its size and position:

- You can dock the taskbar at the top, bottom, or on either side of the desktop.
- When the taskbar is docked at the top or bottom, you can expand the taskbar to be up to half the height of your screen by dragging its border up or down.
- When the taskbar is docked on the left or right, you can adjust its width from nothing (only the border is visible) to up to half the width of your screen.
- You can stipulate that the taskbar should be hidden when you're not using it, or that it should always stay on top of other windows so that it is not accidentally hidden.
- You can lock the taskbar to prevent it from being changed.

Troubleshooting

You cannot move or change the taskbar while it is locked. To lock or unlock the taskbar, right-click an empty area of the taskbar, and click **Lock the Taskbar** on the shortcut menu. A check mark indicates that this option is selected.

Windows XP taskbar buttons change size so that they fit on the taskbar as programs are opened and closed. The maximum number of buttons that can fit on the taskbar varies based on your monitor and display settings. When you exceed the maximum, Windows either tiles the buttons or displays a scroll bar, depending on the current taskbar configuration.

The **notification area** is located at the right end of the horizontal taskbar or at the bottom of the vertical taskbar. By default, the notification area displays the current time. Icons appear temporarily in the notification area when activities such as the following take place:

- The printer icon appears when you send a document to the printer.

- A message icon appears when you receive new e-mail messages.

- The Windows Automatic Update icon appears to remind you to look online for updates to the operating system.

- Information icons appear to give you information about various program features.

- Network connections and Microsoft Windows Messenger icons appear when those features are in use. (Inactive connections are indicated by the presence of a red X on the icon.)

In addition to the items that are visible by default, the taskbar can also display its own set of toolbars. The most frequently used of these is the **Quick Launch toolbar**, which displays single-click links to programs and commands. (This toolbar is hidden by default.)

Tip

The Quick Launch toolbar might be hidden or visible, depending on your taskbar settings.

Windows XP installs links to Microsoft Internet Explorer, Microsoft Windows Media Player, and the Show Desktop command on the Quick Launch toolbar. You can add more program shortcuts to the Quick Launch toolbar at any time by dragging a program or shortcut icon onto it.

In this exercise, you will open several windows and use the taskbar to move among them.

There are no practice files for this exercise.

Follow these steps:

1   Log on to Windows, if you have not already done so.

2   Close any open windows so that no taskbar buttons appear on the taskbar.

Tip

To close an open window, click the **Close** button at the right end of its title bar, or right-click its taskbar button, and then click **Close**. You are prompted to save changes to documents before they close.

start   3   Click the **Start** button to open the **Start** menu.

4 Click **My Documents**.

The My Documents folder opens, and a button appears on the taskbar. The button label is preceded by a folder icon to indicate that the button represents a folder.

Minimize

5 Click the **Minimize** button to hide the folder's window under its taskbar button.

6 On the **Start** menu, click **My Pictures**.

The My Pictures folder opens in a new window, and another button appears on the taskbar. The button label is preceded by a folder icon to indicate the type of window it represents.

7 On the **Start** menu, click **My Music**.

The My Music folder opens in a new window, and a button appears on the taskbar. The button label is again preceded by a folder icon.

You now have three open folder windows, each represented by a taskbar button. The taskbar looks something like this:

The active window's taskbar button
is indicated by a darker color.

8 On the **Start** menu, click **Calculator**.

Calculator opens, and the **Calculator** button appears on the taskbar.

Tip

If your taskbar is getting full, the existing buttons are resized so that there is room for the new button.

9 Drag the Calculator window by its title bar to the center of the screen.

10 On the taskbar, click the **My Pictures** button to make the window for the My Pictures folder active.

The My Pictures window comes to the top of the stack of open windows. On the taskbar, the **My Pictures** button is active instead of the **Calculator** button.

11 If the Quick Launch toolbar is not currently visible, right-click an empty area of the taskbar, point to **Toolbars** on the shortcut menu, and then click **Quick Launch**.

Show Desktop

12 On the Quick Launch toolbar, click the **Show Desktop** button.

All open windows are minimized.

13 On the desktop, double-click the **Recycle Bin** icon.

The Recycle Bin folder opens in a new window. There is not enough room to add the **Recycle Bin** button to the taskbar, so the four folder windows are grouped onto one button. The taskbar now looks like this:

This button's label indicates that it represents four Windows Explorer folder windows.

14 Click the **Windows Explorer** button to display a pop-up list of the windows represented by the button:

15 Click **My Music** on the window list.

The My Music window appears, and the list closes.

16 Right-click the **Windows Explorer** button, and then click **Close Group** on the shortcut menu.

All four folder windows close, and the **Windows Explorer** button disappears. Calculator is now the only open program.

Close

17 Click the **Calculator** button to open Calculator, and then click its **Close** button.

Calculator closes, and the last taskbar button disappears.

Creating Shortcuts

Shortcuts are icons on your desktop or the Quick Launch toolbar that are linked to files, folders, and programs in other locations. Many programs give you the option of creating one or more shortcuts, or in some cases, they create the shortcuts by default, without asking. You can also easily create your own shortcuts, and you can delete any shortcut at any time.

Important

Deleting a shortcut does not delete the program or file that the shortcut is linked to.

In this exercise, you will create a desktop shortcut for an existing program, a desktop shortcut for a Web site, and a Quick Launch shortcut.

Sunset.jpg

The practice file for this exercise is located in the *SBS\WindowsXP\Working \Shortcuts* folder. (For details about installing the practice files, see "Using the Book's CD-ROM" at the beginning of this book.)

Follow these steps:

1   Log on to Windows, if you have not already done so.

Show Desktop

2   On the Quick Launch toolbar at the left end of the taskbar, click the **Show Desktop** button to minimize any open windows.

Tip

If the Quick Launch toolbar is not displayed on the taskbar, right-click an empty area of the taskbar, point to **Toolbars** on the shortcut menu, and then click **Quick Launch**.

3   Right-click an open area of the desktop.

4   On the shortcut menu, point to **New**, and then click **Shortcut**.

The first page of the **Create Shortcut Wizard** appears:

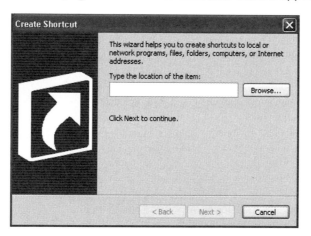

Tip

Wizards are series of pages, similar to dialog boxes, that walk you through the steps necessary to accomplish a particular task. In this case, the wizard will prompt you for the information Windows needs to create a shortcut.

5   Click **Browse** to open the **Browse For Folder** dialog box:

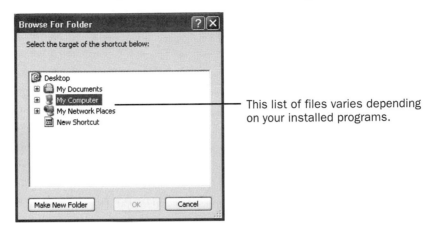

This list of files varies depending on your installed programs.

You use this dialog box to tell the wizard which file or folder you want the shortcut to link to (its target), and where the file or folder is located.

6   Click **My Computer**, then **Local Disk (C:)**, then **SBS**, then **WindowsXP**, then **Working**, and finally **Shortcuts** to browse. Then click the **Sunset** file, and click **OK** to close the dialog box and return to the wizard.

The location, called the path, of the selected file is entered in the **Type the location of the item** box.

7   Click **Next** to move to the **Select a Title for the Program** page:

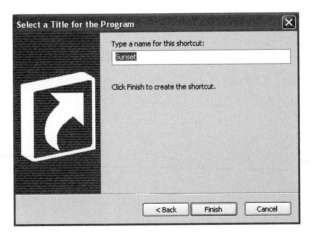

Using information saved with the selected file, the wizard has suggested a name for the shortcut.

8   With the current name selected, type **My Shortcut**.

9   Click **Finish** to close the wizard.

A shortcut is created on the desktop in approximately the place you originally right-clicked. The shortcut is named *My Shortcut*. It is represented by a graphic icon with an arrow in the bottom left corner.

10 Double-click **My Shortcut** to open the Sunset photo that the shortcut links to.

Close

11 Click the photo window's **Close** button to close the window.

12 Right-click **My Shortcut**, and click **Properties** on the shortcut menu.

The **My Shortcut Properties** dialog box appears.

13 Click the **General** tab, and look at the information and available options.

14 Return to the **Shortcut** tab, and click **Change Icon**.

This **Change Icon** dialog box appears:

15 Scroll through the list to see all the available icons.

16 Click your favorite icon, and then click **OK** to close the **Change Icon** dialog box, or click **Cancel** to keep the current icon.

17 Click **OK** to close the **My Shortcut Properties** dialog box and apply your change.

The shortcut's icon changes if you selected a new one.

18 Now you'll create a shortcut for a Web site. Right-click an open area of the desktop, point to **New** on the shortcut menu, and then click **Shortcut**.

The **Create Shortcut** dialog box appears.

19 In the **Type the location of the item** box, type **http://www.msn.com**.

20 Click **Next** to move to the **Select a Title for the Program** page.

The suggested shortcut name is *New Internet Shortcut*.

21 With the current name selected, type **MSN Web Site**.

22   Click **Finish** to close the dialog box and create another shortcut.

23   If you are connected to the Internet, double-click **MSN Web Site** to open the MSN Web site in your default Web browser.

24   Click the **Close** button to close the window.

25   Right-click **My Shortcut**, and drag it to the left of the Quick Launch toolbar.

A thick black line behind the shortcut indicates where it will appear when you release the mouse button.

26   Release the right mouse button when the shortcut is in position on the Quick Launch toolbar, and then click **Copy Here** on the shortcut menu that appears.

A copy of the shortcut appears on the Quick Launch toolbar. A double right arrow now appears at the right end of the toolbar to indicate that more shortcuts are available than can fit on the toolbar.

27   Position the mouse pointer over the new toolbar shortcut.

A ScreenTip displays the shortcut's name.

28   Click the double arrow to view the other available Quick Launch shortcuts.

29   Right-click the taskbar. If **Lock the Taskbar** is checked on the shortcut menu, click it to unlock the taskbar. If **Lock the Taskbar** is not checked, click away from the shortcut menu to close it.

When the taskbar is unlocked, the Quick Launch toolbar is bordered by movable left and right borders, represented by double dotted lines:

The double dotted lines indicate that the taskbar is unlocked.

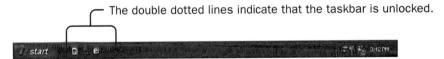

30   Position the mouse pointer over the double dotted lines to the right of the Quick Launch toolbar so that the pointer turns into a double-headed arrow.

31   Drag the double-headed arrow to the right until all the Quick Launch toolbar shortcuts are visible.

32   On the Quick Launch toolbar, right-click your new shortcut, and click **Delete** on the shortcut menu.

The **Confirm File Delete** dialog box appears:

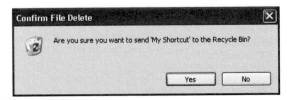

33 Click **Yes**.

The shortcut is deleted from the Quick Launch toolbar.

The two shortcuts you created are still on your desktop. They are used in the next two exercises.

Rearranging Your Desktop

After you have installed several programs and created shortcut icons to put the programs, folders, and files you use most often at your fingertips, your desktop might start to get pretty messy. To cope with the clutter, some people like to line up their icons and shortcuts in regimented rows, some like to arrange them as a sort of frame around the perimeter of their screen, and others like to group them by type in various discrete locations. You can organize your icons and shortcuts manually, or if you are happy with simple arrangements, you can have Windows XP arrange them for you.

In this exercise, you will rearrange the items on your desktop.

My Shortcut
MSN Web site

If you are not continuing from the previous exercise, the practice files for this exercise are located in the *SBS\Windows\XP\Working\Arranging* folder. (For details about installing the practice files, see "Using the Book's CD-ROM" at the beginning of this book.) If you created the desktop shortcuts in the previous exercise, you can use them for this exercise.

Follow these steps:

1 Log on to Windows, if you have not already done so.

Show Desktop

2 If any windows are open, manually minimize them, or on the Quick Launch toolbar, click the **Show Desktop** button.

3 If you did not create the desktop shortcuts in the previous exercise, copy the two shortcuts from the *SBS\WindowsXP\Working\Arranging* folder to your desktop. (See "Using the Book's CD-ROM" for instructions.)

4 Drag your desktop shortcuts to random positions on the desktop.

5 Right-click an open area of the desktop, point to **Arrange Icons By** on the shortcut menu, and then click **Auto Arrange**.

Windows XP neatly arranges your shortcuts on the left side of the desktop.

6 Now try to drag a shortcut to a different position on the desktop.

You cannot move the shortcuts.

7 If you don't like the Auto Arrange feature, right-click an open area of the desktop, point to **Arrange Icons By** on the shortcut menu, and then click **Auto Arrange** to turn it off.

Cleaning Up Your Desktop

Desktop
Cleanup Wizard

new for
WindowsXP

The **Desktop Cleanup Wizard** helps you clean up your desktop by moving rarely used shortcuts to a desktop folder called *Unused Desktop Shortcuts*. The Unused Desktop Shortcuts folder is a temporary holding area for the shortcuts you are not using. You can restore shortcuts from this folder to your desktop, or you can delete the entire folder.

In this exercise, you will use the **Desktop Cleanup Wizard** to clean up your desktop, and you will then delete some desktop shortcuts.

My Shortcut
MSN Web site

If you are not continuing from the previous exercise, the practice files for this exercise are located in the *SBS\Windows\XP\Working\Cleaning* folder. (For details about installing the practice files, see "Using the Book's CD-ROM" at the beginning of this book.) If you created the desktop shortcuts in an earlier exercise, you can use them for this exercise.

Follow these steps:

1   Log on to Windows, if you have not already done so.

Show Desktop

2   If any windows are open, manually minimize them, or on the Quick Launch toolbar, click **Show Desktop**.

3   If you did not create the desktop shortcuts in the earlier exercise, copy the two shortcuts from the *SBS\WindowsXP\Working\Arranging* folder to your desktop. (See "Using the Book's CD-ROM" for instructions.)

4   Right-click any open area of the desktop, point to **Arrange Icons By** on the shortcut menu, and then click **Run Desktop Cleanup Wizard**.

The first page of the **Desktop Cleanup Wizard** appears.

5   Click **Next** to open a **Shortcuts** page like this one:

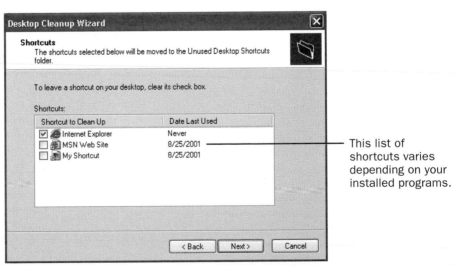

This list of shortcuts varies depending on your installed programs.

6 Make sure the **MSN Web Site** and **My Shortcut** check boxes are selected, clear all other check boxes, and then click **Next**.

The selected shortcuts are displayed on the **Completing the Desktop Cleanup Wizard** page.

7 Click **Finish**.

Windows XP creates a new folder on the desktop called *Unused Desktop Shortcuts* and moves the selected shortcuts into the folder. Notice that the folder icon on the desktop does not have a bent arrow in its bottom left corner, indicating that the icon represents the actual folder rather than a shortcut to the folder.

8 On the desktop, double-click the **Unused Desktop Shortcuts** folder to open it:

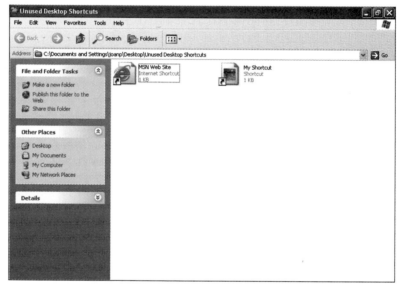

9 Click the **MSN Web Site** shortcut.

10 On the **File and Folder Tasks** menu, click **Move this file**.

The **Move Items** dialog box appears:

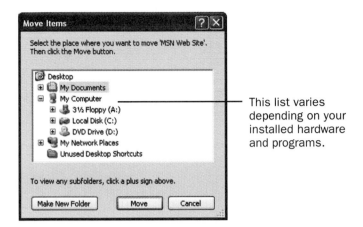

This list varies
depending on your
installed hardware
and programs.

11 If necessary, use the scroll bar to move to the top of the list.

12 Click **Desktop**, and then click **Move**.

The **MSN Web Site** shortcut is moved from the Unused Desktop Shortcuts folder to your desktop.

13 Click the **My Shortcut** shortcut.

14 On the **File and Folder Tasks** menu, click **Delete this file**.

15 In the **Confirm File Delete** dialog box, click **Yes** to delete the shortcut.

Close

16 Click the **Close** button to close the Unused Desktop Shortcuts folder and return to the desktop.

The **MSN Web Site** shortcut has been restored to your desktop.

17 On the desktop, right-click the **MSN Web Site** shortcut, and then click **Delete** on the shortcut menu.

18 In the **Confirm File Delete** box, click **Yes** to delete the shortcut.

19 Right-click the **Unused Desktop Shortcuts** folder, and then click **Delete** on the shortcut menu.

This **Confirm Folder Delete** dialog box appears:

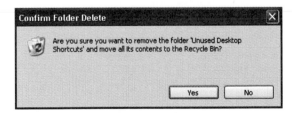

20 Click **Yes** to delete the folder.

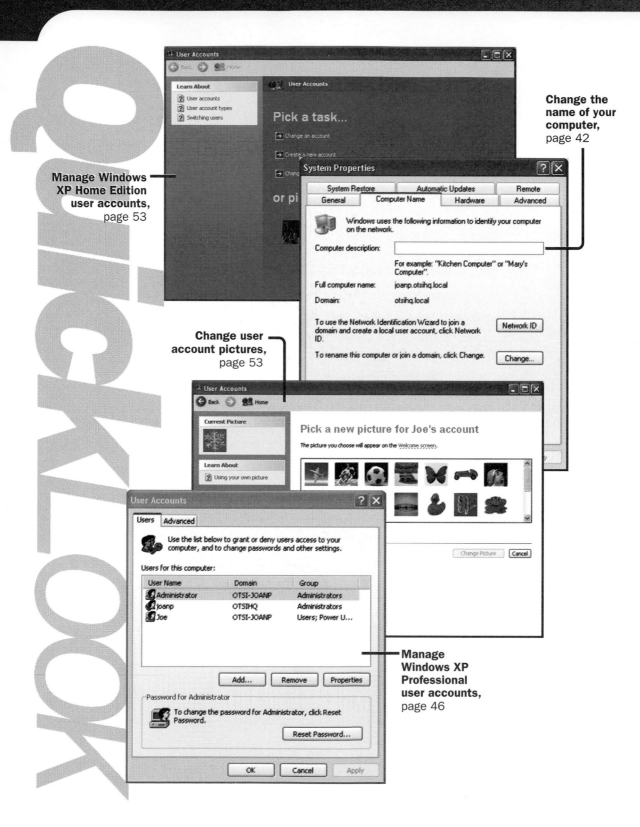

Change the
name of your
computer,
page 42

Manage Windows
XP Home Edition
user accounts,
page 53

Change user
account pictures,
page 53

Manage
Windows XP
Professional
user accounts,
page 46

Chapter 3
Managing Computer Security

After completing this chapter, you will be able to:

✔   Change your computer's name.

✔   Create, modify, and delete user accounts.

✔   Set account passwords.

✔   Represent accounts with pictures.

✔   Set up Fast User Switching so that several people can be logged on simultaneously.

In the old days, computers were isolated, and the only way to get information from one to another was to transfer it on a floppy disk. With the advent of **networks**, information transfer became easier but so did the possibility that the information on a particular computer would be accessed inappropriately or even illegally from another computer. As networks have grown from small to large to huge, concerns about information security have also grown.

Most people think of security in terms of protecting against **viruses** and intruders, or **hackers**. This book doesn't discuss virus protection, which is provided by several commercial software packages and is not included in Microsoft Windows XP. It does discuss protection against intruders.

The most common way of addressing these concerns in a networked computer environment has been through a system of **user accounts** and **passwords**. Microsoft Windows XP extends this account and password system to single stand-alone computers to allow more than one person to use the same machine. For example, if you manage your family's financial records on a home computer that is also used by your children to do their homework, you might want to set up separate accounts for your children so that they can't view or change the critical records you work with while logged on to your account.

The great thing about user accounts and passwords is that they help to keep your information private; that is, you can prevent other users from reading or altering your documents, pictures, music, and other files. You can choose to **share** files by placing them in a folder that is available to other users, but you don't have to. With Windows XP, each user can personalize his or her own working environment and have easy access to frequently used files and applications without worrying about other people making changes.

In this chapter, you will learn how to rename your computer and how to manage user accounts on Windows XP Professional and Windows XP Home Edition computers.

The practice files for this chapter are located in the *SBS\WindowsXP\Computer* folder. (For details about installing the practice files, see "Using the Book's CD-ROM" at the beginning of this book.)

Important

Because management processes are specific to either Windows XP Professional or Windows XP Home Edition, we treat each edition separately, and you should follow the steps for your particular installation. The exercises assume that you have **administrative privileges** on your computer. This means that you are allowed to change basic settings that control access to your computer and the items stored on it. If you are working on a network, a network administrator might have set up your computer so that you cannot change some settings. If this is the case, you can read through the exercises but you won't be able to follow the steps.

Changing Your Computer's Name

Every computer has a name. That might seem like something out of a science fiction story in which computers take over the world, but there is nothing sinister about it. Your computer was named during the Windows XP initial setup process. It might have been named after its user, after its make or model, or based on what it is most commonly used for (for example, *Production*); or it might have been given a whimsical name to give it some sort of personality.

In this exercise, you will locate and change your computer's name.

Important

Many corporations have a standard naming convention for computers on their network to help employees easily locate and identify network resources. If your computer is connected to a network, check with your network administrator before attempting to change your computer's name.

There are no practice files for this exercise.

Follow these steps:

1 Log on to Windows, if you have not already done so.

Important

If your computer is configured to log on to a network domain, you should change the computer name only while you are connected to the domain. Otherwise you might inadvertently change the name to one that is already in use in the domain.

2 On the **Start** menu, click **Control Panel**.

The Control Panel window opens:

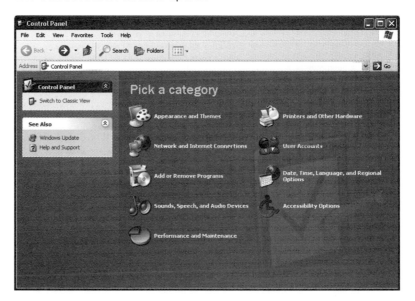

Tip

Control Panel is a central place where you can change many of your computer's settings. These settings are grouped according to category. Clicking the icon of a category displays a window with specific options or starts a wizard that leads you through the process of making changes.

3 Click the **Performance and Maintenance** icon.

The Performance and Maintenance window opens, looking something like this:

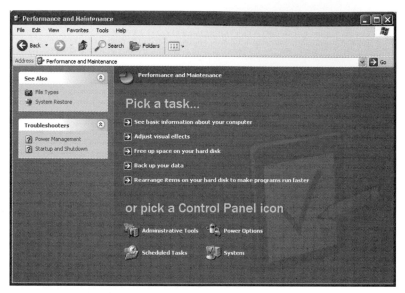

4 Click the **See basic information about your computer** task.

The **System Properties** dialog box appears:

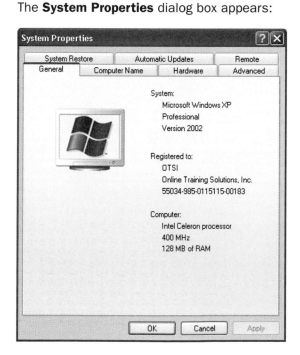

5   Click the **Computer Name** tab to display it:

The names of your computer and, if applicable, your domain or workgroup are displayed in the center of the tab. If you are logged on to a domain, your computer name is represented as *computer name.domain*.

6   Click **Change** to open the **Computer Name Changes** dialog box:

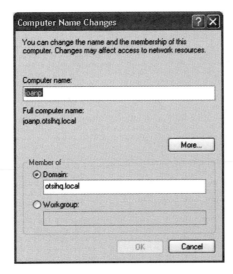

Your current computer name is highlighted.

7 Type your new computer name in the **Computer name** box, and click **OK**.

Troubleshooting

Computer names cannot be longer than 15 characters and must consist of standard characters, which include uppercase or lowercase letters (A–Z or a–z), digits (0–9), and hyphens (-).

If your computer is connected to a network domain, you will be prompted for the user account name and password of a network administrator who has permission to rename the computer in the domain.

8 If you are prompted to do so, enter your user account name and password, and then click **OK**.

9 When Windows XP says you must restart the computer for the changes to take effect, click **OK**.

10 Click **OK** to close the **System Properties** dialog box, and then click **Yes** to restart your computer.

Your computer now has a new name.

Working with User Accounts in Windows XP Professional

If your computer is part of a network, your network administrator must set up a user account or accounts for the computer to be able to access the network. User accounts can be established during the setup process or at any time from Control Panel.

If you have administrative privileges, you can create **local computer** user accounts that allow other people to access your computer. For example, you might want to create a local user account for a friend so that he or she can log on to your computer to check e-mail. Each user account belongs to a **group** with **permissions** to perform certain operations on the computer. The most common groups are:

- *Administrators*, who have unrestricted access to the computer.
- *Power Users*, who have most administrative capabilities but with some restrictions.
- *Users* and *Guests*, who are restricted from making system-wide changes.
- *Backup Operators*, who can override security restrictions for the purpose of backing up or restoring files.

Other groups are available for support personnel, network administrators, and re-mote users. There are also special groups that might be created when a computer is upgraded from other versions of Windows to Windows XP Professional. And finally, anyone assigned to the Administrators group can create custom groups.

In this exercise, you will create a local computer user account, change its privileges, and then delete it.

Tip

You cannot delete the account of a user who is currently logged on to the computer.

There is no working folder for this exercise, but you do need to know your computer's name.

Tip

To find out your computer's name, open Control Panel, click **Performance and Maintenance**, click **See basic information about your computer**, and in the **System Properties** dialog box, click the **Computer Name** tab.

Follow these steps:

1 Log on to Windows, If you have not already done so.

2 Click the **Start** button, and on the **Start** menu, click **Control Panel**. Control Panel appears, like this:

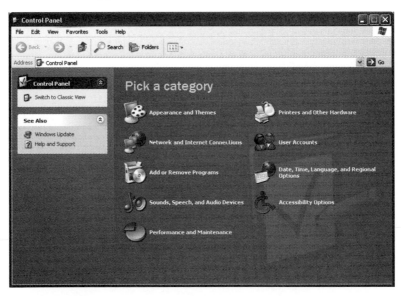

3 In the Control Panel window, click the **User Accounts** icon to open the **User Accounts** dialog box.

4 Click the **Advanced** tab.

5 In the **Advanced user management** area, click **Advanced** to open the Local Users and Groups window.

6 In the left pane of the Local Users and Groups window, click the **Users** folder to display a list of the current user names:

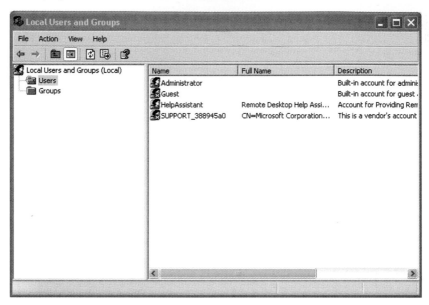

7 On the **Action** menu, click **New User** to open the **New User** dialog box:

8 In the **User name** box, type **Joe**.

9 In the **Full name** box, type **Joe the Dog**.

10 In the **Description** box, type **Man's best friend**.

11 In the **Password** box, type **Woof!**

Tip

Your corporate network policy might require that passwords conform to a minimum length or meet other guidelines. If you are required to create a secure password, use a combination of numeric and alphabetic characters with at least one punctuation mark. Secure passwords must usually be at least eight characters in length.

12 Type the password again in the **Confirm password** box.

13 Ensure that the **User must change password at next logon** and the **Account is disabled** check boxes are cleared, and then click **Create**.

Tip

You clear the first check box because you don't want the user to have to change the password, and you clear the second because you want the account to be active and available.

The account is created, and the input screen is cleared.

14 Click **Close** to return to the Local Users and Groups window.

Joe has been added to the list of users, as shown here:

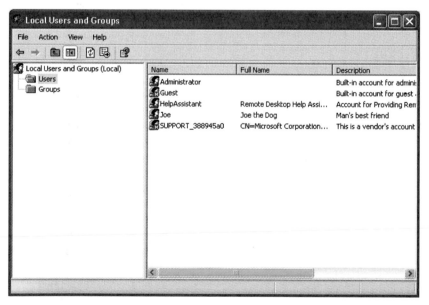

15 In the right pane of the Local Users and Groups window, double-click **Joe** to open the **Joe Properties** dialog box.

16 Click the **Member Of** tab.

Joe is currently shown as a member of the Users group, the default group for new users.

17 Click **Cancel** to close the **Joe Properties** dialog box.

18 To add Joe to another group, click the **Groups** folder to display a list of the available groups in the left pane of the Local Users and Groups window:

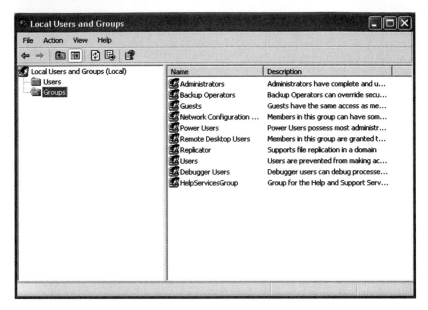

19 In the right pane of the Local Users and Groups window, double-click **Power Users** to open the **Power Users Properties** dialog box.

20 Click **Add**.

21 If you are connected to a network domain, click the **Locations** button, click your computer name, and click **OK**.

22 In the **Enter the object names to select** box, type **Joe**, and click **Check Names**.

Tip

To enter multiple user names, separate the names with a semicolon.

The **Select Users** dialog box looks something like this:

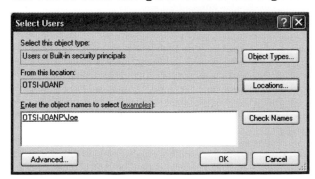

The name you typed is replaced by the *computer name\user name* combination.

Tip

If there are a lot of people named Joe on your network, you might be asked to select the one you want from a list.

23 Click **OK** to add Joe to the Power Users group, and then click **OK** to close the **Power Users Properties** dialog box.

Close

24 Click the **Close** button to close the Local Users and Groups window, and click **OK** to close the **User Accounts** dialog box.

25 On the **Start** menu, click **Log Off**, and then click **Log Off** in the **Log Off Windows** dialog box.

You are logged off of Windows and returned to the logon security screen.

26 Press [Ctrl]+[Alt]+[Del] to access the **Log On to Windows** dialog box.

27 In the **User name** box, type **Joe**.

28 In the **Password** box, type **Woof!** (or the secure password you created in step 11).

The characters of the password are displayed as dots as you type.

29 Click the down arrow to the right of the **Log on to** box, and click your computer in the drop-down list.

30 Click **OK**.

Joe is now logged on to your computer, but not your network domain. The **Start** menu expands, with Joe's full name shown at the top:

Because this is the first time that Joe has logged on to this computer, the desktop is in its default state.

31 On the **Start** menu, click **Log Off**, and then click **Log Off** in the **Log Off Windows** dialog box to log Joe's account off of the computer. Then log back on as yourself, changing the **Log on to** setting to your domain if necessary.

32 Now you'll change the group to which Joe is assigned again. Open Control Panel, and click the **User Accounts** icon to open the **User Accounts** dialog box:

33 In the **Users for this computer** list, click **Joe**, and then click **Properties** to open the **Joe Properties** dialog box.

34 On the **Group Membership** tab, click **Other**, and click **Administrators** in the drop-down list.

35 Click **OK** to change Joe's group membership to Administrators.

36 Now that you've completed this exercise, you don't need this account on your computer, so in the **Users for this computer** list, click **Joe**, and then click **Remove**.

A message box warns you that Joe will no longer be able to use this computer.

37 Click **Yes**.

Joe is removed from the list of users.

38 Click **OK** to close the **User Accounts** dialog box.

Close

39 Click the **Close** button to close Control Panel.

Working with User Accounts in Windows XP Home Edition

Windows XP Home Edition supports two levels of user privileges: computer administrator and limited. Users with computer administrator accounts have permission to do everything, including:

- Create, change, and delete accounts.
- Make system-wide changes.
- Install and remove programs.
- Access all files.

Users with limited accounts have permission to do things that affect only their own account, including:

- Change or remove their password.
- Change their user account picture.
- Change their theme and desktop settings.
- View files they created and files in the Shared Documents folder.

Important

Users with limited accounts can run into difficulties when trying to install new software, because some programs require administrative privileges to install or remove programs. Be sure you have the appropriate privileges before attempting to install or remove new software.

Each Windows XP Home Edition user account is represented on the logon screen by the **user account name** and also by a **user account picture**. Windows XP comes with 23 user account pictures, representing a variety of animals, sports, and interests. You can select the picture that most closely matches your personality or interests. If none of the default pictures is to your liking, you can add a picture you like better.

Tip

Computer administrators can assign or change the picture for any user. Limited account and guest account users can change only their own picture.

Graphics used as user account pictures can be **bitmap (BMP)** files, **Graphic Interchange Format (GIF)** files, **Joint Photographic Expert Group (JPEG)** files, or **Portable Network Graphics (PNG)** files. They can be any size, but they are always displayed at 48 **pixels** high by 48 pixels wide. If you decide to use a picture that does not have the same height and width, it will be stretched or compressed to fit within the user account picture area on the logon screen.

In this exercise, you will create a new user account with administrative privileges, change its privileges, create a password, and choose a custom graphic to represent the user. You will then delete the account.

Tip

You can never delete the account of a user who is currently logged on to the computer.

Joe.bmp

The practice file for this exercise is located in the *SBS\WindowsXP\Computer\ProfileHE* folder. (For details about installing the practice files, see "Using the Book's CD-ROM" at the beginning of this book.)

Follow these steps:

1   Log on to Windows, if you have not already done so.

2   On the **Start** menu, click **Control Panel**.

3   Click the **User Accounts** icon.

The User Accounts window appears:

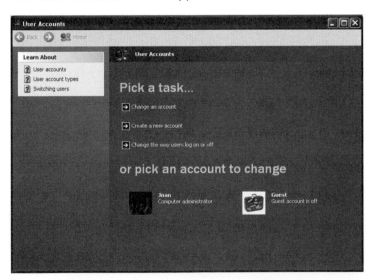

4   Click **Create a new account** to open the **Name the new account** screen.

You are prompted to enter a name for the new account.

5   Type **Joe**, and then click **Next** to move to the **Pick an account type** screen.

You are prompted to specify the account type.

6 Select **Computer administrator**, and then click **Create Account**.

Windows XP creates a new account called *Joe*, and assigns a user account picture to the account, which now appears at the bottom of the User Accounts window.

7 Now you'll customize Joe's account. Click **Joe**.

The options for changing Joe's account are displayed as shown here:

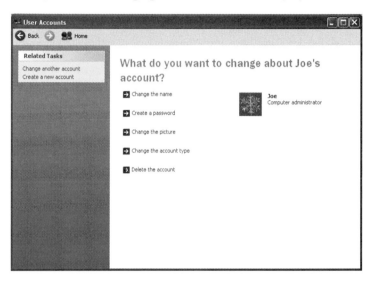

8 Click **Change the picture**.

You are prompted to select from the default pictures shown here:

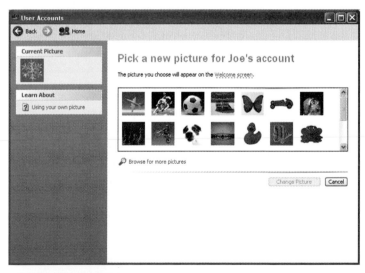

9 Click **Browse for more pictures**.

10 In the Open window, click the down arrow to the right of the **Look in** box, and browse to *SBS\WindowsXP\Computer\ProfileHE*.

11 Click the bitmap named **joe**, and then click **Open**.

A picture of Joe (a puppy) is added to the available pictures; Joe's user account picture is changed, and then you are returned to the account options screen.

12 Click **Change the account type**.

13 On the **Pick a new account type for Joe** screen, click **Limited**, and then click **Change Account Type**.

In the account options screen, the *Limited account* type is now indicated to the right of Joe's user account picture.

14 Click **Create a password**.

You are prompted to enter a password for Joe's account.

15 In the **Type a new password** box, type **BowWow!**, and then press the ⌨Tab key to move to the next field.

To ensure the secrecy of the password, the characters are displayed as dots as you type.

16 In the **Type the new password again to confirm** box, retype **BowWow!**, and then press the ⌨Tab key to move to the next field.

17 In the **Type a word or phrase to use as a password hint** box, type **What does Joe say?**

The screen now looks like this:

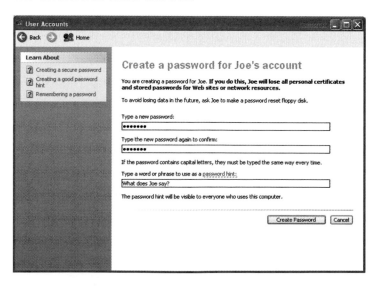

18 Click **Create Password** to save the password as part of Joe's user account profile and return to the account options screen.

The *Password protected* status of Joe's account is now indicated to the right of his user account picture.

19 Now you'll delete Joe's account. Click **Delete the account**.

Troubleshooting

If the account you are trying to delete is currently logged on to the computer, you must switch to that user account and log it off before you can delete it.

You are asked whether you want to keep or delete any files that Joe might have created on the desktop or in the My Documents folder.

20 Joe has not created any files that you care about, so click **Delete Files**, and then click **Delete Account** to delete Joe's account and return to the main **User Accounts** screen.

Joe's account no longer appears among the active accounts.

Close

21 Click the **Close** button to close the User Accounts window, and then close Control Panel.

Switching Quickly Among Users

When you're using Windows XP Professional on a network domain, there is only one way to log onto your computer: by entering your user account name and your password. If you are not on a network domain, whether you are using Windows XP Professional or Home Edition and whether you are working on a network (with no domain) or on a stand-alone computer, you have two logon options:

■ You can select from pictorial representations on the new Windows XP Welcome screen.

■ You can use the classic logon prompt that requires you to enter your user account name as well as your password (if the account is password-protected).

The Welcome screen is the default.

Fast User Switching

new for **Windows**XP

Another new option available in Windows XP on a stand-alone computer is Fast User Switching, which allows multiple users to log on to their user accounts without logging previous users off. This feature saves time and decreases frustration for all users, because open applications don't need to be closed when switching between user accounts.

In this exercise, you will turn on Fast User Switching on your computer.

Tip

Fast User Switching is not available on Windows XP Professional computers that are connected to a network domain.

There is no working folder for this exercise.

Follow these steps:

1 Log on to Windows, if you have not already done so.

2 On the **Start** menu, click **Control Panel**.

The Control Panel window opens.

3 Click the **User Accounts** icon.

The User Accounts window appears, with the current user names displayed at the bottom of the window.

Important

If you have only one user account on your computer, you will need to quickly create at least one other account to be able to use Fast User Switching.

4 Click the **Change the way users log on or off** task.

The **Select logon and logoff options** screen appears.

5 Select the **Use Fast User Switching** check box, and click **Apply Options**.

The change is applied, and you return to the main User Accounts window.

6 With the User Accounts and Control Panel windows still open, click **Log Off** on the **Start** menu.

This **Log Off Windows** dialog box appears:

7 Click **Switch User**. The Welcome screen appears with the current user accounts shown.

8 Click one of the account names to log in with that account.

If the account is password-protected, a password box appears.

Tip

If you don't remember your password, you can click the blue question mark button to see the password hint.

9 Type the password, and click the green arrow button to continue.

You are now logged on to the account, and that account's personal settings are loaded. The **Start** menu expands, with the account's user name and user account picture displayed at the top, like this:

If this is the first time this account has logged in, all the settings are the default settings, and there are no open applications.

10 On the **Start** menu, click **Log Off**.

11 In the **Log Off Windows** dialog box, click **Switch User**.

12 On the Welcome screen, click your own user name, and if your account is password-protected, enter your password.

You are returned to your own user account, where the User Accounts and Control Panel windows are still open. (They might be minimized.)

Close

13 Click the **Close** button to close the User Accounts window, and then close Control Panel.

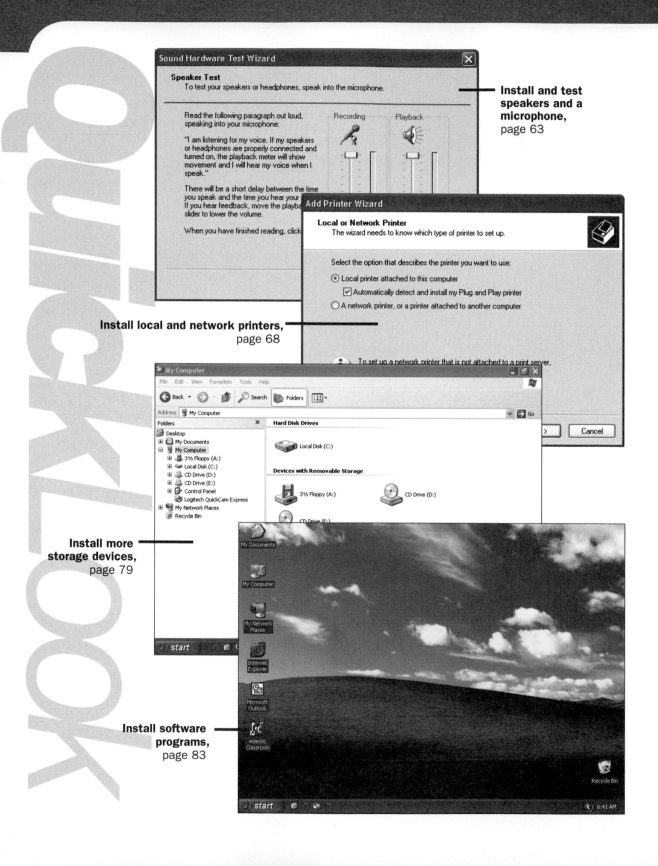

Sound Hardware Test Wizard

Speaker Test
To test your speakers or headphones, speak into the microphone.

Read the following paragraph out loud, speaking into your microphone:

"I am listening for my voice. If my speakers or headphones are properly connected and turned on, the playback meter will show movement and I will hear my voice when I speak."

There will be a short delay between the time you speak and the time you hear your If you hear feedback, move the playba slider to lower the volume.

When you have finished reading, click

Recording

Playback

Install and test speakers and a microphone,
page 63

Add Printer Wizard

Local or Network Printer
The wizard needs to know which type of printer to set up.

Select the option that describes the printer you want to use:

⦿ Local printer attached to this computer

☑ Automatically detect and install my Plug and Play printer

○ A network printer, or a printer attached to another computer

To set up a network printer that is not attached to a print server,

> Cancel

Install local and network printers,
page 68

My Computer

File   Edit   View   Favorites   Tools   Help

Back   ▾   ⚫   ▾   🔍 Search   📁 Folders   ▦ ▾

Address   💻 My Computer   ✔ ➔ Go

Folders   ✕   **Hard Disk Drives**
📁 Desktop
⊞ 📁 My Documents   💾 Local Disk (C:)
⊟ 💻 My Computer
   ⊞ 💾 3½ Floppy (A:)
   ⊞ 💽 Local Disk (C:)   **Devices with Removable Storage**
   ⊞ 💿 CD Drive (D:)
   ⊞ 💿 CD Drive (E:)   💾 3½ Floppy (A:)   💿 CD Drive (D:)
   ⊞ 📷 Control Panel
      Logitech QuickCam Express
⊞ 📁 My Network Places   💿 CD Drive (E:)
🗑 Recycle Bin

Install more storage devices,
page 79

Install software programs,
page 83

🥇 start   6:41 AM

Chapter 4
Adding Hardware and Software

After completing this chapter, you will be able to:

✔ Install speakers and a microphone.

✔ Install local and network printers.

✔ Install a scanner or camera.

✔ Install storage devices.

✔ Install programs and Windows components, and have them start automatically.

People discuss computers in terms of **hardware** and **software**. As you probably know, physical items such as computers and monitors are hardware, and all the programs that enable you to do things with that hardware are collectively known as software.

Whether you're working in an office or at home, you will eventually want to install one or more bits of extra hardware, called **peripheral devices**, on your computer. Some devices, such as the keyboard, monitor, and mouse, usually come with the computer, but you will purchase others separately. The most common devices are speakers and a printer. Other popular devices include scanners, storage devices such as Zip drives, and fax machines. These devices are all **external**—meaning that you can install them without having to open up your computer—but others, such as a CD-ROM burner or a tape backup drive, might be **internal**—meaning that they have to be installed inside your computer's case.

Many peripheral devices fall into a category called **Plug and Play**, which quite literally means that you can plug them in and use them—no setup is required. Others might require that you supply some kind of information, usually through a wizard, or might require a specific **device driver** in order to work properly. Device drivers enable peripheral devices to "talk" to your computer, but they are unfortunately not universal. To hook up a printer, for example, you might need a driver that is not only specific to the printer but also specific to Microsoft Windows XP.

Device Drivers

Device drivers are files that contain information that Windows needs to run your printer, fax machine, scanner, camera, or other device. Drivers can be specific to an individual device or to a family of devices (such as all HP LaserJet printers), and they are often specific to a certain version of Windows.

Device drivers can be found on the Web site of the device manufacturer or on certain Web sites that centralize driver information. If you are looking for current device drivers, try these Web sites:

Manufacturer	Driver Download
Apple	www.info.apple.com/support/downloads.html
Brother	www.brother.com/E-ftp/softwin1.html
Canon	www.usa.canon.com/support/files/
Citizen America	www.citizen-america.com/drivers/
Compaq	www.compaq.com/support/files/
Epson	support.epson.com/filelibrary.html
Fujitsu	www.fcpa.com/cgi-bin/goFrames.cgi/support/su_drivers.html
Hewlett-Packard	www.hp.com/cposupport/software.html
IBM	www.printers.ibm.com/R5PSC.NSF/web/driver/
Kodak	www.kodak.com/global/en/service/software/driverSupport.shtml
Konica	www.kbm.com/Support/Drivers2/
Lexmark	www.lexmark.com/software/software.html
Minolta (business products)	bpg.minoltausa.com/eprise/main/minolta/BPG/support_center /downloads/searchdownload/
NEC	www.nectech.com/css/
Panasonic	www.panasonic.com/support/software/download.html
Ricoh	ricoh-usa.com/download/
Toshiba	copiers.toshiba.com/support/
Xerox	www.xerox.com/go/xrx/template/drivermain.jsp

Other good resources include:

PC Drivers HeadQuarters	www.drivershq.com
The Driver Guide	www.driverguide.com
Totally Drivers	www.totallydrivers.com
WinDrivers	www.windrivers.com

Nowadays you can pretty much walk into a computer store, purchase a computer, plug it in, and start working without installing any software. New name-brand computers usually come with the operating system (in this case, Microsoft Windows XP) already installed. They might also include software programs called applications, which you use to carry out specific tasks, such as word processing. Sooner or later, however, you will want or need to install additional programs, either from a floppy disk, a CD-ROM, a network server, or the Internet. You might also need to install some of the optional components of Windows XP that did not get set up during the operating system's installation.

In this chapter, you will learn how to install hardware and software on your Windows XP computer. The practice files for this chapter are located in the *SBS\WindowsXP\Software* folder. (For details about installing the practice files, see "Using the Book's CD-ROM" at the beginning of this book.)

Installing Speakers and a Microphone

A basic computer system consists of a computer, monitor, keyboard, and mouse. Computer systems that are equipped with sound cards usually come with a set of external speakers so that you can listen to music and other audio files. If you're a real enthusiast, you might want to purchase fancy surround-sound speakers for your computer. Or if you want to listen to audio output privately, you might want to use speakers that have headphone jacks.

Most standard speaker systems consist of two speakers with one cord that connects them to each other, another that connects them to the computer, and a power cord that connects them to the power source. One speaker might have a volume control (independent of the computer-controlled volume control) and a headset jack.

With the rapid evolution of Internet-based communications, digital video, and speech-to-text technologies, microphones are being used more commonly with business and home computer systems. Microphones come in a variety of options: freestanding microphones, microphones that attach to your computer, headset microphones with built-in headphones that allow more private communication and consistent recording quality, boom microphones with a single headset speaker, and many others.

If you will be recording a lot of speech, it is worthwhile to invest in a good-quality microphone. Anything less, and you are likely to find yourself making a return trip to the store. To get the best recorded quality, it is also critical that you choose the type of microphone that best fits your needs. Headset and boom microphones maintain a constant distance between the microphone and your mouth, which helps to maintain a more consistent sound level than a stationary microphone. The headphones built into headset and boom microphones provide the same privacy of conversation as a telephone, because audio output is heard only by the wearer.

In this exercise, you will connect a stereo speaker system and a microphone to your Windows XP computer. You will then test the connection and adjust audio input and output levels appropriately.

There are no practice files for this exercise, but you do need to have a set of speakers and a microphone to complete the steps.

Follow these steps:

1 Log on to Windows, if you have not already done so.

2 Remove the audio devices from their packaging, if you have not already done so.

Tip

If you are using an alternate audio configuration, such as a boom microphone, connect the input and output cables appropriately and then skip to step 8.

3 Link the two speakers using the connector cable.

4 Position the speakers to the left and right of your monitor to provide stereo sound quality.

5 Plug the speakers into a nearby power outlet using the AC adapter cord.

6 Plug the speakers into the speaker jack on the sound card at the back of the computer using the connector cable.

Tip

The speaker jack might be indicated by a small speaker icon or the words *Audio* or *Audio/Out*.

7 Plug the microphone connector cable into the audio input jack on the sound card on the back of your computer.

Tip

The audio input jack might be indicated by a microphone icon or the words *Mic*, or *Microphone*.

8 Click the **Start** button, and then on the **Start** menu, click **Control Panel**.
The Control Panel window appears.

9 Click **Sounds, Speech, and Audio Devices** to open this window:

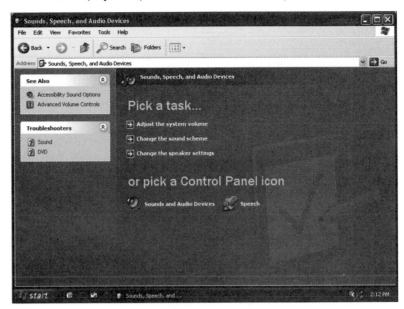

10 Click the **Sounds and Audio Devices** icon.

The **Sounds and Audio Devices Properties** dialog box appears:

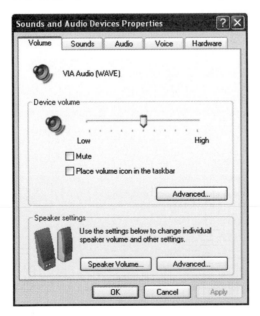

11 Click each of the tabs, and explore the options available.

12 On the **Voice** tab, click **Test hardware**.

The **Sound Hardware Test Wizard** appears:

13 Make sure no programs are open, and then click **Next**.

The wizard runs an automated test of your sound hardware. You will not hear any sounds during this process.

14 After completing the automated test, the wizard prompts you to test the microphone:

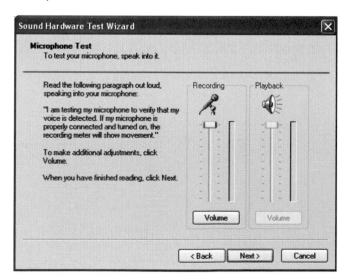

15 Read the microphone test paragraph aloud in your normal speaking voice. Just for fun, you might try singing a couple of lines from your favorite song!

You will not hear any sound from the speakers during the microphone test.

As you speak (or sing), a recording level indicator in the **Recording** area moves in response to your voice. When your voice volume is in an acceptable recording range, the meter is green. If your voice is too loud for the current **Recording** setting, the indicator enters a yellow or red zone, and the **Recording** setting adjusts to a lower level. If your voice is too quiet, the setting adjusts to a higher level to pick up your voice at the most appropriate level for recording.

Troubleshooting

If the **Recording** indicator does not move, your microphone might be incorrectly connected, or it might not be compatible with your computer. If this happens, hold the microphone close to your mouth and scream loudly—if the recording meter moves slightly, the connection is good, and the problem is between your microphone and your computer. You might be able to solve this problem by downloading new device drivers from the microphone manufacturer's Web site, or it might be simpler to replace the microphone.

16 When you have finished reading the paragraph, click **Next** to begin the speaker test:

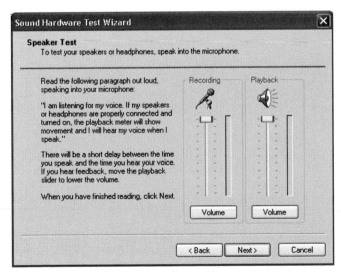

17 Read the speaker test paragraph aloud in your normal speaking voice.

As you speak, the **Recording** and **Playback** indicators will move in response to your voice, and you will hear yourself speaking, with a short delay between your words and the sound. (This can be somewhat distracting.) As with the microphone test, the **Recording** level adjusts to the volume of your voice.

18   Adjust the **Playback** slider control to a comfortable listening level.

Tip

If you are using speakers with a volume control, you can also adjust the volume on the speakers themselves.

19   When you have finished making adjustments, click **Next**, and then click **Finish** to close the **Sound Hardware Test Wizard**.

Close

20   Click **OK** to close the **Sounds and Audio Devices Properties** dialog box, and then click the **Close** button to close the Sounds, Speech, and Audio Devices window.

Installing a Local Printer

A **local printer** is a printer that is connected directly to your computer. The software to run the printer is installed on and run from your computer. When you connect a printer to your Windows XP computer, Windows XP often identifies that the printer has been connected. It then searches through its database of drivers to locate the appropriate software to run the printer. If Windows XP doesn't have the current driver for your particular printer, it asks you to provide the driver.

Troubleshooting

Many printers come with a CD-ROM or floppy disk containing installation files and drivers that were current at the time the printer was manufactured. If you don't have the current **printer drivers**, you can usually locate them on the printer manufacturer's Web site.

In this exercise, you will install a local printer and then test the installation by printing a test page.

There are no practice files for this exercise, but you must have a printer available to complete the steps. If Windows XP does not have the drivers for your printer, you will need to provide them.

Follow these steps:

1 Log on to Windows, if you have not already done so.

2 Connect the printer to the appropriate plug, or **port**, on the back of your computer. Then turn on the printer.

At this point, three things might happen:

- Windows XP might detect the printer and display a **Found New Hardware** alert in the notification area at the right end of the taskbar. In this case, Windows knows what printer drivers to install, so wait while Windows finishes the installation process, and skip the rest of the steps.

- Windows XP might detect the printer but not have all the information it needs to install it, in which case it displays the **Found New Hardware Wizard**. Skip to step 9 to complete the instructions.

- Windows XP might not detect the printer, in which case it does nothing. Go to step 3.

3 If the **Found New Hardware Wizard** does not appear, click **Start**, and then click **Printers and Faxes.**

The Printers and Faxes window appears:

4 On the **Printer Tasks** menu, click **Add a printer**.

The **Add Printer Wizard** opens:

5 Click **Next** to move to the wizard's **Local or Network Printer** page:

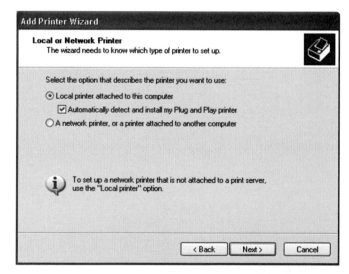

6 Select the **Local printer attached to this computer** option.

7 Clear the **Automatically detect and install my Plug and Play printer** check box.

8 Click **Next** to move to the wizard's **Select a Printer Port** page:

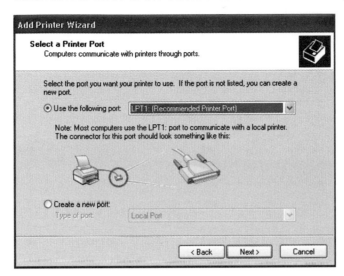

9 Confirm that your printer is connected to the recommended printer port, or select the correct port from the drop-down list, and click **Next** to move to the wizard's **Install Printer Software** page:

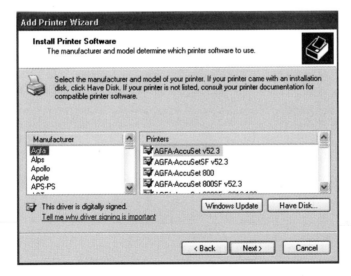

10 If you have an installation CD-ROM or floppy disk, insert it, click **Have Disk**, and follow the instructions on the screen to install your printer.

Important

Your installation CD-ROM or floppy disk must contain updated drivers that are compatible with Windows XP. If your drivers are out of date, download the current drivers from the printer manufacturer's Web site.

11 In the **Manufacturer** list, click the name of the manufacturer of your printer.

The **Printers** list changes to reflect a list of the printer drivers that Windows XP has stored for that manufacturer.

12 In the **Printers** list, select the model of your printer.

Troubleshooting

If your specific model is not listed, select a similar model; or download the necessary drivers from the manufacturer's Web site, return to the **Install Printer Software** page, and click **Have Disk** to install the printer manually.

13 Click **Next** to move to the wizard's **Name Your Printer** page.

14 Type a name for your printer in the **Printer name** box, or accept the default name, and click **Next**.

Tip

Keep the printer name short and easily recognizable, because a long name might not fit in the space provided in some dialog boxes. It's a good idea to use the printer model name or your name to clearly identify the printer, in case you end up with more than one.

15 If you are connected to a network and are asked if you want to share the printer, make sure the **Do not share this printer** option is selected, and click **Next** to open the wizard's **Print Test Page** page:

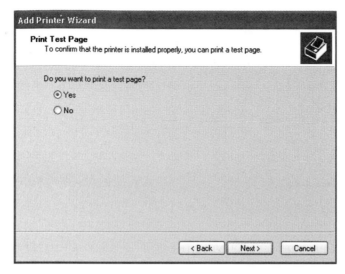

16 Click **Yes**, and then click **Next**.

A completion page something like this one appears:

17 Click **Finish** to print the test page.

After the test page has printed, a confirmation dialog box appears.

18 Click **OK** to close the dialog box and the **Add Printer Wizard**.

Your printer connection displayed in the Printers and Faxes window:

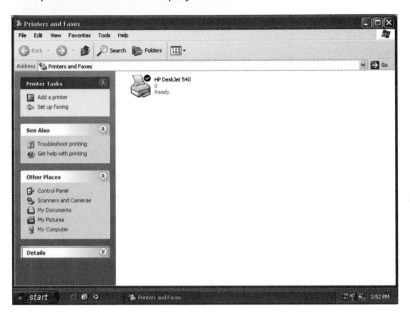

Close

19 Click the **Close** button to close the Printers and Faxes window.

Installing a Network Printer

A **network printer** is a printer that is not connected directly to your computer. Instead, you access the printer over the network, either as a free-standing networked printer, through someone else's computer, through a print server, or through a printer hub.

If the printer you are connecting to is available to everyone on the network, you will not need specific permission to connect to it. If the printer has been made available only to specific people or groups, you will have to ask the printer's "owner" or your network administrator to make the printer available to you.

In this exercise, you will connect to a network printer.

There are no practice files for this exercise, but you must have access to a network printer and know the name of the printer. If the printer is connected to another computer, you must also know that computer's name.

Follow these steps:

1 Log on to Windows, if you have not already done so.

2 On the **Start** menu, click **Printers and Faxes**.

The Printers and Faxes window appears with your currently installed printers shown in the right pane.

3 On the **Printer Tasks** menu, click **Add a printer** to open the **Add Printer Wizard**.

4 Click **Next** to move to the wizard's **Local or Network Printer** page.

5 Select **A network printer, or a printer attached to another computer**, and then click **Next**.

You move to the wizard's **Specify a Printer** page:

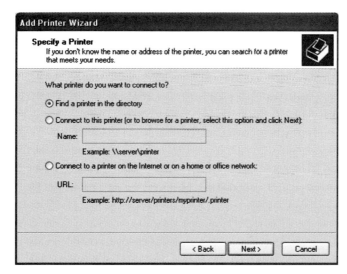

6 Select **Connect to this printer**, and click **Next**.

7 On the **Browse for Printer** page, select the printer you want to use, and click **Next**.

If not everyone on your network is allowed to use this printer, at this point you might be asked for your user account name and password. Enter them, and click OK. If you are allowed to use the printer, you then see the wizard's next page. If you are not, you will have to specify a different printer.

8 If the dialog box appears, enter your user account name and password, and then click **OK** to close the dialog box and make the connection.

If you have more than one printer installed, you are prompted to specify whether you would like this one to be the printer Windows XP uses unless you specify differently:

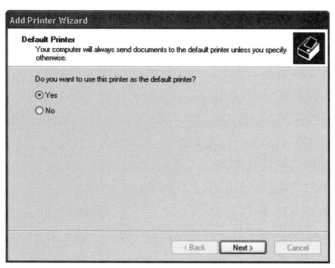

9 If this page appears, make your selection, and then click **Next**.

A completion page appears:

The name of the computer to which the printer is attached would be shown here.

10 Click **Finish** to close the dialog box.

Tip

If you are prompted to print a test page, do so because this is a good opportunity to test your connection.

Your new printer connection is now displayed in the Printers and Faxes window:

The check mark identifies the default printer.

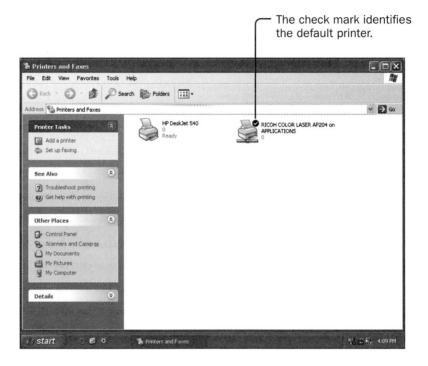

Close

11 Click the **Close** button to close the Printers and Faxes window.

When you print anything from one of your applications, your computer will use the default printer unless you specifically select a different printer.

Configuring the Fax Service

Fax service

new for
WindowsXP

Good news: You no longer need to spend money on a free-standing fax machine to send and receive faxes! You can now use the Microsoft Fax service to send and receive faxes using a fax/modem or a fax board installed in your computer, or via your corporate LAN. You can fax a document from any application, send a cover fax page, and track and monitor your fax activity. New wizards make configuring and sending faxes simple. To configure the Fax service:

1   On the **Start** menu, click **Control Panel**, and then click **Printers and Other Hardware**.

2   In the Printers and Other Hardware window, click the **Printers and Faxes** icon.

3   In the Printers and Faxes window, click **Set up faxing**.

Installing a Scanner or Camera

Scanners are devices you use to convert printed information—words, drawings, photographs, and so on—into digital data that can be processed by your computer. If you have an **optical character recognition (OCR)** program, scanned documents can often be converted to word processor or spreadsheet files. Scanned photos, drawings, and graphics can be saved as graphic files for use on a Web site or in other documents. The digital image can be opened and enhanced in a graphic processing program.

Computer-compatible cameras come in various shapes and sizes, including handheld digital cameras and digital video cameras (such as "eyeball" cameras).

Most modern scanners and digital video cameras are Plug and Play peripheral devices. To install a scanner or camera, you can simply plug it into the appropriate port on your computer. Windows XP recognizes the device and installs it on your computer. However, some peripheral devices come with special software that enables the features of the hardware, and some manufacturers recommend that you install the software before connecting the hardware to your computer; this is one case where it's a good idea to read the manual first!

After the scanner or camera is installed, you can use the **Scanner and Camera Wizard** in Windows XP to easily create, download, and process images from a scanner, digital camera, or video camera.

In this exercise, you will install and access a Plug and Play scanner or camera.

There are no practice files for this exercise, but you must have a scanner or camera available to complete the steps.

Follow these steps:

1   Log on to Windows, if you have not already done so.

2   Plug your scanner or camera into the appropriate port on your computer.

Windows XP detects the device and displays a *Found New Hardware* message in the notification area of the taskbar while it installs the hardware.

Important

The installation of the scanner or camera may take several minutes. Wait for the notification to go away before continuing with this exercise.

3   On the **Start** menu, click **Control Panel**.

4   In the Control Panel window, click the **Printers and Other Hardware** icon.

5   In the Printers and Other Hardware window, click the **Scanners and Cameras** icon.

Your installed scanners and cameras are displayed on the right pane of the Scanners and Cameras window.

6   Double-click the icon for your scanner or camera to open the **Scanner and Camera Wizard**.

You can now start working with your installed device.

Installing a Storage Device

A variety of **data storage devices** are available; the most common are hard disk drives and floppy disk drives. Every computer has at least one hard disk drive, and almost all computers come with a floppy disk drive installed. However, when you need extra storage space, you don't have to buy a new computer or even upgrade your hard drive. It is quite simple to install an internal or external storage device on your Windows XP computer, and there are plenty of options to choose from, such as **Zip disk drives**, **Jaz disk drives**, and **tape drives**. As the cost of CD-Read-Write (CD-RW) drives decreases, they are also becoming increasingly common.

In this exercise, you will install an external storage device.

There are no practice files for this exercise, but you must have a Plug and Play Zip drive or similar storage device available to complete the steps.

Follow these steps:

1   Log on to Windows, if you have not already done so.

2   Plug the storage device into the appropriate port and into a power source, if necessary.

Windows XP detects the device and displays a *Found New Hardware* message in the notification area of the taskbar while it installs the hardware.

The storage device is now listed as one of your available storage locations when you open, save, or look for a file on your computer.

Need More Ports?

Most computers come equipped with a standard set of **ports** that you use to connect a keyboard, mouse, monitor, or printer. If your computer has a sound card and a network card, you also have audio and network ports. Many desktop and laptop computers now also have **USB ports** to handle the growing number of devices that are designed to work with this method of connection.

When you install several peripheral devices on the same computer, you might find that you don't have enough ports to connect them all. All is not lost! Here are three options for expanding your connection capacity:

■   Install extra ports. After turning off your computer, you can remove its cover and insert a card with more ports, which you can purchase in any computer store, into one of the available **expansion slots**. When you turn the power back on, Windows XP detects and installs the new ports without further ado.

■   Daisy-chain multiple devices. Many devices that connect to the computer via its **parallel port** can be "daisy-chained" together to form a linked network of devices. For example, you might connect a Zip drive to your computer's parallel port and then connect a printer to the Zip drive's parallel port. Data you send to the printer will pass through the Zip drive.

■   Use a hub. Multiple devices can be connected to a hub that is in turn connected to your computer, enabling all the devices to share that single connection. Hubs are available for network, peripheral devices, and USB devices. If you want to make a physical connection to multiple peripheral devices but you don't need to use more than one at a time, you can use a switch box, which looks similar to a hub but allows only one active connection at a time.

Installing Internal Devices

Although many hardware components can be added to your system through the somewhat simple use of ports and cables, other devices might require that components be installed inside the computer's case. The internal component might be in the form of a card that provides a new connection at the back of the computer, or it might be a new hard disk drive, floppy disk drive, CD-ROM drive, or tape backup drive that is accessed from the front of the computer.

To install an internal device, you need to remove the cover from your computer and delve into its innards. This is not a book on hardware configuration, but we do want to demonstrate the manner in which Windows XP assimilates new hardware as it is added to your system.

In this exercise, you will install an internal CD-RW drive.

There are no practice files for this exercise, but you must have an internal CD-RW drive and a screwdriver available to complete the steps.

Follow these steps:

1 Turn off your computer, and disconnect the power cord.

2 Remove the computer's cover, and install the internal device according to the manufacturer's instructions.

3 Replace the cover, and reconnect the power cord.

4 Turn on the computer, and log on to Windows XP.

Windows detects and installs the internal device.

Troubleshooting

If Windows XP does not detect the device, it is likely that you need to download updated device drivers from the manufacturer's Web site.

5 Right-click the **Start** button, and then click **Explore**.

6 In the left pane, click **My Computer**.

Windows displays a list of the internal and external storage devices installed on your computer, something like this:

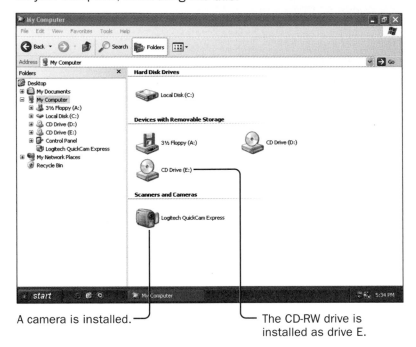

A camera is installed. ⎯⎯⎯

The CD-RW drive is installed as drive E.

Burning Your Own CDs

CD burning

new for
WindowsXP

With CD-Recordable (CD-R) burners and CD-ReWritable (CD-RW) drives now becoming more budget-friendly options, Windows XP provides an easy CD burning feature that enables you to copy (or **burn**) your files, photos, music, and software to a compact disc (CD) without the need for third-party software. Most CDs have a data capacity of approximately 650 MB.

To burn data to your installed CD-RW drive:

1 Insert a blank CD in the CD-RW drive.

2 On the **Start** menu, click **My Computer**.

3 Browse to the folder containing the files you want to copy to CD, and click the **Copy this folder** task.

4 In the **Copy Items** dialog box, click the CD drive, and then click **Copy**.

5 Click the balloon note that tells you files are waiting to be copied.

6 On the **CD Writing Tasks** menu, click **Write these files to CD**.

7 Follow the **CD Writing Wizard's** instructions to complete the process.

Installing a New Software Program

Software programs can be installed from a variety of sources: a CD-ROM, a floppy disk, a file on your computer, over a network, or over the Internet.

Regardless of the sources of the installation files, almost all software programs are installed by running an executable file that is usually called *Setup.exe*. Many software manufacturers use files called autorun files, which are located in the **root** directory of the place from which the program is being installed—usually a CD-ROM. When you insert the CD-ROM into its drive, your computer checks the drive, and if it finds an autorun file, it starts it. The autorun file in turn starts an executable file that either leads you through the setup process or simply starts the program contained on the CD-ROM. Autorun files take the guesswork out of the setup process, because they don't require you to browse to a specific location, find a specific file, run a specific program, or make any sort of decision about which installation action to take.

Troubleshooting

With Windows XP, only a user with **administrative privileges** can install certain programs on your computer. If you do not have administrative privileges for the computer on which you want to install new software, you might find that the installation procedure simply fails. The software setup program might just appear to crash, and you might not suspect that the wrong privileges are the culprit until your third unsuccessful attempt! Check with your network administrator or the person who created your user account if you can't install a program.

Many companies supply free software or software upgrades that can be downloaded or installed from the Web. To install a program from the Internet, click the link that is provided. Depending on the type of installation file, you might be offered two options—to run the installation file from its current location on the Internet or to download the installation file to your own computer and run it **locally**. If you have a high-speed Internet connection through a **DSL** modem or a **cable modem**, it is simplest to run the installation file from the Internet. If your connection is not very fast or is unreliable, it is usually easier to download the file and run it locally.

Depending on the location from which you are installing the program, you might have to enter a unique registration code, called a **product key** or **CD key**, during the setup process:

- If you are installing the program from a CD-ROM, the product key is usually located on a sticker on the back of the CD-ROM jewel case.

- If you work for a company that keeps the most current versions of their licensed software on one or more **servers** rather than distributing it on CD-ROM to their employees, your network administrator will be able to supply the product key.

- If you are installing the program from the Internet, you might not need a product key, but the software supplier might request or require you to register with the company before installing the software. The main purpose of this requirement is to add you to software manufacturers' mailing lists so that they can follow up with marketing materials and other information. The E-mail User Protection Act (HR 1910) requires that companies provide you with a means to remove yourself from mailing lists, and you can generally find a removal link or instructions at the bottom of the e-mail messages you receive from the company if you would prefer not to receive further messages.

Product keys are one of the methods software manufacturers use to try to prevent **software piracy**. A program that requires a product key for installation can't be installed without it. If you lose your product key, you won't be able to install the program in the future, unless you have registered your copy of the software and can successfully appeal to the software manufacturer for a replacement product key.

Many programs offer multiple installation options, such as *default*, *complete*, or *custom*. Some programs that are installed from a CD-ROM offer the option of copying large files to your computer or accessing them from the CD-ROM when needed. You might have the option of waiting to install rarely used program features the first time you need them to save space on your hard disk for the features that you do need. When choosing your installation type, consider the way in which you will use the application, the amount of space required by the application, and how much space is available on your hard disk. Also think about whether the installation source will be available to you later, in case you need to access files that aren't installed to your computer or want to re-install the application. In most cases, the default installation fits the needs of the average user and is the best choice.

When you start the installation process, most programs offer you the opportunity to accept or change the installation location, which by default is usually a product-specific subfolder within the Program Files folder on your drive C. A progress bar might be displayed to keep you informed about what is going on during the installation process, and depending on the program, you might be informed of specific actions and file installations as they occur. When the installation is complete, you might be required to restart your computer; in fact, some large program installations require multiple restarts. Restarting the computer allows the installation program to replace older versions of files that are in use and to clean up after itself.

Tip

You can change a program's settings or remove the program altogether through the **Add or Remove Programs** dialog box, which is available from Control Panel.

In this exercise, you will install and uninstall a program from a folder on your hard drive.

Setup

The program you will install in this exercise is located in the *SBS\WindowsXP \Software* folder. (For details about installing the practice files, see "Using the Book's CD-ROM" at the beginning of this book.) This program will lead you through a tour of a computer-based training product called *eclecticClassroom*.

Follow these steps:

1 Log on to Windows, if you have not already done so.

2 On the **Start** menu, click **My Computer**.

3 Browse to the *SBS\WindowsXP\Adding\Software* folder.

4 Double-click **Setup** (the one with the computer icon).

The installation program starts, and walks you through the process of installing the eclecticClassroom Tour on your computer.

5 Click **Next** on each page to accept all the default installation options.

When the setup program is complete, an icon representing the program appears on your desktop:

Icon for new program

6   Double-click the **eclecticClassroom** icon to start the program.

Close

7   When you have finished exploring the program, click the **Close** button to close the program's window.

8   If you would like to remove the program, on the **Start** menu, click **Control Panel**.

9   In the Control Panel window, click **Add or Remove Programs**.

The Add or Remove Programs window opens, displaying a list of your currently installed programs.

10   Click **eclecticClassroom Tour**.

The eclecticClassroom program listing expands.

11   Click the **Remove** button.

The eclecticClassroom uninstall program starts.

12   Accept the default uninstall options to remove the program from your computer.

When the uninstall process is complete, the icon no longer appears on your desktop.

Installing Windows Components

Windows XP comes with a variety of components that are installed automatically during a typical installation. Others are available but are not installed unless you specifically add them to your system.

The **Windows Components Wizard** walks you through the process of installing, configuring, and removing Windows XP components, which include:

- Accessories, utilities, and games
- Function-specific programs including Fax Services, Indexing Service, Internet Information Services (IIS), Message Queuing, Networking Services, and other network file and print services
- Microsoft Internet Explorer and MSN Explorer
- Management and monitoring tools
- Automatic updating of root certificates

To start the **Windows Components Wizard**, in the Control Panel window, click **Add or Remove Programs**, click **Add/Remove Windows Components**, and follow the directions.

Starting Programs Automatically

If you use certain programs every day, you can easily have Windows start them for you whenever you log on to Windows. For example, some people start their e-mail program first thing in the morning and don't quit it until just before they go home. Other people might work all day in a particular accounting program. You might want to open your company's intranet site each morning to look for updates, or you might want to open your favorite Web site to check your horoscope. Whatever the reason, you shouldn't have to go through a repetitive sequence each day when Windows can do it for you.

Tip

If the program you're starting requires a user account name and password, you will still have to enter that yourself.

To specify that a particular program should start automatically, you place a shortcut to the program in the Startup folder. Each user has his or her own Startup folder, and there is also a Startup folder that applies to all users, so you can choose to make a program start automatically for everyone, or just for you.

You can access the Startup folders through the **Start** menu, or through Windows Explorer. You cannot access another user's individual Startup folder, but you can access the folder that pertains to all of the people who use your computer.

In this exercise, you will specify that a program be started automatically when anyone logs on to your computer. This example uses **Microsoft Paint**, but you can substitute any other program.

There are no practice files for this exercise.

Follow these steps:

1   Log on to Windows, if you have not already done so.

2   On the **Start** menu, point to **All Programs**, right-click **Startup**, and then click **Explore All Users** on the shortcut menu.

Tip

You can click **Explore** to open your own Startup folder, or click **Open** to open the Startup folder with the **Folders** list closed.

Windows Explorer opens to the *C:\Documents and Settings\All Users \Start Menu\Programs\Startup* folder, with the Folders list open:

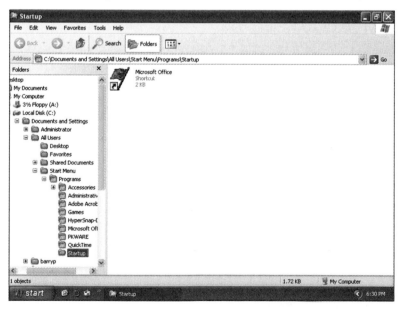

3   In the **Folders** list, click **Accessories** to expand the Accessories folder:

4 Move the left pane's vertical scroll bar until the Startup folder is visible.

5 In the right pane, point to the shortcut to the **Paint** program, hold down the right mouse button, and drag the program to the **Startup** folder in the left pane.

When you release the mouse button, a shortcut menu appears.

Troubleshooting

The shortcut menu appears because you used the secondary mouse button to drag the file, rather than the primary mouse button. If you use the primary mouse button to drag the file, it moves to the folder, and you don't see the shortcut menu.

6 Click **Copy Here** on the shortcut menu.

A copy of the shortcut is created in the Startup folder for all users of your computer to access.

7 In the **Folders** list, click the **Startup** folder to display your new shortcut.

Close

8 Click the **Close** button to close the Startup window.

9 On the **Start** menu, click **Log Off**, and then click **Log Off** in the **Log Off Windows** dialog box. Then log back on again.

After Windows starts up, a new Paint window opens.

10 Click the **Close** button to close Paint.

11 You probably don't want Paint to start every time you open Windows, so repeat step 2 to open the Startup folder, delete the Paint shortcut, and close the folder to return your system to its original condition.

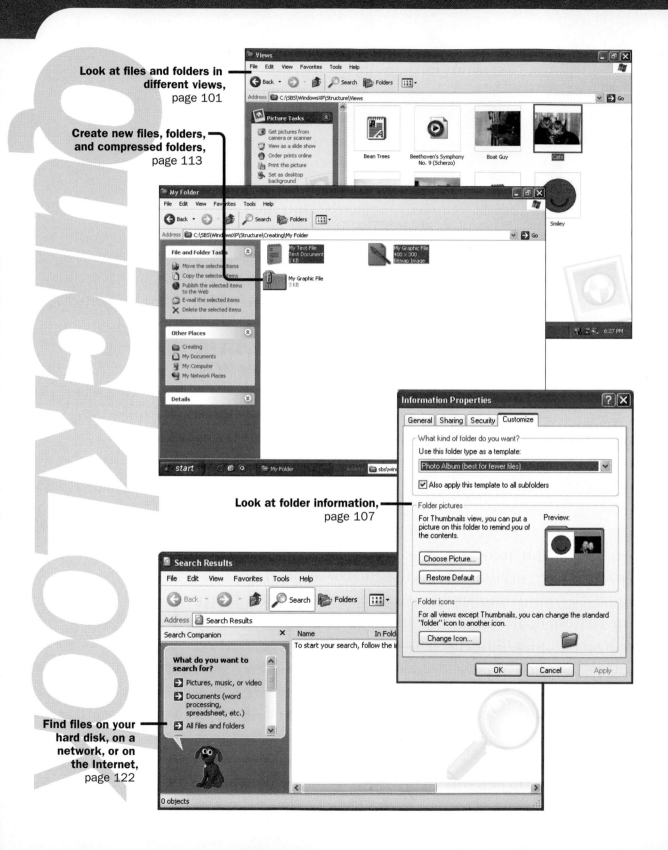

Look at files and folders in different views, page 101

Create new files, folders, and compressed folders, page 113

Look at folder information, page 107

Find files on your hard disk, on a network, or on the Internet, page 122

Chapter 5
Working with Files and Folders

After completing this chapter, you will be able to:

✔ Find your way around your computer.

✔ Look at different views of your files and folders.

✔ Create, edit, delete, move, and rename files and folders.

✔ Find files and folders.

Your computer stores information in the form of files. There are many different types of files. Some are used to run programs, some are created by programs, and some are created by you. The files used or created by programs include **executable files** and **dynamic-link libraries (DLLs)**. These files are sometimes hidden to prevent accidental deletion of important data. The files you create include documents, spreadsheets, graphics, text files, slide shows, audio clips, video clips, and other things that you can open, look at, and change using one of a variety of applications.

Files are organized on your computer in folders. When Microsoft Windows XP is installed on a computer, it creates four **system folders**:

- *Documents and Settings.* This folder contains a subfolder for each **user profile**—each user who has logged on to the computer or who has logged on to a network domain through the computer. Windows XP may create multiple profiles for one person if that person logs on in different ways. For example, you might have one folder for when you are logged on to the domain and another folder for when you are not logged on to the domain.

- *Program Files.* This is the folder where most programs install the files they need in order to run. When you install a new program, you are generally given the opportunity to change the installation folder; if you accept the default, the program is installed in this location.

- *temp.* The operating system and various other programs might store temporary files in this folder.

- *WINDOWS* or *WINNT*. Most of the critical operating system files are stored in this folder. You can look, but unless you really know what you are doing, don't touch!

Within each profile subfolder in the Documents and Settings folder, Windows XP creates three folders:

■ *My Documents*. This folder is a convenient place to store documents, spreadsheets, and other files you want to access quickly.

■ *My Pictures*. This subfolder of My Documents has special capabilities for handling picture files.

■ *My Music*. This subfolder of My Documents has special capabilities for handling music files.

You shouldn't ever need or want to touch the folders used and created by your programs, but knowing how to organize the files you create is essential if you want to be able to use your computer efficiently.

All files have names, and all file names consist of two parts—the name and the extension—separated by a period. The type of file or the program in which it was created is indicated by the extension. The extension is a short (usually three letters, sometimes two or four) abbreviation of the file type. By default, Windows XP hides file extensions. If you would prefer to see your file extensions, open My Documents (or any folder) in Windows Explorer, and on the **Tools** menu, click **Folder Options**, and display the **View** tab. Clear the **Hide extensions for known file types** check box, and then click **OK** to close the dialog box and apply your settings.

Tip

When discussing file types, people often refer to them by their extensions only, as in "I'm going to e-mail you some docs for your review."

Files also have icons, which are graphic representations of the file type. Depending on the way you're looking at your files, you might see a large icon, a small icon, or no icon.

 In this chapter, you will learn how to view and manipulate your files and folders. The practice files for this chapter are located in the *SBS\WindowsXP\Structure* folder. (For details about installing the practice files, see "Using the Book's CD-ROM" at the beginning of this book.)

More About Extensions and Icons

Whether or not you can see extension and icons, every file has one of each assigned to it. Some of the most common file type extensions and icons include the following:

File type	Extension	Icon	File type	Extension	Icon
Bitmap image	.bmp		Dynamic-link library	.dll	
Microsoft Access database	.mdb		Microsoft Excel spreadsheet	.xls	
Microsoft PowerPoint presentation	.ppt		Microsoft Word document	.doc	
Zipped file	.zip		Text file	.txt	
Web file	.htm or .html		Wave sound file	.wav	

Exploring Your Computer

You can use Windows Explorer to view all the files, folders, drives, and peripherals on your computer, as well as those on any computers you are connected to through a network. Windows Explorer now has two views:

- *Folders view* displays the hierarchical structure of files, folders and subfolders, drives, and peripheral storage devices on your computer. It also shows any network drives that have been mapped to drive letters on your computer.

Context-sensitive tasks
new for
WindowsXP

- *Tasks view* displays links to tasks and places that are related to the folder you're currently looking at. The tasks and places are updated automatically based on the contents of the folder.

You can open a specific folder in Windows Explorer by using the **Start** menu options, the Windows Explorer Address Bar, or the Address toolbar on the taskbar.

In this exercise, you will start Windows Explorer in Folders view, explore the files and folders on your computer in different views, and practice navigating between folders.

There are no practice files for this exercise.

Follow these steps:

1   Log on to Windows, if you have not already done so.

2   On the **Start** menu, point to **All Programs**.

The **All Programs** menu expands:

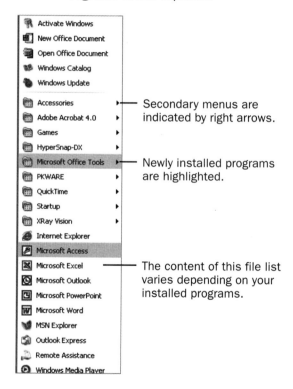

Secondary menus are indicated by right arrows.

Newly installed programs are highlighted.

The content of this file list varies depending on your installed programs.

3 On the **All Programs** menu, point to **Accessories**.

The **Accessories** menu expands:

All the programs on this menu are part of a typical Windows XP installation.

4 On the **Accessories** menu, click **Windows Explorer**.

Tip

You can quickly display Windows Explorer by right-clicking the **Start** button and clicking **Explore**. If you have a ⊞ key on your keyboard, you can hold down this key and press E. You also can create a shortcut to Windows Explorer on your desktop to make it easily accessible. Right-click a blank area of the desktop, point to **New**, and then click **Shortcut**. In the **Type the location of the item** box, type **explorer.exe**, and click **Next**. In the **Type a name for this shortcut** box, type **Explorer** (or accept the default), and click **Finish**. To make the shortcut accessible when open windows obscure the desktop, you can drag the shortcut to the Quick Launch toolbar on the taskbar.

Windows Explorer opens your My Documents folder in Folders view, looking something like this:

The menus on the menu bar group commands in categories.

The toolbar provides buttons for common actions associated with the window's contents.

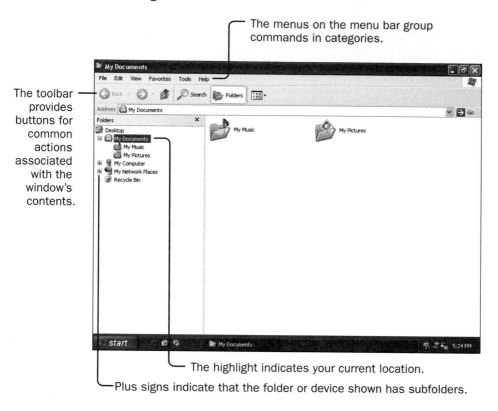

The highlight indicates your current location.

Plus signs indicate that the folder or device shown has subfolders.

Tip

Your specific Windows Explorer display can vary depending on the hierarchical structure of your computer and whether you have explored its contents before. For example, the Address Bar might not be visible in your Windows Explorer window.

Below the title bar, most windows have a **menu bar** with several categories of actions, called **menus**. Each menu lists a number of **commands** that you can carry out on the files and folders displayed in the window. Below the menu bar you see one or more **toolbars** of various types. These toolbars provide **buttons** that enable you to carry out common actions, often with a single mouse click.

Folders view displays the folder structure on the left and the contents of the selected folder on the right. For example, in the screen graphic on the facing page, the My Documents folder is selected on the left and its contents are shown on the right. This is the traditional Windows way of looking at things.

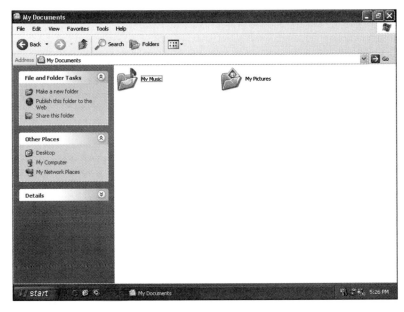

5 On the toolbar, click the **Folders** button.

The Windows Explorer window changes to look like this:

The right pane still displays the contents of the current folder, but the left pane now displays a list of tasks and places that are relevant to the currently selected folder or file. This is the Windows XP way of looking at things.

Tip

Clicking the **Folders** button toggles the Folders pane open and closed. Folders view appears over Tasks view and has a **Close** button. You can close Folders view by clicking this button, revealing the hidden Tasks view. You cannot click a **Close** button to close Tasks view.

6 Click the **Folders** button again to return to Folders view.

7 In the left pane, click **My Computer** to see the list of drives and removable storage devices that your computer contains.

8 Click **Local Disk (C:)** to see the list of folders stored there.

Important

The folders and files stored directly on a drive are said to be stored in that drive's **root directory**. The first time you attempt to display the contents of the root directory, you might see a warning message telling you to click a link to display the files. This is because the root directory often contains system files that should not be modified or moved in any way.

9 If the right pane does not display the contents of the root directory, click **Show the contents of this folder**.

The left pane now displays the folders created by Windows and the SBS folder in which the practice files from this book's CD-ROM are installed, as well as any other folders you have created in the root directory.

Tip

The *SBS* folder will be visible only if you installed the practice files in the default folder. If you did not install the practice files, or if you installed them in an alternate location, you will not see them here.

The right pane displays the contents of the root directory. As you can see here, the subfolders displayed in the right pane are the same as those listed in the left pane:

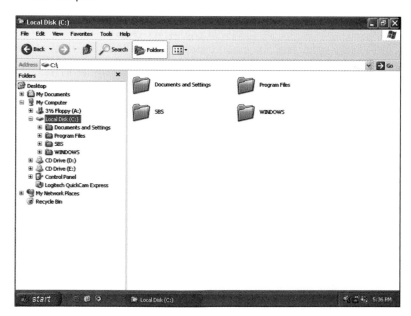

Important

Never delete files from the root directory or any of the system folders created by Windows unless you are absolutely sure you know what you are doing.

10 In the left pane, click **Documents and Settings** to expand the folder.

11 Click **All Users** to expand that folder.

The All Users folder contains four subfolders: *Desktop*, *Favorites*, *Shared Documents*, and *Start Menu*. Files, programs, and shortcuts contained in these folders are available to everyone using this computer.

12 In the left pane, click each of the folders and subfolders in the All Users folder to view the contents of that folder.

13 Click the minus sign next to the All Users folder to contract the folder structure.

14 Click your own user name to expand your user profile.

In Home Edition, click your name, not the *user name.computer name*.

15 In the right pane, double-click the **My Documents** folder.

In Home Edition, click your personalized folder (for example, **Joan's Documents**).

The folder is highlighted in the left pane, and its contents are displayed in the right pane. The folder name appears on the window's taskbar button, and the full path to the folder is displayed in the Address Bar.

Tip

The **path** of a folder or file gives the address where the folder or file is stored on your hard disk. A typical path starts with the drive letter and lists the folders and subfolders you have to go to, separated by backslashes (\), to find the folder or file. If the Address Bar is not visible, you can turn it on by right-clicking the toolbar and clicking **Address Bar** on the shortcut menu. You might then have to right-click the toolbar and click **Unlock the Toolbars** to be able to drag the Address Bar below the toolbar.

16 In the right pane, double-click the **My Pictures** folder.

The folder contains a shortcut to a Sample Pictures folder, whose icon displays previews of up to four pictures in the folder:

In Home Edition, you might not see these pictures.

17 Double-click the **Sample Pictures** folder.

The contents of the folder are displayed:

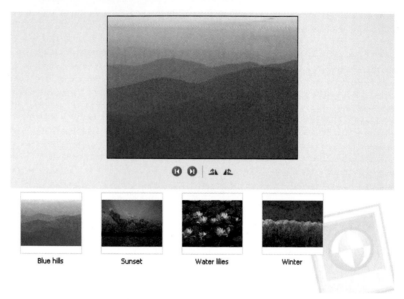

| Blue hills | Sunset | Water lilies | Winter |

When you double-click the shortcut, you link to the folder to which the shortcut points. In this case, the shortcut links to the All Users folder. The Address Bar reflects link's target location.

18 On the toolbar, click the **Back** button.

You return to your last location, your own My Pictures folder.

Forward

19 On the toolbar, click the **Forward** button.

You return to the Sample Pictures folder.

Up

20 On the toolbar, click the **Up** button.

You move up one folder to the *C:\Documents and Settings \All Users.WINDOWS\Documents\My Pictures* folder.

Close

21 Click the **Close** button at the right end of the window's title bar to close the window.

Viewing Files and Folders in Different Ways

New ways of viewing files and pictures

new for WindowsXP

On the right side of the Windows Explorer window, you can view your files and folders in several different ways. You can view thumbnails or slideshows of graphic files, display file and folder types as tiles or icons, or view a detailed or not-so-detailed file list. The view options for each folder are available on that folder window's toolbar, and they vary depending on the contents of the folder. Available views include the following:

- *Details view* displays a list of files or folders and their properties. The properties shown by default for each file or folder are Name, Size, Type, and Date Modified. For pictures, the defaults also include Date Picture Taken and Dimensions. You can display a variety of other properties that might be pertinent to specific types of files, including Date Created, Data Accessed, Attributes, Status, Owner, Author, Title, Subject, Category, Pages, Comments, Copyright, Artist, Album Title, Year, Track Number, Genre, Duration, Bit Rate, Protected, Camera Model, Company, Description, File Version, Product Name, and Product Version.

- *Filmstrip view* displays the currently selected picture at the top of the window above a single row of smaller versions of all the pictures in the current folder. This option is available only for the My Pictures folder and its subfolders.

- *Icons view* displays the icon and file name for each file or folder in the current folder.

- *List view* displays a list of the files and folders in the current folder, with no additional information other than the file name and a small icon representing the file type.

- *Thumbnails view* displays up to four miniature representations of the files contained in each folder. These thumbnails are displayed on top of a folder icon that is about an inch and a half square. Thumbnails of individual files display a miniature of the file if it is an appropriate type (such as a graphic), or an icon representing the type of file. The file or folder name is displayed below the thumbnail.

- *Tiles view* displays a large file type icon or folder icon, the file or folder name, and up to two additional pieces of information for each file in the current folder. The additional information varies depending on the type of file.

In this exercise, you will open a folder in Windows Explorer, navigate to another location using the Address Bar, and then view a group of files in several different ways.

The practice files for this exercise are located in the *SBS\WindowsXP\Structure \Views* folder. (For details about installing the practice files, see "Using the Book's CD-ROM" at the beginning of this book.)

Follow these steps:

1   Log on to Windows, if you have not already done so.

2   On the **Start** menu, click **My Computer**.

The My Computer folder opens in Windows Explorer:

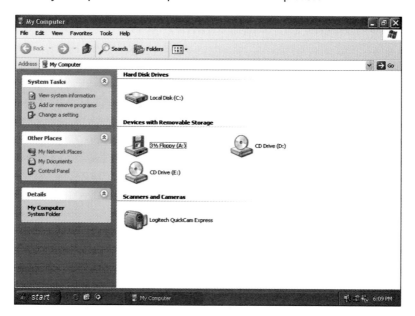

The right pane displays the drives and folders contained in My Computer. The left pane displays a list of tasks and places that are relevant to My Computer.

3   Click in the **Address** box on the Address Bar.

Tip

If the Address Bar is not visible in your current view of Windows Explorer, right-click the toolbar, and click **Address Bar** on the shortcut menu. You might then have to right-click the toolbar and click **Unlock the Toolbars** to be able to drag the Address Bar below the toolbar.

My Computer is highlighted, and anything you type will now replace it.

4   Type **C:\SBS\WindowsXP\Structure\Views**. (If practice files are not stored on drive C, substitute the correct drive letter.)

5 Click the **Go** button.

You move to the specified folder.

6 Click **Cats** to preview this picture:

The left pane links to tasks and places related to this folder.

The current view displays file type-specific tiles for each file, along with the file name and selected file information.

Tip

If you have changed the default folder view, your window might look different from this one.

Views

7 On the toolbar, click the **Views** button.

A drop-down menu displays the view options available for this folder:

The menu indicates that Tiles view is currently selected.

8 On the menu, click **Thumbnails**.

The folder content is displayed in Thumbnails view:

The associated tasks and locations do not change, because you have changed only how you see the folder's content, not the content itself.

9   On the toolbar, click the **Views** button again, and then on the drop-down menu, click **Icons** to switch to Icons view:

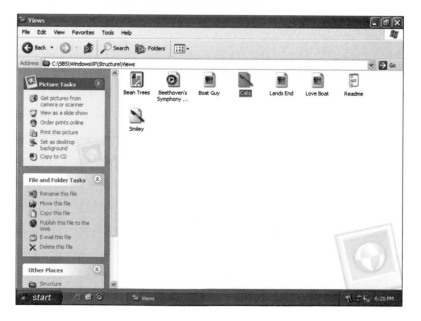

10 On the **Views** drop-down menu, click **List** to switch to List view:

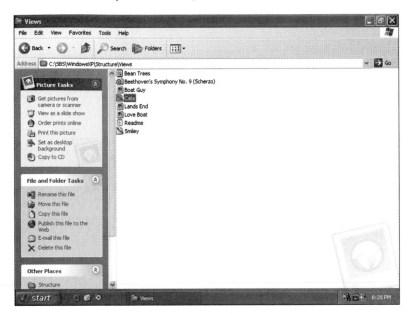

11 On the **Views** drop-down menu, click **Details** to switch to that view:

The up arrow indicates that the files are sorted in ascending alphabetical order by name.

12 Move the pointer over the column headings (Name, Size, Type, and Date Modified).

As the pointer passes over each header, the header changes color to indicate that it is currently selected.

13 Click **Size**.

The eight files are re-sorted in ascending order by file size, as indicated by the up arrow next to Size.

14 Click **Size** again.

The eight files are re-sorted in descending order by file size, and the arrow changes direction to indicate the change of order.

15 Right-click any of the column headings to display this shortcut menu:

The columns currently displayed on the right side of the window are indicated by check marks. *Name* is gray because the file name must be displayed.

16 On the shortcut menu, click **Author**.

A check mark appears next to your selection. When the menu closes, a new column called *Author* is displayed, and the names of the people who created the files are listed, for files that have associated authors.

17 Right-click a column heading, and click **More** on the shortcut menu.

The **Choose Details** dialog box appears:

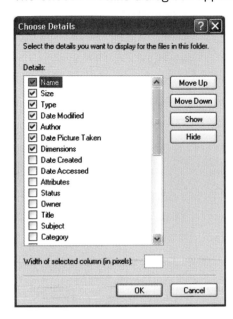

The currently displayed columns appear at the top of the list.

18 Scroll through the list of available columns.

19 Clear the **Author** check box, and click **OK**.

The **Choose Details** dialog box closes.

Close

20 Click the **Close** button to close Windows Explorer.

Looking at File and Folder Information

Each file and folder has a variety of information associated with it, including its name, size, author, and many other items. You can view the information for all the files or subfolders in a folder by looking at the folder contents in Details view. You can look at the information for a specific file or folder by viewing its properties. You can also edit some file and folder properties.

Windows XP has a variety of special folder types. Storing files of the corresponding type in one of these folders enables you to use features that are desirable for that type, such as playing music clips or viewing photographs. Folder types include:

- Documents
- Pictures
- Photo Album
- Music
- Music Artist
- Music Album
- Videos

In this exercise, you will add the Address toolbar to the taskbar, navigate to a directory using the Address toolbar, view the properties of a file, view the properties of the folder, and change the picture shown on the front of the folder.

Smiley

The practice file for this exercise is located in the *SBS\WindowsXP\Structure \Information* folder.

Follow these steps:

1 Log on to Windows, if you have not already done so.

2 Right-click the taskbar. If **Lock the Taskbar** is selected on the shortcut menu, click it to unlock the taskbar.

3 Right-click the taskbar again. On the taskbar shortcut menu, point to **Toolbars**, and then click **Address**.

The Address toolbar is added to the taskbar. It is currently minimized, like this:

The dotted lines and double top border
indicate that the taskbar is unlocked.

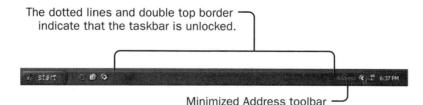

Minimized Address toolbar

4 Position the pointer over the double dotted line to the left of the Address toolbar until the pointer changes to a double-headed arrow. Then drag the line to the left until you can see the entire Address toolbar:

5 Click in the **Address** box, and type **C:\SBS\WindowsXP\Structure \Information**.

6 Click the **Go** button.

You move to the specified folder, which looks like this:

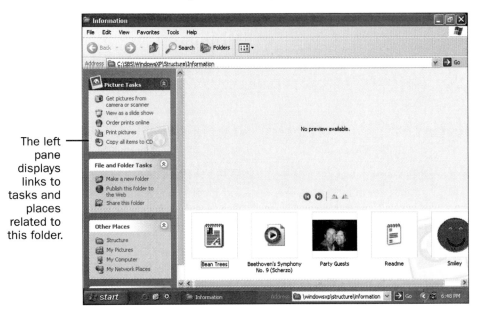

The left pane displays links to tasks and places related to this folder.

The folder opens in Filmstrip view because the folder has been set up as a Photo Album.

Troubleshooting

If your folder does not look like this, click the **Views** button on the toolbar, and click **Filmstrip**.

7 In the filmstrip at the bottom of the right pane, click **Smiley**.

A preview of that file is displayed in the center of the window, as shown on the next page.

109

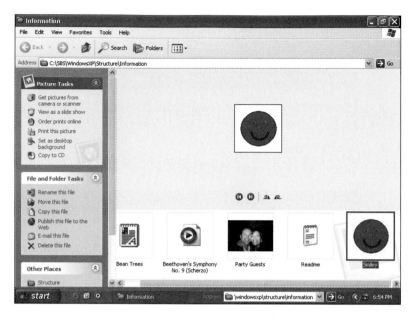

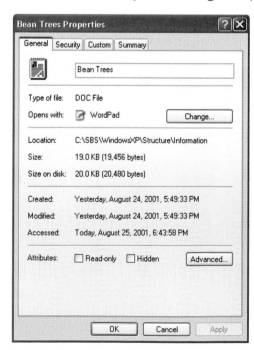
8 Click the **Views** button on the toolbar, and then click **Tiles**.

The contents of the current folder are displayed in Tiles view.

9 Right-click the **Bean Trees** file, and click **Properties** on the shortcut menu.

This **Bean Trees Properties** dialog box appears:

10 Click each tab, and look at the information. Then click **Cancel**.

11 On the **Other Places** menu, click **Structure** to move up one level.

The subfolders of the **Structure** folder are displayed:

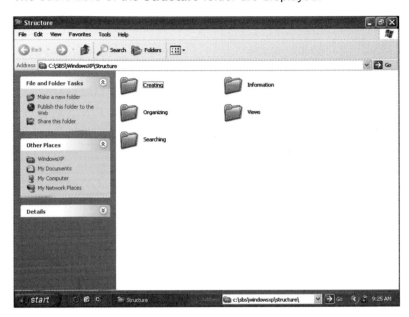

12 On the **Views** menu, click **Thumbnails**.

The contents of the folder are displayed in Thumbnails view:

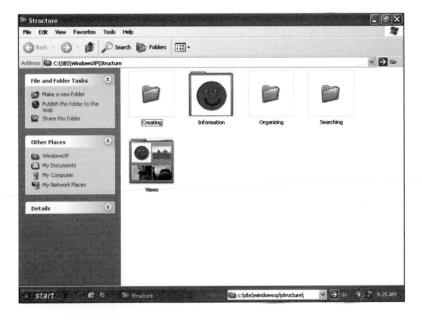

For all the folders that contain graphics, a selection of their graphics is displayed on the folder thumbnails.

13 Right-click the **Information** folder, and then click **Properties** on the shortcut menu.

The **Information Properties** dialog box appears.

14 Look at the information on the **General**, **Sharing**, and **Security** tabs.

In Home Edition, the dialog box does not have a **Security** tab. The information on the tabs is identical to that in a file's **Properties** dialog box.

15 Click the **Customize** tab:

16 Click the down arrow to the right of the **Use this folder type as a template** box to view the list of available folder templates.

The **Photo Album** type is currently selected.

17 Click the down arrow again to contract the list.

18 In the **Folder pictures** section, click **Choose Picture**.

The **Browse** dialog box appears, displaying the graphic files contained in the Information folder.

19 Click **Smiley**, and then click **Open** to close the dialog box and apply your selection.

20 Click **OK** to close the **Information Properties** dialog box and save your changes.

The Preview picture changes to display only the smiling face drawing.

Close

21 Click the **Close** button to close the window.

Creating, Editing, and Deleting Files and Folders

Each application on your computer creates files of a particular type. For example, Microsoft Word creates documents (DOC files), Microsoft Excel creates spreadsheets (XLS files), Microsoft Access creates databases (MDB files), and so on. You can also create and edit simple text documents and graphics using the tools that come with Windows XP.

As you create these files, you will want to create folders in which to organize the files for easy retrieval.

Compressed (zipped) folders

new for **Windows**XP

When you buy a computer these days, it likely comes with a hard disk that will store several **gigabytes (GB)** of information. A gigabyte is 1 billion **bytes**, and a byte is a unit of information that is the equivalent of one character. Some of your files will be very small—1 to 2 **kilobytes (KB)**, or 1000 to 2000 bytes—and others might be quite large—several **megabytes (MB)**, or several million bytes. If you create enough files that you start to get concerned about running out of hard disk space, you might want to **zip** folders. A zipped folder is a folder whose contents are compressed. The folder can contain the files you have created, program files, or even other folders. Compressed content takes up less space and is easier to copy or move from one place to another, especially if you are doing the copying via e-mail. Zipped folders are indicated by a zipper on the folder icon. You can protect a zipped folder with a password.

In this exercise, you will create a new folder and two new files: a text document and a picture. You will then compress your two new files into a zipped folder and delete all the files and folders you created in the exercise.

There are no practice files for this exercise, but you must have installed the practice files from this book's CD-ROM so that you have the *SBS\WindowsXP\Structure \Creating* folder on your hard disk.

Follow these steps:

1 Log on to Windows, if you have not already done so.

2 If the Address toolbar is not open on the taskbar, open it by right-clicking the taskbar, pointing to **Toolbars** on the shortcut menu, and clicking **Address**. Then resize the toolbar by dragging the dotted line to the left.

Important

The taskbar must be unlocked for you to be able to resize the Address toolbar. (If necessary, right-click the taskbar, and click **Lock the Taskbar** on the shortcut menu.)

3 Click in the **Address** box, and type **C:\SBS\WindowsXP\Structure \Creating**.

4 Click the **Go** button.

The window for the specified folder opens in Windows Explorer. The folder is empty.

Views

5 Click the **Views** button, make sure that **Tiles** is selected on the drop-down menu, and then click away from the menu to close it.

6 Read the list of tasks currently available on the **File and Folder Tasks** menu.

Because the folder doesn't contain any files, all three available options are related to folders.

7 On the **File and Folder Tasks** menu, click **Make a new folder**.

A new folder is created with the name *New Folder*. The file name is selected so that you can change it:

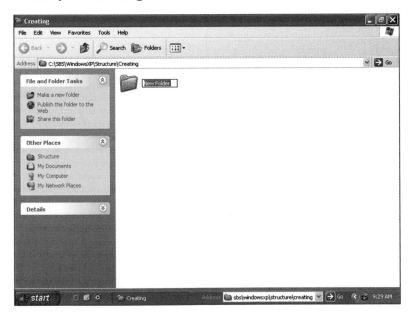

8 Type **My Folder**, and then press ⌷Enter⌷.

9 Double-click your new folder to open it.

10 Right-click the empty right pane, and on the shortcut menu, point to **New**, and then click **Text Document**.

A new text document is created with the name *New Text Document*. The file name is selected so that you can change it.

11 Type **My Text File**, and then press ⌷Enter⌷.

The file is renamed, and the file name, file type, and file size are displayed next to the file's icon. Because the file is empty, the size is 0 KB.

The **File and Folder Tasks** menu changes to reflect the addition of your new file.

12 Double-click the file icon.

The text document opens in the Notepad program, where you can edit it.

Tip

Notepad is a text-editing program that comes with Windows XP.

13 Type **This is a text file that I created in Windows Notepad.**

Close

14 Click the file's **Close** button to close the file, and click **Yes** when you are prompted to save your changes.

The file information changes to reflect a new file size of 1 KB.

Tip

This file doesn't really contain 1000 characters. The file size next to a file is rounded up to the nearest whole kilobyte.

15 Right-click an empty area of the right pane, and on the shortcut menu, point to **New**, and then click **Bitmap Image**.

A new graphic file is created with the name *New Bitmap Image*. The file name is selected so that you can change it.

16 Type **My Graphic File**, and then press ⌷Enter⌷.

The file is renamed, and the file name and file type are displayed next to the file's icon.

17 Right-click the graphic file, and click **Edit** on the shortcut menu.

The file opens in the Microsoft Paint program:

Because it is a new file, the canvas is empty.

Maximize

18 Click the **Maximize** button to make the window fit the screen.

Tip

Paint is a simple graphics program that comes with Windows XP. You can use Paint to create simple **bitmap** images and to edit graphics in the bitmap format. Bitmaps represent images as dots, or **pixels**, on the screen.

19 Experiment with the Paint tools as you paint a picture of any kind. (Click a tool, move the pointer over the blank canvas, and drag the pointer to use the tool.) When you're done, click the Paint window's **Close** button, and click **Yes** when you are prompted to save your changes.

The file information changes to reflect the size of the graphic; in this case, the file is 400 pixels wide x 300 pixels high.

20 Click the text file to select it, hold down the [Ctrl] button, and then click the graphic file to select it as well.

As you select each file or combination of files, the **File and Folder Tasks** menu changes to reflect the currently valid options.

21 Right-click the selection, and on the shortcut menu, point to **Send To**, and then click **Compressed (zipped) Folder**.

22 If you are prompted to associate ZIP files with compressed (zipped) folders, click **Yes**.

A zipped folder named after one of the selected files is created:

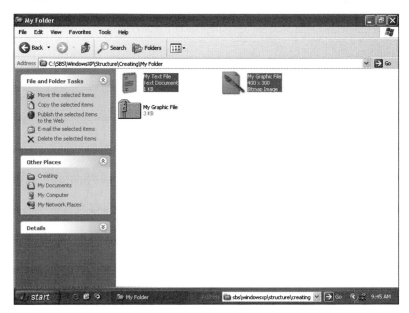

23 Double-click the zipped folder to open it.

You can see your files inside.

Up

24 On the toolbar, click the **Up** button two times to return to the *SBS \WindowsXP\Structure\Creating* folder.

25 Click the **My Folder** folder to select it.

26 On the **File and Folder Tasks** menu, click **Delete this folder**, and click **Yes** when you are prompted to confirm the deletion of the folder and its contents.

Tip

If you want to save your text file or graphic file, skip step 26.

27 Click the window's **Close** button to close it.

Working with Files and Folders on Multiple Computers

If you regularly work on more than one computer, you probably need a simple way of moving files back and forth between computers. You can use **Briefcase** to help avoid the confusion of having different versions of the same file in different places. You can store files in Briefcase, carry Briefcase to another computer, and then carry Briefcase back to your main computer, where Briefcase will synchronize the working version with the originals. To use Briefcase:

1   Right-click the desktop, or right-click an empty area of the right pane in Windows Explorer.

2   On the shortcut menu, point to **New**, and then click **Briefcase**.

A new folder named *New Briefcase* is created.

3   Right-click the briefcase icon, click **Rename** on the shortcut menu, and give the briefcase any name you want.

4   Double-click the briefcase icon to open it in Windows Explorer. (If you see an information window, read the information, and click **Finish**.)

5   Drag your files into the briefcase.

A copy of each file is created inside the briefcase. The copy is linked to the original file, and the location of the original file and its status (whether the files are synchronized) is displayed.

6   Move the briefcase folder to a floppy disk or other portable storage medium, or copy the briefcase folder to your laptop computer over the network or via a direct cable connection.

7   Work on the original files or the files inside the briefcase.

8   After you make changes, insert the disk containing the briefcase into your main computer, or reconnect your laptop computer to your main computer, and click **Update All** on the **Briefcase** menu to bring your files up to date.

Moving and Renaming Files and Folders

When you have accumulated enough files that you need to organize them in some way, you can easily make copies of existing files and folders, move files and folders from one location to another, and rename files and folders. The organization methods of copying, pasting, moving, and renaming are the same for both files and folders.

In this exercise, you will make copies of files and folders using four different methods and then move files between folders using two different methods.

My Graphic File

The practice file for this exercise is located in the *SBS\WindowsXP\Structure \Organizing* folder. (For details about installing the practice files, see "Using the Book's CD-ROM" at the beginning of this book.)

Follow these steps:

1 Log on to Windows, if you have not already done so.

2 If the Address toolbar is not open on the taskbar, open it by right-clicking the taskbar, pointing to **Toolbars**, and then clicking **Address**. Then resize the toolbar by dragging the dotted line to the left.

Important

The taskbar must be unlocked for you to be able to resize the Address toolbar. (If necessary, right-click the taskbar, and click **Lock the Taskbar** on the shortcut menu.)

3 Click in the **Address** box, and type **C:\SBS\WindowsXP\Structure \Organizing**.

Go

4 Click the **Go** button.

The *SBS\WindowsXP\Structure\Organizing* folder opens in Windows Explorer. The folder contains two subfolders named *Folder 1* and *Folder 2*. Folder 1 contains a file called *My Graphic File*. Folder 2 is currently empty.

Views

5 Click the **Views** button, and make sure that **Tiles** is selected.

6 Click **Folder 1** to select it. On the **File and Folder Tasks** menu, click **Copy this folder**.

This **Copy Items** dialog box appears:

7 In the dialog box, browse to the *C:\SBS\WindowsXP\Structure\Organizing* folder, and then click **Copy**.

Windows creates a copy of the folder, called *Copy of Folder 1*.

8 Right-click the new folder, and click **Rename** on the shortcut menu.

The folder name is selected for editing.

9 Type **Folder 3**, and press [Enter].

The folder is renamed.

10 Double-click **Folder 3** to open it.

Folder 3 opens. The folder contains a file called *My Graphic File*.

11 Now you'll create a copy of this file. Right-click the file, and click **Copy** on the shortcut menu.

12 Right-click an empty area of the right pane, and click **Paste** on the shortcut menu.

Windows creates a copy of the file, called *Copy of My Graphic File*.

13 To create a second copy, click the original file to select it, and on the **Edit** menu, click **Copy**. Then on the **Edit** menu, click **Paste**.

Windows creates a copy with the name *Copy (2) of My Graphic File*.

14 To create a third copy, click the original file to select it, and then press [Ctrl]+[C], the keyboard shortcut for the **Copy** command.

Up

15 On the toolbar, click the **Up** button to return to the *C:\SBS\WindowsXP\Structure\Organizing* folder.

16 Double-click **Folder 2** to open it, and press [Ctrl]+[V], the keyboard shortcut for the **Paste** command, to paste the copy in that folder.

Windows creates a copy of the file. Because it is the first copy in this location, it is named *My Graphic File* without a copy number.

Tip

Keyboard shortcuts provide a quick way of carrying out actions from the keyboard instead of using the mouse. If a command has a keyboard shortcut, the shortcut appears next to the command on its menu. For a list of keyboard shortcuts, search the Help file for *Windows keyboard shortcuts overview*.

17 On the toolbar, click the **Back** button two times to return to Folder 3.

18 Click **Copy (2) of My Graphic File** to select it.

19 On the **File and Folder Tasks** menu, click **Move this file**.

The **Move Items** dialog box appears with the *C:\SBS\WindowsXP\Structure\Organizing* folder highlighted:

20 Click **Organizing**, click **Folder 2**, and then click **Move** to move the file to Folder 2.

The file disappears from Folder 3.

21 Click the **Up** button, and then double-click **Folder 2** to open it.

The file is now in this folder.

22 On the toolbar, click the **Folders** button to change to Folders view.

The left pane displays the hierarchical structure of your computer, expanded to show the current folder:

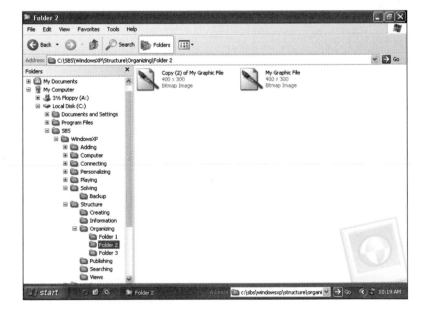

23 Drag **Copy (2) of My Graphic File** from the right pane, and drop it in Folder 1 in the left pane.

The file disappears from Folder 2.

24 In the left pane, click **Folder 1** to open it.

The file is now in this folder.

Close

25 Click the window's **Close** button to close it.

Finding Files

Search Companion

new for
WindowsXP

You can search for all types of objects, including files, printers, and computers, using a feature of Windows XP called **Search Companion**. You can search for files on your own computer, on other computers on your network, or even on the entire Internet. You can search for computers on your organization's network, and you can also search for people on your network or on the Internet.

Search Companion is user-friendly and comes equipped with a guide, in the form of an animated screen character. The default character is Rover the dog, but you can change the character to Merlin the wizard, Courtney the tour guide, or Earl the surfer. If you want, you can remove the character entirely.

Included in Search Companion is **Indexing Service**, which indexes the files on your computer while your computer is idle, improving search speed. (Indexing creates a database of file names and contents so that Search Companion can search the database instead of having to search the files themselves.)

In this exercise, you will search for a text file called *Find this file* on your computer, turn on Indexing Service to speed up future searches, and change the Search Companion animated screen character.

Find this file

The practice file for this exercise is located in the *SBS\WindowsXP\Structure \Searching* folder. (For details about installing the practice files, see "Using the Book's CD-ROM" at the beginning of this book.)

Follow these steps:

1 Log on to Windows, if you have not already done so.

2 On the **Start** menu, click **Search**.

The **Search Results** window opens, with Search Companion displayed on the left side:

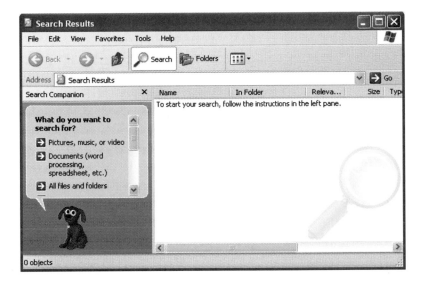

Maximize

3 Click the window's **Maximize** button so that you can see all the options at once.

4 In the list of search options, click **All files and folders**.

Search Companion's next page prompts you to enter identifying characteristics, called **search criteria**, for the file or folder you are searching for:

5 In the **A word or phrase in the file** box, type **Windows XP Step by Step**.

Tip

In searches, the asterisk (*) is a **wildcard** that represents any number of characters (including zero). The question mark (?) is a wildcard that represents one character. For example, enter *.txt* to search for any text file; enter *s*.txt* to search for any text file with a file name that begins with the letter *s*; and enter *s??.txt* to search for any text file that has a three-letter file name beginning with the letter *s*.

6 In the **Look in** box, make sure that **Local Hard Drives** is selected in the drop-down list, and then click **Search**.

Search Companion searches your computer for all files containing the search phrase and displays a list of the files in the right pane. The search might take some time, but entering a specific phrase helps to narrow the results.

When the search is complete, Search Companion's next page asks whether your desired file was found. It should now be easy to spot the file you're looking for, Find This File.

7 In the left pane, click **Yes, but make future searches faster**.

8 On the next page, click **Yes, enable Indexing Service**, and then click **OK**.

There is no apparent change when you turn on Indexing Service, but from that point on, it will run continuously on your computer.

9 Click the Rover character to open this page:

10 Just for fun, click **Do a trick** a few times to see how talented Rover is.

11 When you're done, click **Choose a different animated character**.

12 On the selection page, click **Next** to cycle through the available options, and when you find a character you like, click **OK**.

Rover wanders off, and your selected character takes his place.

Tip

If having Indexing Service turned on seems to slow down your computer, you can turn it off by clicking **Search** on the **Start** menu, then **Change preferences**, then **Without Indexing Service**, and then **No, do not enable Indexing Service**. Then click **OK**.

Close

13 Click the **Close** button in the Search Companion title bar to close the pane.

Accessing Your Entire Network

Windows Explorer gives you access not only to drives and resources on your own computer, but also to drives and resources across your entire network and the Internet through the My Network Places folder.

To browse to another computer or resource on your network, open Windows Explorer in either Tasks view or Folders view, and click **My Network Places**.

If you want to access a particular network drive or resource on a regular basis—for example, if you regularly connect to a specific server—you can **map** the drive in Windows Explorer to make it more easily available. When you map a drive, you assign it a **local** drive letter so you can easily browse to it. You can also instruct Windows to reconnect to that drive every time you log on.

To map a drive in Windows Explorer:

1 Open Windows Explorer in Tasks view or Folders view.

2 On the **Tools** menu, click **Map Network Drive**.

3 Specify the drive letter you would like to use for this drive.

4 Browse to the folder, specify your connection options, and click **Finish**.

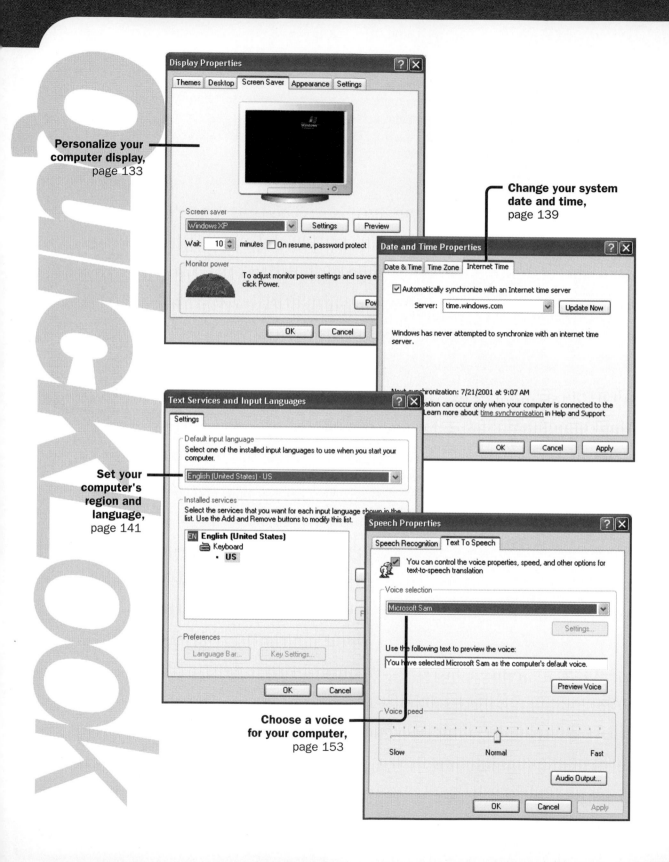

Personalize your computer display, page 133

Change your system date and time, page 139

Set your computer's region and language, page 141

Choose a voice for your computer, page 153

Chapter 6
Personalizing Windows XP

After completing this chapter, you will be able to:

✔ **Change the look of your working environment.**

✔ **Change your system's date, time, regional, and language settings.**

✔ **Make Windows XP easier to see and use.**

✔ **Choose a voice for your computer.**

✔ **Train your computer to recognize your voice.**

The way programs look on your computer screen and the way you use them are determined to a large extent by the Microsoft Windows XP user interface. Some elements of the interface, such as the graphics, fonts, and colors used, are cosmetic. Other aspects, such as how much you can see on the screen, how the computer handles numeric values, and the language it uses, affect the way you work. In this chapter, you will learn how to personalize your computer to fit the way you work.

Until recently, the only way most people could communicate with their computers was by reading, typing, and mouse clicks. With Windows XP, talking to your computer is no longer science fiction. You will learn how to train your computer to recognize your voice and how to select the voice you want the computer to use to talk to you.

For some people, talking to the computer might be a way of working around physical limitations. Many special devices are available to people with disabilities to give them full access to the capabilities of their computers. Microsoft is at the forefront of efforts to make technology more accessible and works closely with other companies and organizations to ensure that its technology fully supports the devices they develop. In this chapter, you will learn about the various options that you have for assisting you to better see, hear, or control your Windows XP computer.

 The practice files for this chapter are located in the *SBS\WindowsXP\Personalizing* folder. (For details about installing the practice files, see "Using the Book's CD-ROM" at the beginning of this book.)

Changing the Look and Feel of Windows

You can easily change the look of the Windows interface by applying a different **theme**. Each theme includes a desktop background color or picture; a color scheme that affects title bars and labels; specific fonts that are used on title bars, labels, and buttons; icons to graphically represent common programs; sounds that are associated with specific actions; and other elements. Previous versions of Windows came with a long list of available themes, and additional themes could be downloaded from the Internet. Windows XP has simplified the theme-selection process by offering only two basic themes—Windows XP and Windows Classic—and making all the other themes available online.

In this exercise, you will switch between the Windows XP and Windows Classic themes. If you want, you can explore the online options on your own at a later time.

There are no practice files for this exercise.

Follow these steps:

1 Log on to Windows, if you have not already done so.

2 On the **Start** menu, click **Control Panel**.

The Control Panel window appears:

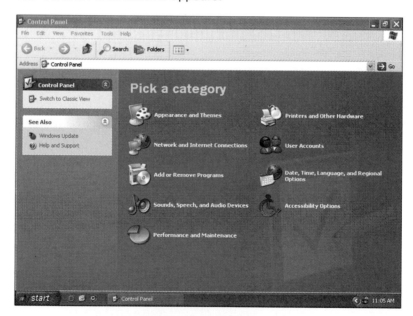

3 Click the **Appearance and Themes** icon.

The Appearance and Themes window opens:

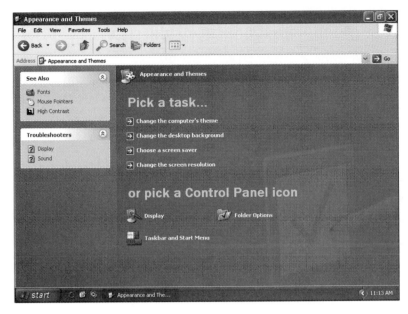

4 Click the **Change the computer's theme** task.

The **Display Properties** dialog box appears, with the **Themes** tab selected.

A preview of the current theme is displayed in the Sample window.

5 Click the down arrow to the right of the **Theme** box, and click **Windows Classic** in the drop-down list.

The Sample window changes to reflect your selection:

6 Click **OK** to close the dialog box and apply your settings.

You are returned to the **Appearance and Themes** dialog box, which now has a white background. The taskbar and **Start** menu have also changed.

Close

⊠

7 Click the window's **Close** button to return to the desktop.

The classic desktop looks quite boring compared to the Windows XP desktop!

8 Repeat steps 2 through 4 to return to the **Themes** tab of the **Display Properties** dialog box.

9 Click the down arrow to the right of the **Themes** box, and click **Windows XP** in the drop-down list.

10 Click **OK** to close the dialog box and return to the Appearance and Themes window, which now has the Windows XP look and feel.

11 Click the **Close** button to close the Appearance and Themes window.

Applying a Custom Desktop Background

The default desktop background for Windows XP Professional is an outdoor scene, with the Windows XP logo and version in the bottom right corner. If this background doesn't appeal to you, you can easily change it. Your choice of background usually reflects your personal taste—what you'd like to see when your program windows are minimized or closed. Some people prefer simple backgrounds that don't interfere with their desktop icons, and others like photos of family members, pets, or favorite places.

Windows XP comes with over 30 desktop backgrounds to choose from. Some of them are photographs; others are geometric patterns. If you prefer, you can opt for a plain background and then set its color. You can also choose a photograph of your own.

In this exercise, you will first switch to a plain, colored background, choose a background photograph, and then return to the default background.

There are no practice files for this exercise.

Follow these steps:

1 Log on to Windows, if you have not already done so.

2 On the **Start** menu, click **Control Panel**.

The Control Panel window appears.

3 Click the **Appearance and Themes** icon.

The Appearance and Themes window opens.

4 Click the **Change the desktop background** task.

The **Display Properties** dialog box appears with the **Desktop** tab selected:

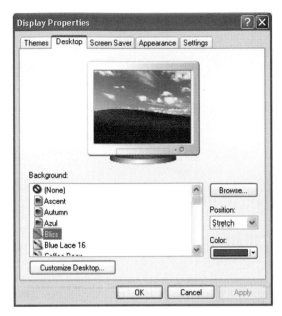

A preview of the current desktop background is displayed at the top of the dialog box.

The **Background** box contains a list of background options.

Tip

You can quickly open the **Display Properties** dialog box by right-clicking an empty area of the desktop and clicking **Properties** on the shortcut menu.

5 Click each of the available backgrounds.

As you select each background, it is displayed on the preview screen at the top of the dialog box.

6 In the **Background** box, click **None**.

The preview screen now displays a plain, colored background.

7 Click the down arrow to the right of the **Color** box, and click the purple square in the drop-down list.

Your choice is reflected on the preview screen.

8 Click **Apply** to apply your background selection.

Minimize

9   Click the Appearance and Themes window's **Minimize** button so that you can see your new background behind the dialog box, like this:

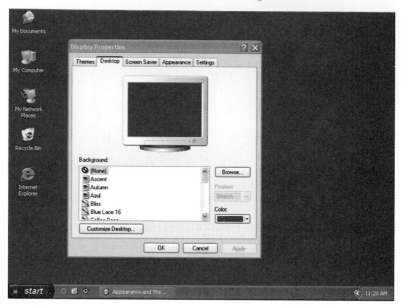

10   In the **Background** box, click **Azul**, and then click **Apply**.

The selected background is visible behind the dialog box, like this:

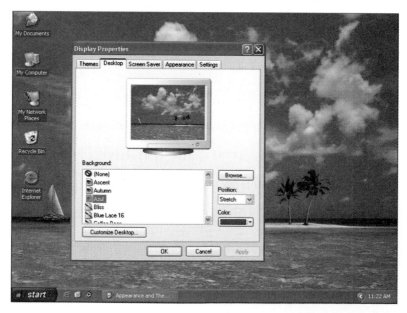

Note that the icon label backgrounds are still purple because icon label colors are determined by the background color setting.

11 Click the down arrow to the right of the **Color** box, click the aqua square in the drop-down list, and then click **Apply** to bring the color of the background photo and icon labels more in line with each other.

12 Click **OK** to close the **Display Properties** dialog box.

13 Now return the desktop to the default state. Right-click a blank area of the desktop, and click **Properties** on the shortcut menu.

14 Click the **Desktop** tab.

15 In the **Background** box, click **Bliss**.

16 Click the down arrow to the right of the **Color** drop-down list, click **Other**, and then click the smoky blue that is in the third square down in the fifth column in the **Basic colors** area.

17 Click **OK** to close the **Color** dialog box.

18 Click **OK** to close the **Display Properties** dialog box.

19 Right-click the **Appearance and Themes** button on the taskbar, and then click **Close** on the shortcut menu to close the window.

Selecting a Screen Saver

Screen savers are static or moving images that are displayed on your computer after some period of inactivity. The original concept behind screen savers was that they prevented your computer's monitor from being permanently "imprinted" with a specific pattern when it was left on for too long without changing. Modern monitors are not as susceptible to this kind of damage, but it is still a good idea to use a screen saver or to have your monitor automatically use power-saver mode after a given period with no activity.

Using a screen saver is an excellent way to protect your computer from prying eyes when you are away from your desk. To further protect your data, you can require that your password be entered to unlock the screen saver after it is set in motion.

In this exercise, you will select a screen saver that consists of a slideshow of photographs.

The practice files for this exercise are located in the *SBS\WindowsXP\Personalizing \ScreenSaver* folder. (For details about installing the practice files, see "Using the Book's CD-ROM" at the beginning of this book.) However, if you have a folder of your own favorite photos on your computer, feel free to use that folder instead.

Follow these steps:

1   Log on to Windows, if you have not already done so.

2   On the **Start** menu, click **Control Panel**.

The Control Panel window appears.

3   Click the **Appearance and Themes** icon.

The Appearance and Themes window opens.

4   Click the **Choose a screen saver** task.

The **Display Properties** dialog box appears with the **Screen Saver** tab selected:

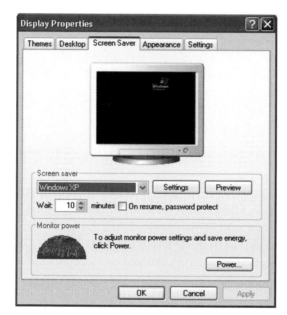

5   Click the down arrow to the right of the **Screen saver** box.

6   In the drop-down list, click **My Pictures Slideshow**.

The preview screen displays a slideshow of the pictures in your My Pictures folder, if there are any pictures there.

7   Click the **Settings** button.

The **My Pictures Screen Saver Options** dialog box appears:

8   Click **Browse**.

The **Browse for Folder** dialog box appears.

9   Browse to the *SBS\WindowsXP\Personalizing\ScreenSaver* folder, and click **OK**.

10   Click **OK** to close the **My Pictures Screen Saver Options** dialog box, and then click **Preview** on the **Screen Saver** tab to see what your slideshow will look like as a screen saver.

Notice the variety of transitional effects used between photos. (Don't move the mouse or the preview will stop.)

11   Move the mouse or press any key on the keyboard to finish previewing the slideshow.

Tip

To use a password to get out of your screen saver in Windows XP Professional, select the **On resume, password protect** check box on the **Screen Saver** tab.

12   Click **OK** to close the dialog box and apply your settings.

Close

13   Click the **Close** button to close the Appearance and Themes window.

14   If you want to turn off the screen saver, repeat steps 2 through 5, click **Windows XP** in the **Screen Saver** drop-down list, click **OK** to close the **Display Properties** dialog box, and then close the Appearance and Themes window.

Changing Specific Interface Elements

In addition to making major changes to your theme and background, you can also make finer adjustments to various parts of your working environment, such as the following:

■ You can choose either Windows XP–style or Windows Classic–style windows and buttons.

■ You can choose from 3 Windows XP color schemes or 22 Windows Classic color schemes.

■ You can choose normal, large, or extra large display fonts.

■ You can stipulate a fade or scroll transition effect for menus and ScreenTips.

■ You can smooth the edges of screen fonts using standard or ClearType technology.

■ You can use large icons.

■ You can show shadows under menus.

■ You can show the contents of a window while you are dragging it.

■ You can hide keyboard shortcuts on menus.

All these options can be set on the **Appearance** tab of the **Display Properties** dialog box.

Changing Your Monitor Settings

When you purchase a computer monitor, one of the things you consider is its size or display area, which is measured like a television screen: diagonally in inches. After the monitor is set up, you are more likely to be concerned about its resolution or **screen area**, which is measured in **pixels** and is expressed as *pixels wide* by *pixels high*.

When personal computers first became popular, most computer monitors were capable of displaying a screen area of only 640 pixels wide by 480 pixels high (known as 640 × 480). Now most computer monitors can also display at 800 × 600 pixels and 1024 × 768 pixels, and some can display a screen area of 1600 × 1200 pixels (or perhaps by the time this book is published, even higher). In effect, as the screen resolution increases, the size of the pixels decreases, and a larger screen area can be shown in the same display area.

Most computer users have a choice of at least two different screen resolutions. Some people prefer to work at 640 × 480 because everything on their screen appears larger; others prefer to fit more information on their screen with a 1024 × 768 display.

Current resolution statistics indicate that approximately 5 percent of Internet users have their screen resolution set to 640 × 480, and approximately 51 percent have a screen resolution of 800 × 600. The fastest-growing segment of the market, approximately 42 percent of Internet users, have a screen resolution of 1024 × 768 or greater.

In this exercise, you will change your screen area to the maximum and minimum sizes supported by your computer.

Troubleshooting

Screen resolution capabilities are partly dependent on your specific monitor. The settings shown or specified in this exercise might not be available on your computer.

There are no practice files for this exercise.

Follow these steps:

1 Log on to Windows, if you have not already done so.

2 On the **Start** menu, click **Control Panel**.

The Control Panel window appears.

3 Click the **Appearance and Themes** icon.

The Appearance and Themes window opens.

4 Click the **Change the screen resolution** task.

The **Display Properties** dialog box appears with the **Settings** tab selected:

5 Point to the marker on the **Screen resolution** slider, hold down the mouse button, and drag the marker all the way to the right to change to the maximum resolution.

The change is reflected on the preview screen.

Tip

As you move the resolution slider to the right, the color quality setting might change. Often the maximum resolution will not support the highest color quality.

6 Click **Apply**.

Your screen resolution changes. The **Monitor Settings** dialog box appears, prompting you to indicate whether you like the change:

You have 15 seconds to make your decision. If you click **Yes**, the resolution is retained; if you click **No** or don't click either button, the resolution returns to its previous setting.

7 Click **Yes**.

The dialog box closes, and your screen is at its maximum resolution:

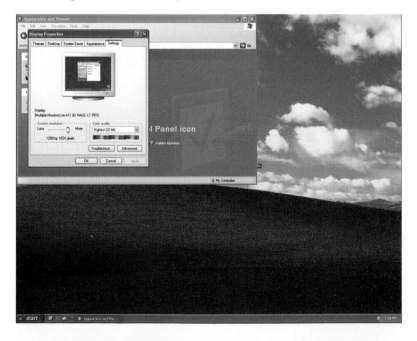

8 In the **Display Properties** dialog box, move the **Screen resolution** slider all the way to the left to change to the minimum resolution.

The change is reflected on the preview screen.

9 Click **OK**, and then if prompted, click **Yes** in the **Monitor Settings** dialog box to complete the change.

10 If necessary, repeat the process to select your favorite screen resolution, and then close the Appearance and Themes window.

Changing Your System's Date and Time

By default, Windows XP displays the **system time** in the notification area at the right end of the taskbar. When you point to the time, the **system date** is displayed as a ScreenTip. The system time controls a number of behind-the-scenes settings and is also used by Windows and your programs to maintain an accurate record of happenings on your computer.

Tip

If you prefer to not display the time, right-click a blank area of the taskbar, click **Properties** on the shortcut menu, and clear the **Show the clock** check box in the **Taskbar and Start Menu Properties** dialog box.

Internet Time
Synchronization
new for
WindowsXP

You can set the system date, system time, and time zone manually, or if your computer is part of a network domain, a **time server** can be used to synchronize your computer clock automatically. If your computer is not part of a network domain, you can synchronize your system time with an Internet-based time server. If you have a continuous Internet connection, you can program your computer to be synchronized automatically once a week.

In this exercise, you will manually reset your system time and then connect to an Internet time server for an automatic update.

Troubleshooting

Many corporate and organizational **firewalls**, and some personal firewalls, prevent your computer from connecting to time-synchronization services. If you have a personal firewall and you cannot access an Internet time server, read your firewall documentation for information about unblocking network time protocol (NTP) or switch to the **Microsoft Internet Connection Firewall**.

There are no practice files for this exercise, but you must have an active Internet connection to complete all the following steps. If your computer is part of a network domain, you will not be able to complete steps 10 through 12.

Follow these steps:

1   Log on to Windows, if you have not already done so.

Your taskbar looks something like this:

Clock

Notification area

The current system time is displayed in the notification area.

2   Position the mouse pointer over the clock.

The current system date is displayed as a ScreenTip.

3   Right-click the notification area, and then click **Adjust Date/Time** on the shortcut menu.

The **Date and Time Properties** dialog box appears:

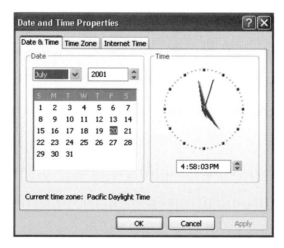

Your current system date is displayed on a calendar on the left. Your current system time is displayed in both analog and digital formats on the right, and both clocks are changing once a second. Your current time zone is displayed at the bottom of the tab.

4   Drag the mouse pointer over the hour setting displayed in the digital clock to select it, and then use the spinner (the up and down arrows) to the right of the clock to change the hour.

The analog clock reflects your change, and both clocks stop advancing.

5   Repeat step 4 for the minutes setting, and for the AM/PM setting.

6   Click **OK** to close the dialog box and update your settings.

The clock on the taskbar changes to reflect your new time setting.

7 Double-click the clock on the taskbar.

The **Date and Time Properties** dialog box appears.

8 Click the **Internet Time** tab, which looks like this:

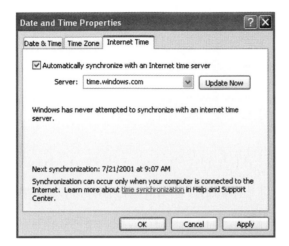

If the contents of the tab are dimmed, the Internet Time Synchronization feature is not currently available.

9 If Internet Time Synchronization is not available, manually reset the time on the **Date & Time** tab, and then skip to step 13.

10 Select the **Automatically synchronize with an Internet time server** check box.

11 Select a server in the drop-down list, and then click **Update Now**.

Your computer connects to the selected time server via the Internet, and updates your system time.

12 Click the **Date & Time** tab to see your updated setting.

13 Click **OK** to close the **Date and Time Properties** dialog box.

The clock once again reflects the current time.

Tip

The Internet time servers currently available in the **Server** drop-down list might not update your system time if the system date is incorrect.

Changing Your Regional and Language Settings

Different countries express numeric values, such as dates, times, currencies, decimals, and so on, in different formats. Your computer was set by its manufacturer to express these values in keeping with the area in which the computer will probably be used. Most people will never need to change these settings. However, if you are located in a country for which the manufacturer's settings are not correct—or if you move, work with international customers, or want to experiment just for fun—you might want to change your regional settings. Windows XP provides number, currency, time, date, and language settings for over 90 regions of the world (including 13 different English-speaking regions).

In this exercise, you will change your regional settings to those of Sweden and then restore them to your original settings.

Tip

If you are already working with Swedish settings, substitute another country in this exercise.

There are no practice files for this exercise.

Follow these steps:

1 Log on to Windows, if you have not already done so.

2 Quit any open programs, and close any open windows.

3 On the **Start** menu, click **Control Panel**.

The Control Panel window opens.

4 Click the **Date, Time, Language, and Regional Options** icon.

The Date, Time, Language, and Regional Options window opens:

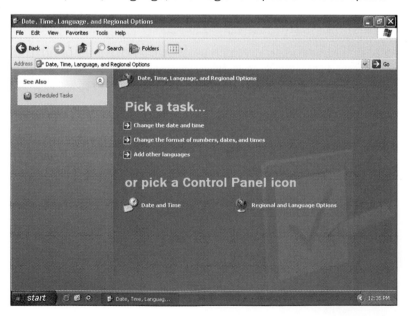

5 Click the **Regional and Language Options** icon.

The **Regional and Language Options** dialog box appears:

6 In the **Standards and formats** area, click the current country to open the drop-down list.

7 Scroll through the list until you find *Swedish*.

8 Click **Swedish**.

The settings in the **Samples** area change to reflect the appropriate number, currency, time, and date expressions for the Swedish language.

9 In the **Location** area, click the current country to open the drop-down list, and click **Sweden**.

10 Click the **Languages** tab.

11 In the **Text services and input languages** area, click **Details**.

This **Text Services and Input Languages** dialog box appears:

If you have additional languages installed on your computer, they are listed in your dialog box.

12 Click **Add**.

The **Add Input Language** dialog box opens.

Important

Make a note of your current **Input language** and **Keyboard layout/IME** settings before changing the input language.

13 Click the down arrow to the right of the **Input language** box, and click **Swedish** in the drop-down list.

The keyboard selection changes to match your language selection.

14 Click the down arrow to the right of the **Keyboard layout/IME** box, and click your original setting in the drop-down list to ensure that your keyboard will still work as expected.

15 Click **OK** to close the dialog box.

Swedish is added to your list of installed services and to the **Default input language** drop-down list. Your original language is still selected as the default, as indicated both in the drop-down list and by the bold font in the **Installed services** box.

Personalizing Windows XP **6**

Note that each language in the **Installed services** box is represented by a specific two-letter combination in a small green square.

16 Click the down arrow to the right of the **Default input language** box, and click **Swedish** in the drop-down list.

Swedish is selected as the default, as indicated both in the drop-down list and by the bold font in the **Installed services** box.

17 In the **Preferences** area, click **Language Bar**.

The **Language Bar Settings** dialog box appears:

18 Review the Language bar settings, and then click **Cancel** to close the dialog box.

19 Click **OK** to close the **Text Services and Input Languages** dialog box, and then click **OK** to close the **Regional and Language Options** dialog box and apply your settings.

The clock in the notification area of the taskbar now displays the time in 24-hour format.

20 Position the mouse pointer over the clock.

The day and date are displayed in Swedish.

The Language bar is displayed at the right end of the taskbar.

21 Return to the **Regional and Language Options** dialog box by clicking the **Regional and Language Options** icon.

22 On the **Regional Options** tab, select your original language and location settings.

23 On the **Languages** tab, click **Details** to open the **Text Services and Input Languages** dialog box.

24 In the **Installed services** box, click **Swedish**, and then click **Remove**.

25 Click **OK** to close the **Text Services and Input Languages** dialog box, and click **OK** to close the message that Swedish won't be removed until your computer restarts.

26 Click **OK** to close the **Regional and Language Options** dialog box, and then close the Date, Time, Language, and Regional Options window.

145

Making Windows XP Easier to See and Use

If you have trouble seeing and using some of the elements of your computer screen, you can adjust many of the features of Windows XP to make those elements clearer or easier to use. For example, you can change the size of the font used in the title bars and menus; make icons larger; change the width of the insertion point and the rate at which it blinks; and make the scroll bars and window borders wider.

Because it can be difficult to undo some of these options after you have set them, this topic will briefly describe the Windows XP accessibility tools without having you actually change anything. These tools are available when you click **Accessibility Options** in Control Panel and are intended to provide a minimum level of functionality for users with special needs. Most users with disabilities will need utility programs with more advanced functionality for daily use.

Windows XP includes these programs to assist people with visual disabilities:

■ The **Accessibility Wizard** leads you through the process of configuring basic accessibility settings.

■ The **Utility Manager** starts, stops, or checks the status of the Accessibility programs. If you have administrator-level access, you can have programs start when Utility Manager starts.

Tip

To start the Utility Manager, press ⊞+U. You can start Accessibility programs before logging on to your computer by pressing ⊞+U at the Welcome to Windows screen.

■ **Microsoft Magnifier** opens a magnification panel in which the screen under the mouse pointer is displayed, magnified up to nine times. You can adjust the size and location of the magnification panel.

■ **Microsoft Narrator** works with Windows setup, the Windows desktop, Control Panel programs, Internet Explorer, **Notepad**, and **WordPad** as a text-to-speech tool. It reads menu commands, dialog box options, and other screen features out loud, telling you what options are available and how to use them. It also reads your keystrokes to you as you type and tells you your location as you move around. You can also choose to have the mouse pointer follow the active item on the screen. Narrator speaks in the voice of a character named *Microsoft Sam*. You have some control over the features of Sam's voice, including speed, volume, and pitch, but Narrator speaks only in English.

■ **SoundSentry** flashes a part of the screen that you specify every time the system's built-in speaker plays a sound.

■ **ShowSounds** instructs programs that usually convey information only by sound to also provide visual information, such as displaying text captions or information icons.

If you think any of these tools will help you see your computer a little more clearly, you can activate them through **Accessibility Options** in Control Panel.

Inputting Text Without Using the Keyboard

The traditional method of entering information into a computer document is by typing it using the keyboard. However, if you have mobility problems, you might find it difficult to use the keyboard to type. Windows XP provides a variety of tools to help, including the following:

■ **On-Screen Keyboard** allows you to select the full range of keys using your mouse or other device. This keyboard can be used to enter text into any application.

■ **StickyKeys** makes it easier to use the keyboard with one hand by making the Ctrl, Shift, and Alt keys "stick" down until you press the next key.

■ **FilterKeys** causes Windows to ignore brief or repeated keystrokes, or slows the repeat rate.

■ **ToggleKeys** sounds a tone when you press the Caps Lock, Num Lock, or Scroll Lock keys. A high-pitched sound plays when the keys are switched on, and a long-pitched sound plays when the keys are switched off.

■ **MouseKeys** allows you to use the numeric keypad to control the mouse pointer.

If you have Microsoft Office XP Handwriting Recognition installed, you have access to other methods of inputting text, including the On Screen Standard Keyboard, an alternative point-and-click keyboard that works only with Office applications; Writing Pad, a handwriting input window where words you write with your mouse or a stylus on a special line are converted to typed words in the current document; Write Anywhere, a handwriting utility you can use to write words across any portion of a document and have them converted to text; and Drawing Pad, a quick way to create a simple drawing and insert it into a Microsoft Office document. Handwriting Recognition can be installed during a custom installation of Office XP. If Office XP was installed on your computer without the handwriting recognition option, you can use the **Add or Remove Programs** dialog box, which is available through Control Panel, to change the Office XP installation options.

Training Your Computer to Recognize Your Voice

Not so long ago, if an executive didn't know how to type or how to type fast enough, he or she could dictate letters and memos to a secretary, who would type them. Similarly, if a student had a broken arm and couldn't take notes in class or write out his or her homework assignment, another student would be assigned to do the writing or take dictation.

Dictation has naturally evolved to trigger the development of speech recognition software. This technology enables you to dictate to your computer in a normal speaking voice and have your information recorded as text. Although as of the date this book was written Windows XP does not come with its own speech recognition software, if you install the **Microsoft Speech Recognition** that comes with Office XP, you can then control this feature from within Windows XP.

Tip

The Microsoft Speech Recognition engine can be installed during a custom installation of Office XP. If Office XP was installed on your computer without the speech recognition option, you can add it from within Microsoft Word 2002 by starting Word, and on the **Tools** menu, clicking **Speech** and then **Yes**.

Each person who uses your computer can create a speech profile so that the Speech Recognition engine recognizes his or her speech pattern accurately. You might also want to create specific speech profiles for different environments. For example, if you are going to talk to your computer both in a relatively noisy work environment and in a relatively quiet home office environment, you would want to create separate profiles to ensure that the ambient noise is handled appropriately. After you've decided which profiles you will need, an easy-to-use wizard guides you through a series of sessions that train the Speech Recognition engine to recognize your particular voice. The accuracy of the Speech Recognition engine increases as you complete more of these training sessions.

Tip

The accuracy of speech recognition is dependent on the quality of your microphone, the way you speak, and the amount of ambient noise. If you are serious about using this technology, invest in a good headset microphone. If you have a fast computer (over 400 MHz), consider using a USB headset.

In this exercise, you will configure the Office XP speech recognition software to recognize your voice, and you will dictate a simple text document.

Buzzy Bee

The practice file for this exercise is located in the *SBS\WindowsXP\Personalizing \SpeechToText* folder. (For details about installing the practice files, see "Using the Book's CD-ROM" at the beginning of this book.) To complete this exercise, you need to have speakers and a microphone, and approximately 45 minutes of uninterrupted time in a reasonably quiet environment. You also need to have Word 2002 installed.

Follow these steps:

1 Log on to Windows, if you have not already done so.

2 On the **Start** menu, click **Control Panel**.

3 In the Control Panel window, click **Sounds, Speech, and Audio Devices**.

4 In the Sounds, Speech, and Audio Devices window, click the **Speech** icon.

The **Speech Properties** dialog box opens, with the **Speech Recognition** tab selected.

Tip

If there is no **Speech Recognition** tab in the **Speech Properties** dialog box, this feature has not been Installed. To install it, open Word 2002, and on the **Tools** menu, click **Speech**, and then click **Yes** to install it. During installation, you will work through the steps in the **Microphone Wizard**, just as you would do here, to add a new profile. If you are installing Speech Recognition now, skip to step 8 after you start the installation process.

5 In the **Recognition Profiles** area, click **New**.

The **Profile Wizard** opens with your logon information shown.

6 Accept the logon information, or type your name and environment in the **Profile** box.

7 Click **Next**.

The **Microphone Wizard** starts:

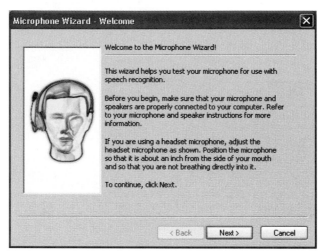

8 Follow the instructions for positioning your microphone, and then click **Next** to move to this **Test Microphone** page:

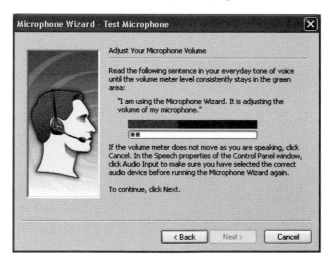

9 Read the sample text aloud in a normal voice.

The volume meter moves in response to your voice; the microphone sensory equipment automatically adjusts to record your voice at the most appropriate level.

10 Click **Next** to move to this **Test Positioning** page:

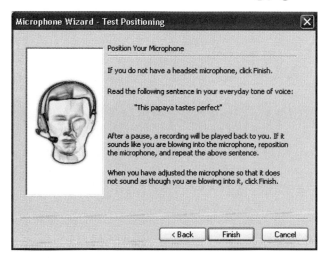

The sample text on this page is designed to test the recording of "spitting" sounds, such as *p*, *s*, and *t*.

11 Read the sample text aloud in a normal voice.

After a short delay, your words are repeated back to you.

12 If the sounds are unclear, adjust the distance of the microphone from your mouth, and repeat the process until you are satisfied with the results.

13 Click **Finish**.

The **Voice Training Wizard** starts.

14 Follow the instructions to complete the vocal exercises.

Remember to speak in a normal tone of voice so that the Speech Recognition Engine can accurately profile your specific speech pattern. This process takes approximately 10 minutes, depending on how fast you speak.

As you work through the training session, you will learn more about the way the Speech Recognition Engine works. As you read the sample text aloud, the **Voice Training Wizard** highlights the words it recognizes. If it doesn't hear the word it is expecting, it stops highlighting and returns to the last recognized pause. You should then stop reading and return to the beginning of the unrecognized text. When you successfully finish reading each page of sample text, the **Voice Training Wizard** moves to the next page.

15 When you finish with the first training session, *Introduction to Microsoft Speech Recognition*, click **Finish** to return to the **Speech Recognition** dialog box.

Your new profile is now selected in the **Recognition Profiles** area.

16 Click **OK** to close the dialog box.

The Language bar opens, making the dictation options available.

17 Click the **Folders** button, browse to the *SBS\WindowsXP\Personalizing \SpeechToText* folder, and open the *Buzzy Bee* document.

18 If the **Dictation** and **Voice Command** options are not visible on the Language bar, click **Microphone** to display them.

The first time you use the microphone from within Office, the **Office Voice Training Wizard** opens and leads you through a voice training session that is similar to the one you have already completed.

19 On the Language bar, click **Dictation**.

The Speech Message changes to reflect first that Dictation is on and then that it is listening to you.

20 Position the insertion point at the end of the Buzzy Bee document.

21 Read the story paragraph aloud, including the punctuation. Say *comma*, *period*, *semicolon*, *quote*, and so on for the punctuation marks. At the end of the paragraph, say *new paragraph*.

As you read, a highlighted series of dots appears, like an expanding ellipsis. As the Speech Recognition Engine completes its deliberations, it translates each dot into a word. Don't expect your first attempt at speech translation to come out perfectly—it generally requires at least three training sessions to come up with something that is intelligible.

22 On the Language bar, click **Tools**, and then click **Training**.

23 Walk through another training session. When you complete the training session, re-read the story paragraph.

When you compare the two computer-generated paragraphs, the results are much closer to the actual words in the second version.

24 Complete one more training session, and then re-read the story paragraph and compare the results to the first two versions.

The computer should be generating something close to the actual text at this point.

You can see that the speech-recognition capabilities increase as you complete additional training sessions. If you are going to use speech recognition, you might choose to complete further sessions at this point, or as time permits, in order to ensure the greatest possible accuracy.

Close

25 Click the document's **Close** button to close the document; save your changes if you want to.

Tip

If you installed speech or handwriting recognition and would like to remove them, you can do so through **Add or Remove Programs** in **Control Panel**.

Choosing a Voice for Your Computer

Software products are available to enable your computer to "read" documents to you. For example, your computer can let you know when you receive a new e-mail message and can read the message so that you don't have to. These products work with the Windows **text-to-speech (TTS)** software, which can "speak" in a variety of voices and languages. Windows XP comes with three voices: LH Michael, LH Michelle, and Microsoft Sam. (LH is for Lernout & Hauspie, the original creator of the voice translation software.) The default voice is Microsoft Sam.

In this exercise, you will switch to a different voice and adjust the speed of the voice.

There are no practice files for this exercise.

Follow these steps:

1 Log on to Windows, if you have not already done so.

2 On the **Start** menu, click **Control Panel**.

3 In the Control Panel window, click **Sounds, Speech, and Audio Devices**.

4 In the Sounds, Speech, and Audio Devices window, click the **Speech** icon.

In the **Speech Properties** dialog box, the **Text To Speech** tab displays these options:

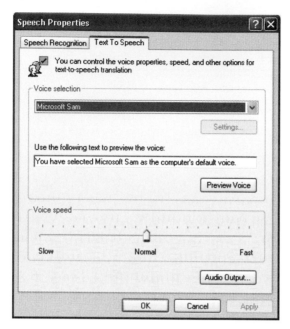

Tip

If you don't have Office XP and Speech Recognition installed, you will not have a **Speech Recognition** tab or additional voices.

5   Click **Preview Voice**.

The text in the preview box is read aloud in the Microsoft Sam voice.

6   In the **Voice selection** drop-down list, click **LH Michelle**.

The text in the preview box changes to reflect your selection, and the computer reads it aloud in the LH Michelle voice.

7   In the **Voice selection** drop-down list, click **LH Michael**.

The text in the preview box changes to reflect your selection, and the computer reads it aloud in the LH Michael voice.

8   Select the text in the preview box, and type **This is Oz, the Great and Terrible. Who are you, and what do you want?**

9   Click **Preview Voice**.

The computer reads your text aloud in the Microsoft Sam voice.

10   Select the voice you prefer to use on your computer.

11 Adjust the voice speed selector to **Fast**, and click **Preview Voice**.

12 Adjust the voice speed selector to **Slow**, and click **Preview Voice**.

13 Adjust the selector, and click **Preview Voice** until you find the speed you like best for this voice.

14 Click **OK** to close the dialog box and save your settings.

Close

15 Click the **Close** button to close the Sounds, Speech, and Audio Devices window.

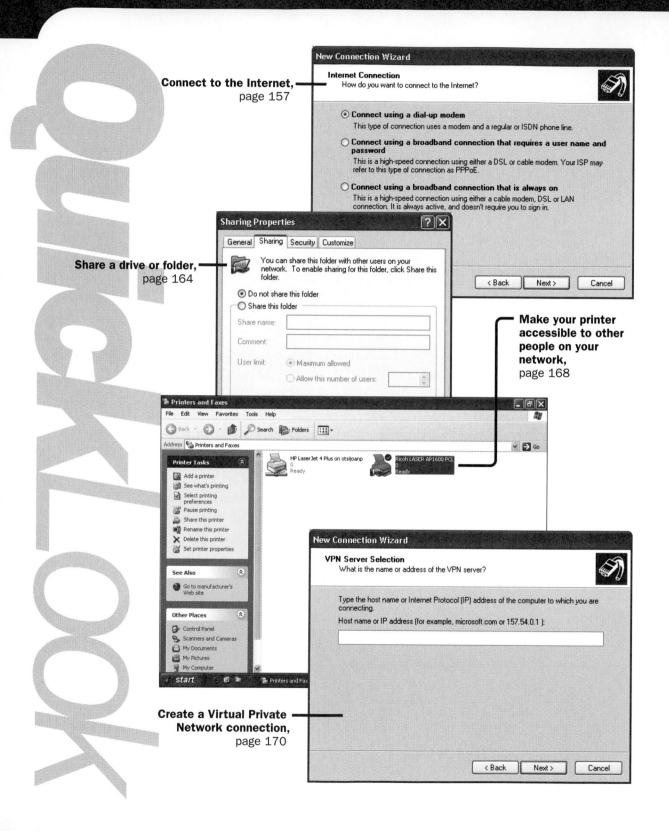

New Connection Wizard

Internet Connection
How do you want to connect to the Internet?

○ **Connect using a dial-up modem**
This type of connection uses a modem and a regular or ISDN phone line.

○ **Connect using a broadband connection that requires a user name and password**
This is a high-speed connection using either a DSL or cable modem. Your ISP may refer to this type of connection as PPPoE.

○ **Connect using a broadband connection that is always on**
This is a high-speed connection using either a cable modem, DSL or LAN connection. It is always active, and doesn't require you to sign in.

< Back   Next >   Cancel

Sharing Properties

General | Sharing | Security | Customize

You can share this folder with other users on your network. To enable sharing for this folder, click Share this folder.

○ Do not share this folder
○ Share this folder

Share name:

Comment:

User limit: ○ Maximum allowed

      ○ Allow this number of users:

Printers and Faxes

File   Edit   View   Favorites   Tools   Help

Back   ·   Search   Folders

Address   Printers and Faxes

Printer Tasks
- Add a printer
- See what's printing
- Select printing preferences
- Pause printing
- Share this printer
- Rename this printer
- Delete this printer
- Set printer properties

HP LaserJet 4 Plus on otsijoanp
0
Ready

Ricoh LASER AP1600 PCL
0
Ready

See Also
- Go to manufacturer's Web site

Other Places
- Control Panel
- Scanners and Cameras
- My Documents
- My Pictures
- My Computer

start   Printers and Fax

New Connection Wizard

VPN Server Selection
What is the name or address of the VPN server?

Type the host name or Internet Protocol (IP) address of the computer to which you are connecting.

Host name or IP address (for example, microsoft.com or 157.54.0.1):

< Back   Next >   Cancel

Chapter 7
Making Connections

After completing this chapter, you will be able to:

✔ Connect to the Internet via a dial-up or broadband connection.

✔ Understand what's needed to create a network of computers.

✔ Share printers, drives, and folders with other people.

✔ Create a Virtual Private Network connection.

Computers can be connected in a variety of ways that enable them to communicate across a room or across the world. Until recently, computer connections, servers, routers and gateways were the domain of techies. But now connecting computers has become easy enough that almost anyone can take advantage of the convenience and efficiency that can result from sharing the resources of one computer with another.

In this chapter, you will learn about three types of computer connections that can enhance your computing capabilities. First you see how to set up a connection between your computer and the Internet. Then you learn a bit about the Microsoft Windows XP tools available to set up a connection between your computer and one or more other computers, and you explore how to share your computer's resources after the network is established. And finally, you see how these two types of connections can be combined to enable you to connect your computer remotely to a network via the Internet.

 The practice files for this chapter are located in the *SBS\WindowsXP\Connecting* folder. (For details about installing the practice files, see "Using the Book's CD-ROM" at the beginning of this book.)

Connecting to the Internet

In the past, many employers thought that giving their employees access to the Internet from their work computers would mean a loss of productivity, as people received and sent personal e-mail messages or indulged in surreptitious surfing of the Web. These days, more and more employers are coming to the conclusion that Internet access can actually enhance the productivity of people in some jobs, and many provide organization-wide access. If you work for such an employer, Internet access has likely been set up for you. If you don't, and you can't persuade your boss that Internet access would be an advantage, you'll have to be content with setting up access on a computer at home. In fact, Internet access is fast becoming one of the primary reasons for buying a home computer, and setting up access is easier than ever with Windows XP.

As an individual, you cannot connect to your computer directly to the Internet; you must access the Internet through a computer or network of computers that acts as a go-between. To connect your computer to this go-between, you might use a **local area network (LAN)**; a high-speed **broadband connection** such as **cable**, **ISDN**, or **DSL**; or a **dial-up connection**. Whichever type of connection you use, the **New Connection Wizard** can help you with the necessary setup work:

- If you are connecting to the Internet via a LAN, you are actually connecting to the computer on a network that has been set up to provide Internet access.

- If you have set up a user account with an **Internet service provider (ISP)** in order to gain access through that company's computers, you can use the **New Connection Wizard** to simplify the connection configuration process.

- If you are connecting via a dial-up connection, you are making a connection from your computer to another computer using two **modems** and an ordinary telephone line. The remote computer usually belongs to the ISP with whom you have set up your user account.

If you are connecting via a dedicated cable or DSL connection—one that doesn't require a user account name or password—you do not need to use the **New Connection Wizard**; no additional configuration should be required.

To create an Internet connection through an ISP, you need to set up a user account. The ISP will then provide the information the wizard will ask for during the connection process, such as:

- The specific **IP address** or the address of the **DHCP server**
- **DNS** addresses and domain names
- **POP3** or **IMAP** settings for incoming e-mail
- **SMTP** settings for outgoing e-mail

In this exercise you will use the **New Connection Wizard** to connect to the Internet via a broadband or dial-up connection.

There are no practice files for this exercise. If you are connecting via a dial-up connection, you must have the name and phone number of your ISP, your user account name, and your password. If you are connecting via a password-protected broadband connection, you must have the name of your ISP, your user account name, and your password.

Follow these steps:

1   Log on to Windows, if you have not already done so.

2   On the **Start** menu, click **Control Panel**, and then click the **Network and Internet Connections** icon.

The Network and Internet Connections window opens:

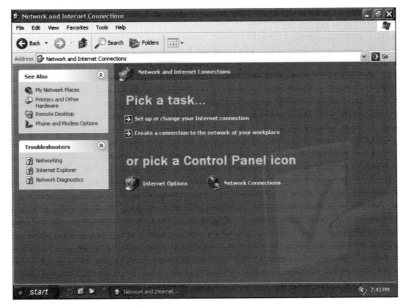

3   Click the **Set up or change your Internet connection** task.

The **Internet Properties** dialog box appears with the **Connections** tab displayed:

4 Click **Setup** to open the **New Connection Wizard**.

Important

The first time you use the **New Connection Wizard**, the **Location Information** dialog box is displayed so that you can enter the local area code and a few other pieces of information that should be common to any connection you create.

5 If the **Location Information** dialog box appears, click **OK**, provide the requested information, and then click **OK** again.

6 Click **Next** to move to the wizard's **Network Connection Type** page:

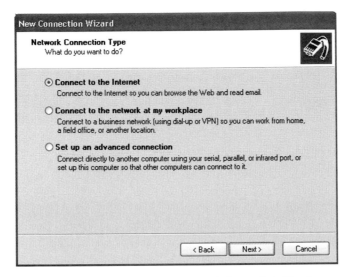

7 Click **Connect to the Internet**, and then click **Next**.

8 On the **Getting Ready** page, click **Set up my connection manually**, and then click **Next** to display the connection options:

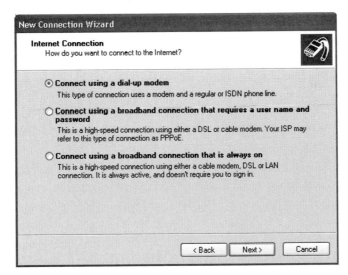

9 If you are connecting using a modem and phone line, select the first option, and click **Next**. You will then be prompted for the name and phone number of your ISP, your user account name, and your password. You must also specify whether to turn on the **Internet Connection Firewall** (a security feature that comes with Windows XP) for this connection and who can use the connection.

Accessing Your Computer Remotely

Remote
Desktop

new for
WindowsXP

If you travel a lot or often work at home, you don't necessarily have to take all your files and folders with you. Instead, you can work, via the Internet, on your own computer using **Remote Desktop**, a new Windows XP feature.

To use Remote Desktop, both the computer you are currently working on and the one you want to access must be running Windows XP. You must have **administrative permissions** on the computer you want to be able to access remotely in order to turn on Remote Desktop.

To set up your computer so that it can be accessed using Remote Desktop:

1   On the **Start** menu, click **Control Panel**.

2   In the Control Panel window, click **Performance and Maintenance**, and then click the **System** icon.

3   In the **System Properties** dialog box, click the **Remote** tab.

4   In the **Remote Desktop** area, select the **Allow users to connect remotely to this computer** check box.

5   When the **Remote Sessions** message box appears, read the message, and then click **OK** to close it.

6   You are automatically authorized as a remote user of your own computer. If you want to authorize additional remote users, click **Select Remote Users**, add users in the **Remote Desktop Users** dialog box, and then click **OK**.

7   Click **OK** to close the **System Properties** dialog box, and then close the Performance and Maintenance window.

To access your computer from another Windows XP computer via Remote Desktop:

1   On the **Start** menu, point to **All Programs**, point to **Accessories**, point to **Communications**, and then click **Remote Desktop Connection**.

2   Click **Options** to expand the dialog box if necessary.

3   Enter the connection information on the **General** tab.

4   Specify the display information on the **Display** tab.

5   Specify any other pertinent information, and then click **Connect**.

To turn off Remote Desktop access on your computer:

1   On the **Start** menu, click **Control Panel**.

2   In the Control Panel window, click **Performance and Maintenance**, and then click the **System** icon.

3 On the **Remote** tab, clear the **Allow users to connect remotely to this computer** check box.

4 Click **OK** to close the **System Properties** dialog box, and then close the Performance and Maintenance window.

For more information, search for *Remote Desktop* in the Help and Support Center.

10 If you are connecting using a password-protected broadband connection, select the second option, and click **Next**. You will then be prompted for the name of your ISP, your user account name, and your password. You must also specify whether to turn on the Internet Connection Firewall for this connection and the name(s) of any other user(s) who has permission to use the connection.

11 If you are connecting using a dedicated, or constant, broadband connection, select the third option, and click **Next**. You will not have to provide any additional information.

12 Click **Finish** to close the wizard and create the connection.

Close

X

13 Click the **Close** button to close the Network and Internet Connections window.

If you created a connection that requires you to sign in to your user account, a shortcut is added to your desktop.

Networking Two or More Computers

If you have two or more computers in your office or at home that are currently stand-alone, you can connect them together to form a simple network. You can then share the resources on one computer, such as an Internet connection, a printer, or a scanner, with any other computer on the network. Networking also makes it easy to share files and folders.

A discussion of how to install the hardware and software necessary to create a network is beyond the scope of this book. If you are interested in this topic, you might want to read *Home Networking with Microsoft Windows XP Step by Step* by Matthew Danda and Heather T. Brown (Microsoft Press, 2001).

After you physically connect the computers using hardware and cables designed for this purpose, you can use the tools that come with Windows XP to easily set up a simple network:

Network Setup Wizard

■ The **Network Setup Wizard** walks you through the process of establishing the necessary software connections between the computers after they are physically connected.

Internet Connection Sharing

■ **Internet Connection Sharing (ICS)** lets all the computers on your network share one Internet connection. After ICS is turned on, you can use programs such as Microsoft Internet Explorer 6 and Microsoft Outlook Express from all the computers on your network as though they were connected directly to the Internet.

Internet Connection Firewall

■ A **firewall** is a security system that acts as a protective barrier between a computer and the outside world. **Internet Connection Firewall** is firewall software that provides a secure information pipeline between your network and the outside world, specifying what information can be communicated from your computer or network to the Internet and from the Internet to your network or computer.

Network Bridge
new for **Windows**XP

■ In the past, special hardware was required to allow communication between segments of a network that used different types of **network adapters**, such as **Ethernet**, home phoneline network adapter (HPNA), wireless, and IEEE 1394. **Network Bridge** connects (bridges) these segments using software. To bridge two or more segments, a single Windows XP computer must contain an adapter card of each type. A single bridge can be used with as many different types of network adapters as the computer is physically able to accommodate.

When these tools are in place, you can take advantage of any resource available on the network, no matter where it might be physically located.

Sharing Drives and Folders

Whether you work on your computer in a work or a home environment, you might need to share documents with other people on your network. Rather than sending copies of documents to everyone who might need them, you can place the documents on a **shared drive** or in a **shared folder**.

You can share folders and drives from within Windows Explorer or from the **Computer Management** administrative tool. When you share a drive or a folder on your computer, you allow other people to access the documents the drive or folder contains whenever they need them (as long as your computer is turned on). The icon of a shared drive or folder has an outstretched hand beneath it.

Tip

You can share the entire contents of your hard drive or the contents of a removable storage device such as a ZIP drive.

When you share a drive or a folder, the default setting allows any other user on the network to have full access to the files it holds. Another user can see the contents of the drive or folder, open files, save changes, create new files on the drive or in the folder, and delete files from the drive or folder. You can limit access so that only selected people or groups of people can work with the contents, and you can limit the types of access that each person or group has.

Tip

Windows XP computers that are not connected to a network domain have a Shared Documents folder that contains the Shared Pictures and Shared Music folders. The contents of these shared folders are available to anyone using the computer, meaning that multiple users of the same computer can share files with each other by placing the files in these folders.

In this exercise, you will share a folder on your computer from within Windows Explorer and give access to the shared folder to a specific group of people.

The practice files for this exercise are located in the *SBS\WindowsXP\Connecting \Sharing* folder. (For details about installing the practice files, see "Using the Book's CD-ROM" at the beginning of this book.)

Follow these steps:

1   Log on to Windows, if you have not already done so.

2   On the **Start** menu, click **My Computer**.

The My Computer folder opens in Windows Explorer:

The drivers and devices displayed here vary depending on your computer's configuration.

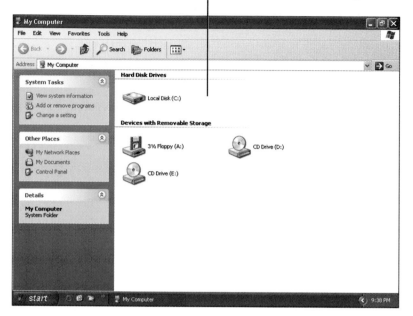

3 Click the down arrow to the right of the **Address** box to display the folder hierarchy in the drop-down list.

Tip

If the Address Bar is not visible in the Windows Explorer window, right-click the tool-bar, and click **Address Bar** on the shortcut menu.

4 Browse to the *C:\SBS\WindowsXP\Connecting\Sharing* folder.

The selected folder opens in Windows Explorer:

5 On the **File and Folder Tasks** menu, click **Share this folder**.

The **Sharing Properties** dialog box appears:

6 Click **Share this folder**.

The dialog box options become available. The default share name is the folder name.

7 Click **Permissions**.

The **Permissions for Sharing** dialog box appears:

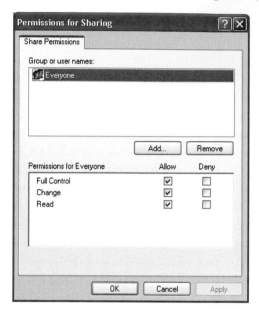

You can add or remove users and change permissions in this dialog box.

8 Click **Cancel** to close the dialog box without making changes.

9 Click **OK** to share the folder.

Up

10 Click the **Up** button to move up one level to the *SBS\WindowsXP\Connecting\Sharing* folder.

The hand below the Sharing folder's icon now indicates that the folder is shared.

Close

11 Click the **Close** button to close the window.

Sharing a Printer

To be able to print from a stand-alone computer, you must have a printer physically connected to one of the computer's ports. When two or more computers are networked, multiple computers can use the same printer.

You can share a printer that is attached to your computer with the entire network or with a select group of people. When you share your printer, you assign it a name.

This name might be based on the manufacturer or model of the printer (such as *HP LaserJet*), some special feature (such as *Color*), or perhaps the physical location of the printer (such as *Front Office*). Regardless, simple names work best because they are more likely to be easily identified by everyone who needs to use the printer.

Tip

Some printers suggest their own printer name during the sharing process. You can either accept the suggested name or replace it with one you choose.

In this exercise, you will share a printer that is attached to your computer.

There are no practice files for this exercise, but you must have a printer attached to and properly installed on your computer. You do not need to be connected to a network in order to complete this exercise, but your shared printer will be available to another computer user only when you are.

Follow these steps:

1 Log on to Windows, if you have not already done so.

2 On the **Start** menu, click **Printers and Faxes**.

The Printers and Faxes window opens:

3 In the right pane, click the printer you want to share.

4 On the **Printer Tasks** menu, click **Share this printer**.

The printer's **Properties** dialog box appears with the **Sharing** tab selected.

5 Click **Share this printer**.

6 In the **Share name** box, type a simple name for the printer.

7 Click **OK** to close the dialog box and turn on sharing for the specified printer.

You return to the Printers and Faxes window, where the printer's icon now indicates that it is shared:

The outstretched hand indicates that this printer is shared.

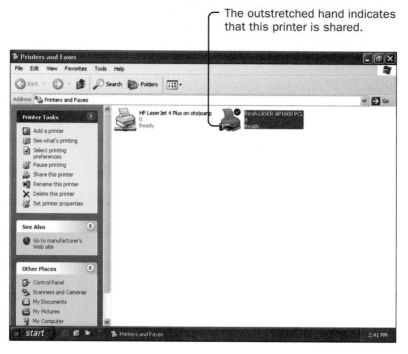

Close

8 Click the **Close** button to close the Printers and Faxes window.

Connecting to a Virtual Private Network

Another type of network connection that is becoming increasingly common in the corporate world is a **Virtual Private Network (VPN)** connection. A VPN connection uses the Internet to access a private (corporate or institutional) network, thus extending the private network so that you are virtually, if not physically, part of it.

If your organization has set up a **remote access server**, you can create a VPN connection to your network over the Internet. Using this connection, you have full use of network resources while you are away from the office, which is extremely useful when you are traveling or working from home.

Naturally, the speed of your VPN connection is limited by the speed of your Internet connection. On one hand, if you are using VPN with a dial-up connection, you might find that you run out of patience while waiting for your computer to access common network resources. On the other hand, VPN with a broadband connection can be nearly as good as being there!

In this exercise, you will create a VPN connection over the Internet.

There are no practice files for this exercise, but you must know the **host name** or **IP address** of your organization's remote access server and your user account name and password for your organization's network.

Troubleshooting

If you do not have access to a remote access server, you can't complete this exercise.

Follow these steps:

1 Log on to Windows, if you have not already done so.

2 On the **Start** menu, click **Control Panel**, and then click **Network and Internet Connections**.

The Network and Internet Connections window opens.

3 Click the **Create a connection to the network at your workplace** task.

The **New Connection Wizard** opens:

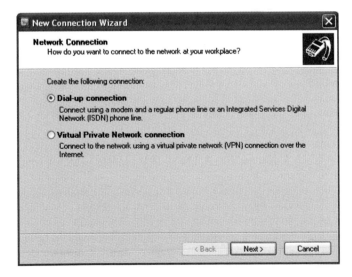

4 On the **Network Connection** page, click **Virtual Private Network connection**, and then click **Next**.

The **Connection Name** page opens:

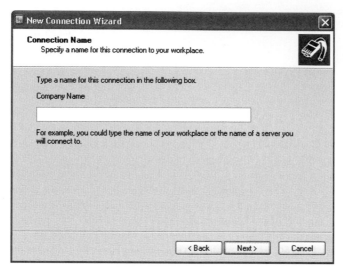

5 Type a name for your connection in the **Company Name** box, and click **Next**.

You will usually name the connection after the organization to which you are connecting.

6 If you don't have a full-time Internet connection, the **Public Network** page opens to give you the option of dialing an existing connection before making the VPN connection:

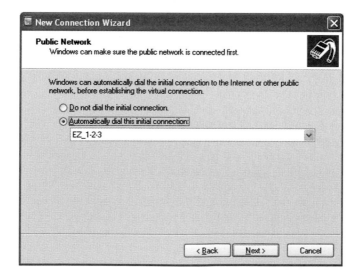

Make your selection, and click **Next**.

Whether or not you have a full-time Internet connection, you now see the **VPN Server Selection** page:

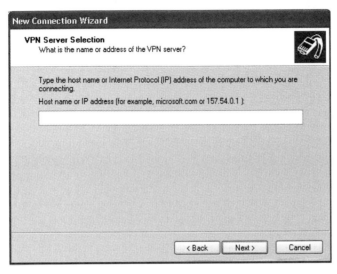

7 Type the remote access server's host name or IP address in the box, and click **Next** to move to the **Connection Availability** page:

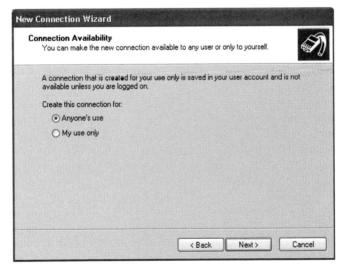

8 Specify whether you want to make the connection available to other users of your computer or keep it to yourself.

9 Click **Next** to move to the wizard's last page:

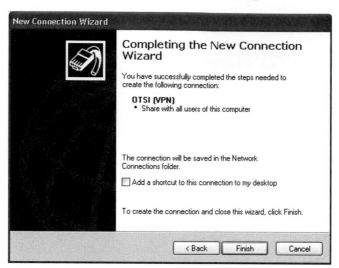

10 Select the **Add a shortcut to this connection to my desktop** check box, and then click **Finish** to create the connection.

Close

11 Click the **Close** button to close the Network and Internet Connections window.

12 On the desktop, double-click the icon for your new connection.

If you have to start your Internet connection, you are prompted to do so now. You are prompted to enter the user account name and password for the connection:

13 Enter your user account name and password for the network to which you are connecting.

14 Select the **Save this user name and password for the following users** check box, and then make sure that the **Me only** option is selected.

15 Click **Connect**.

You connect to the network. The network verifies your user account name and password, and then logs you on.

When you are connected to the network, a network icon appears in the notification area, and you can connect to the same network resources as you could if you were sitting at your desk at work.

16 To close the VPN session, right-click the network icon, and click **Disconnect**.

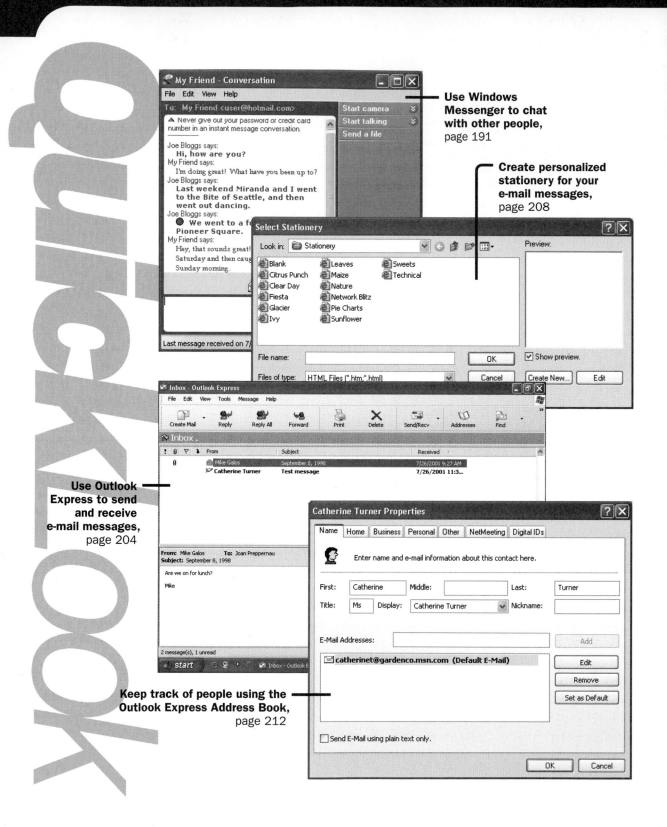

Use Windows Messenger to chat with other people, page 191

Create personalized stationery for your e-mail messages, page 208

Use Outlook Express to send and receive e-mail messages, page 204

Keep track of people using the Outlook Express Address Book, page 212

Chapter 8
Communicating with Other People

After completing this chapter, you will be able to:

✔ **Create a Passport account.**

✔ **Configure and use Windows Messenger for Internet-based instant messaging.**

✔ **Configure and use Outlook Express for server-based e-mail.**

With computer communications, the world has become a much smaller place. Where it once took months for a letter to travel from one side of the world to the other, it can now take minutes for an electronic letter to make the same trip. And with instant messaging, real-time conversations between people who are physically located miles apart are becoming common.

In this chapter, you venture beyond your own computer and communicate with the outside world by using an instant messaging service and an e-mail program.

There are no practice files for this chapter.

Creating a Passport Account

Passport is an Internet-based user account system that provides four main services:

- **Passport** enables you to sign in to a variety of Microsoft and commercial Web sites using a single user account name and password.

- **Passport Wallet** is a secure personal database where you can store Visa, MasterCard, American Express, Discover, Diner's Club, and other account information, as well as **Microsoft Network (MSN)** online gift certificates. You can then use your virtual wallet to provide information for online purchases, rather than typing it each time.

- **Kids Passport** helps you protect and control your children's online privacy by specifying what information your children can share with participating Web sites and what those sites can do with that information. For example, children under 12 years old need a Kids Passport to use Windows Messenger. Kids Passports require the consent of a parent or guardian.

Tip

For more information about Kids Passports, use your Web browser to visit the Web site at *kids.passport.com*.

- ■ **Public Profile** allows you to create a public page of information about yourself.

The concept behind Passport is that you have a single user account name and password that you can use all over the Web, instead of having to set up separate accounts with each Web site that requires one. Your personal information and preferences are stored as part of your Passport, so you don't have to re-enter them each time you visit a site. Because your information is stored on a central server, it is available to you whether you connect to the Internet from your own computer or another one.

If you use the Passport Wallet service, you can store your credit card information in your Passport and use it to make "one-click" purchases with a variety of online retailers. Passport started out as a Microsoft service, but now more and more companies are using it, including 1-800-FLOWERS, Costco, Godiva, Radio Shack, and Victoria's Secret. Sites that use Passport display the Passport logo, which looks like this:

How personal information—especially credit card numbers—is stored and used is a big concern for most online consumers, and Passport has taken strict measures to ensure that the information is secure. Many of the methods that Web sites use to verify your identity do not use advanced security technologies, making it easier for an unauthorized person to access your personal information. Passport, on the other hand, uses powerful Internet security technologies to prevent unauthorized people from accessing your personal sign-in profile. Here's how:

- ■ Even though you can use your Passport on numerous sites, your password is stored only in the secured Passport database. When you sign in, the password you type is shared only with Passport to verify your identity. Your password is never shared with any of the participating Passport sites. This reduces the number of avenues hackers can use to gain access to your personal information.

- ■ When you sign in to Passport, your sign-in name and password are sent over the Internet using a secure connection. This means that only Passport is authorized to access the data sent across the connection.

- ■ After you sign in to a participating Passport site and leave the secure connection, the site keeps track of who you are by using a computer-generated key rather than your Passport sign-in name. Participating sites regularly refresh this key to make it difficult for anyone else to pose as you at these sites.

■ If you or someone else makes several incorrect attempts at guessing your password during sign in, Passport automatically blocks access to your account for a few minutes. This makes it significantly more difficult for password-cracking programs to try out thousands of common passwords using your sign-in name.

■ Each time you log on to your Passport account, Passport stores your session information in a small encrypted text file (called a **cookie**) on your computer. When you log off of your Passport account, the cookie (and all your personal information) is deleted from the computer, which means that you can safely use your Passport account from any computer, even a public or shared computer.

Your personal information—including your e-mail and mailing addresses—is also protected by strict privacy policies, and you're always in control of which sites have access to it.

.NET Passport
Wizard
new for
WindowsXP

So how do you set up a Passport account? If you have a Hotmail or MSN e-mail account, you already have one or both of these e-mail services Passport-enabled. If you don't have one of these accounts, the **.NET Passport Wizard** makes it easy to get one. You can set up a Passport-enabled e-mail address through Hotmail, or you can create a simple Passport account that does not include e-mail.

In this exercise, you will use the .NET Passport Wizard to add a Passport account to your Windows XP user profile. If you don't already have a Passport-enabled account, such as a Hotmail or MSN e-mail account, the wizard will help you create one.

Tip

These steps assume that you use Windows XP in a networked environment. The steps for setting up a Passport account on a stand-alone computer are slightly different. If your computer is not on a network domain, you will be able to follow along with the majority of these steps, and the differences should be self-evident.

There are no practice files for this exercise, but you must have an active Internet connection to complete it.

Follow these steps:

1 Log on to Windows, if you have not already done so.

2 On the **Start** menu, click **Control Panel**.

The Control Panel window opens:

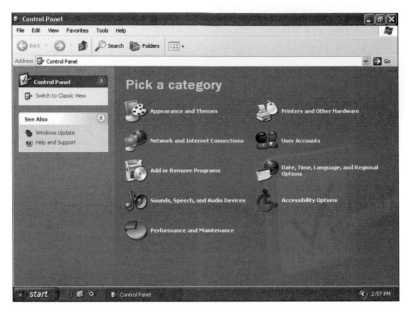

3 Click **User Accounts**.

4 In the **User Accounts** dialog box, click the **Advanced** tab.

5 In the **Passwords and .NET Passports** area, click **.NET Passport Wizard**.

The **.NET Passport Wizard** appears:

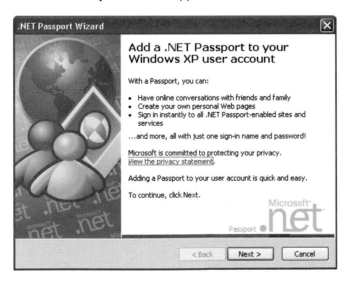

6   Click **Next** to display the wizard's next page:

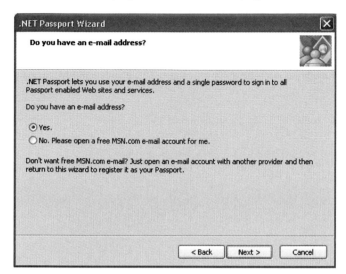

Tip

From this point on, you are working on the Web. Because Web sites can and do change, the dialog boxes you see and the interactions between you and the Web site might differ from those described here.

The wizard prompts you to specify an existing e-mail account or to create a new Hotmail account.

7   If you already have an e-mail account, click **Yes**, click **Next**, and then skip to step 13.

8   If you don't have an existing e-mail account, click **No. Please open a free MSN.com e-mail account for me**, and then click **Next**.

The Hotmail registration page opens.

9   Complete the profile and account information, and then click **Sign Up**.

Tip

If someone else has already selected your requested user name, Hotmail suggests other possibilities based on your first and last names.

Hotmail creates your new user account.

10   Click **Continue at Hotmail**, and take a look at the Hotmail window.

Close

☒

11   When you are ready, click the **Close** button to close your Web browser and return to the **.NET Passport Wizard**.

Important

To maintain an active Hotmail account, you must sign in at least once within the first 10 days and at least once every 60 days thereafter. Using your Passport on any of the Passport-enabled sites counts as signing in.

12 Click **Next**.

13 Enter your Hotmail or e-mail address into the **E-mail address or Passport** box, and then click **Next**.

14 Enter your password into the **Password** box.

15 If you would like to sign in automatically on the computer you are using, select the **Sign me in automatically** check box, and then click **Next**.

Tip

If you regularly use a Passport service such as Windows Messenger, you might want to automatically sign in to your Passport account each time you log on to the computer, rather than signing in manually.

Your Windows XP user account is now configured with your .NET Passport:

16 Click **Finish**.

17 Click **OK** to close the **User Accounts** dialog box.

18 Click the Control Panel window's **Close** button to close it.

Creating Strong Passwords

No computer system is ever completely secure. You can help keep your information secure by using a strong password. Here are some tips for creating strong passwords:

- Use a combination of uppercase and lowercase letters, numbers, symbols, and punctuation marks.

- Don't use single words—merge two or more words or misspell them.

- Don't choose words or numbers that might be easy to guess, such as your birthday, your spouse's name, or your phone number.

- Change your password at least every three months.

Setting Up Windows Messenger

Windows Messenger is an instant messaging program that you can use to **chat** with friends or co-workers via the Internet. You can monitor which of your contacts are online and exchange instant messages with up to four other people within the same message window. You can even send files and photos. Earlier versions of this program were called *MSN Messenger*.

In addition to chatting, with Windows Messenger you can monitor your e-mail account, track stocks, and invite other people to participate in a teleconference or play a game. If you have speakers and a microphone installed, you can place phone calls from your computer to another computer, to a telephone, or to a mobile device without paying long-distance charges.

Instant messaging and e-mail are both good electronic communication methods, and while they are in many ways similar, they have a few significant differences. An instant message can be initiated only when both the sender and receiver are online and logged in to Windows Messenger. Unless you specifically save a Windows Messenger session, the contents of the discussion are gone when you close the discussion window, and they can't be pulled up for later reference.

To use Windows Messenger, you must have already set up a Passport account (or a Kids Passport account for children under 12). MSN Internet Access accounts and Hotmail accounts are already part of the Passport system, so if you have one of these accounts, you can use Windows Messenger.

When you use Windows Messenger, the people you communicate with see your **display name** in their **Contact** list. When you select your display name, keep in mind that the people with whom you exchange instant messages might have lots of names on their **Contact** lists. If your display name does not clearly identify who you are, they might end up talking to the wrong person. For example, a display name of *J* might be for Jan, Jeff, Jim, Joan, or Joe. A display name of *Joan* might be for Joan X or Joan Y. Also keep in mind that all your instant-message buddies will see your display name, so keep it respectable!

Another way to establish a distinct online presence and imbue your online presence with your own personality is to jazz up the appearance of your messages. You can specify the name, size, style, and color of the font in which your messages appear to differentiate them from those of other conversation partners.

You can tailor your Windows Messenger sessions in a variety of ways:

- You can make your contact phone numbers available to other Windows Messenger users.

- By default, Windows Messenger starts automatically when you log on to your computer. (You can disable this feature if you find it distracting.)

- You can specify how long you can be away from your computer before Windows Messenger shows your status as Away. The default is 10 minutes.

- Windows Messenger can display pop-up messages or play sounds to alert you to new chat messages, new e-mail messages, or the arrival of one of your contacts online.

- You can choose who can see your online status and who has permission to send you messages. When another Windows Messenger user adds you to his or her **Contact** list, you receive an instant message the next time you sign on, asking if you would like to allow that person to see your online status. Whenever you're online, you can see a list of the people who have added you to their **Contact** list and either allow them to see you or block them from seeing you.

Protecting Children's Privacy

In November 1998, the U.S. Congress passed the Children's Online Privacy Protection Act (COPPA), which requires that operators of U.S.-based online services or Web sites obtain parental consent prior to the collection, use, disclosure, or display of the personal information of children under the age of 13. COPPA went into effect on April 21, 2000, and is governed by regulations established by the Federal Trade Commission.

More information about COPPA, including parents' pages, kids' pages, and public service announcements, is available at *www.ftc.gov/opa/1999/9910/childfinal.htm*.

In this exercise, you will configure some of your Windows Messenger options.

There are no practice files for this exercise, but you must have an active Internet connection and a Passport account to complete it. The exercise assumes that you have not used Windows Messenger before and that Windows XP is not configured to start Windows Messenger automatically when your computer starts.

Follow these steps:

1   Log on to Windows, if you have not already done so.

2   On the **Start** menu, point to **All Programs**, and then click **Windows Messenger**.

Windows Messenger signs you in:

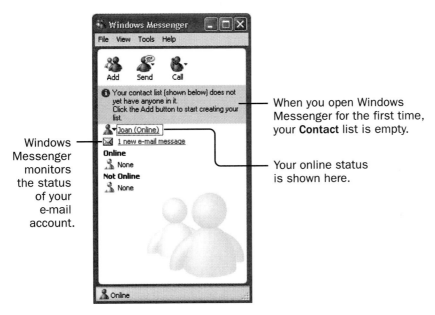

Windows Messenger monitors the status of your e-mail account.

When you open Windows Messenger for the first time, your **Contact** list is empty.

Your online status is shown here.

3   On the **Tools** menu, click **Options**.

The **Options** dialog box appears with your personal information displayed:

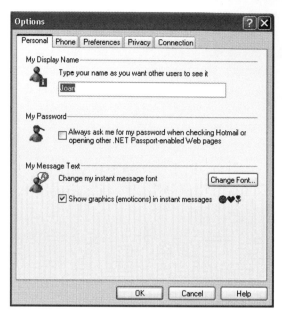

4 In the **My Display Name** area, type the name you want other Windows Messenger users to see when you are online.

5 Click the **Change Font** button to open this **Change My Message Font** dialog box:

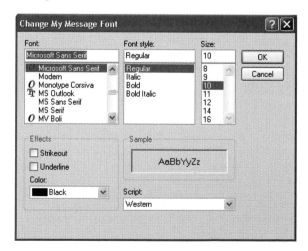

6 Make the following selections:

- In the **Font** box, click **Verdana**.
- In the **Font style** list, click **Bold**.
- In the **Font size** list, click **8**.
- In the **Color** drop-down list, click **Purple**.

The **Sample** box changes to display each of your selections.

7 Click **OK** to close the dialog box and save your changes.

8 Click each of the tabs in turn to examine your other options.

9 When you are done, click **OK** to close the dialog box.

Close

10 Click the **Close** button to close Windows Messenger.

A dialog box appears, telling you that the service will continue to run in the background.

11 Select the **Don't show me this message again** check box, and then click **OK**.

The dialog box closes. The Windows Messenger icon is displayed in the notification area of the taskbar. It remains there as long as you are signed in and changes to reflect your online status.

Windows
Messenger

12 Click the **Windows Messenger** icon, and click **Exit** on the pop-up menu to close the program.

Adding Contacts to Windows Messenger

As long as you know someone's e-mail address or Passport name, you can easily add that person to your **Contact** list. If you don't have a person's contact information but he or she is enrolled in the Hotmail Member Directory, you can look up his or her contact information online as part of the process.

When you add someone's Hotmail, MSN, or Passport account to your **Contact** list, Windows Messenger notifies that person like this:

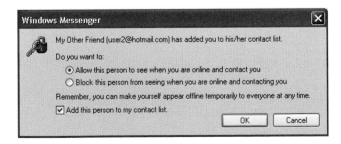

New contacts can allow you to see their status or not, and they can choose whether to add you to their own **Contact** list.

Until new contacts agree to allow you to see them, they are listed as *Not Online*. If they choose to block your access, you won't know it; they simply won't ever be listed as *Online*. After contacts agree to allow you to see them, they appear as either *Online* or *Not Online*, depending on whether or not they are logged on to their account. When you add contacts with non–Passport-enabled accounts (such as regular corporate e-mail addresses) to your **Contact** list, Windows Messenger does not notify the contacts, and they are always displayed as *Not Online*. You can't send instant messages to contacts listed as *Not Online*, but you can send them e-mail messages via your Passport-enabled e-mail account.

The following icons indicate the status of your Windows Messenger contacts:

Icon	Status	Icon	Status
👤	Online	👤	Not Online
👤	Busy	👤	Away

In this exercise, you will add people to your Windows Messenger **Contact** list using their e-mail addresses.

There are no practice files for this exercise. You must have an active Internet connection and have configured Windows Messenger to complete this exercise. In addition, you need to know the address of at least one other person who has a Passport account.

Tip

You can create a Hotmail or Passport account to practice with if you don't have another person's account handy.

Follow these steps:

1   Log on to Windows, if you have not already done so.
2   On the **Start** menu, point to **All Programs**, and then click **Windows Messenger**.
3   If you did not select the automatic logon option, log on now using your Passport account.

Windows Messenger starts, displaying your name, e-mail account status, and **Contact** list:

Add

4   Click the **Add** button.

The **Add a Contact Wizard** appears:

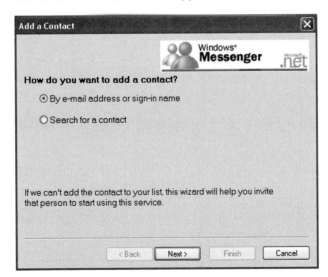

5   Click **By e-mail address or sign-in name**, and click **Next**.

6   On the wizard's second page, type the e-mail address you are practicing with in the box, following the examples shown, and then click **Next**.

When the contact has successfully been added, you see a confirmation message like this one:

Windows Messenger offers to send your new contact an e-mail message (in any of 26 languages) explaining how to install the Windows Messenger software, if he or she doesn't already have it. You can personalize this e-mail message before it is sent.

7   Click **Next**, and then click **Finish** to close the wizard.

The contact is added to your list and shown as *Not Online*. After the contact agrees to allow you access, his or her name moves to the **Online** list:

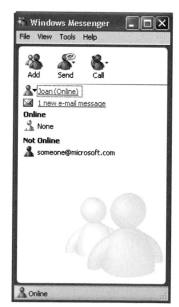

Tip

To delete a contact from your **Contact** list, select the contact's name, and press ⌫.

8   On the **File** menu, click **Close**.

      Windows Messenger is still displayed as an icon in the notification area of the taskbar.

Windows
Messenger

9   Click the **Windows Messenger** icon, and then click **Exit** on the pop-up menu to close the program.

Sending and Receiving Instant Messages

Chatting by sending and receiving instant messages is a great way to exchange information with co-workers and friends without making inconvenient telephone calls or crowding already overflowing Inboxes with e-mail messages. You start the conversation with one person, and you can then add up to two more people after it has started, up to a maximum of four people.

Instant message conversations are held in a conversation window that you can resize by dragging its frame. Unless you explicitly save it, the text in the conversation window is lost when you close the window.

In this exercise, you will send and receive instant messages with one or more online contacts.

There are no practice files for this exercise. You must have an active Internet connection and have configured Windows Messenger with at least two online contacts to complete this exercise.

Follow these steps:

1   Log on to Windows, if you have not already done so.

2   On the **Start** menu, point to **All Programs**, and then click **Windows Messenger**.

3   If you did not select the automatic logon option, log on now using your Passport account.

Windows Messenger starts, displaying your name, e-mail account status, and **Contact** list:

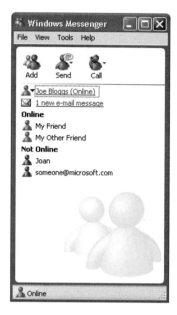

4   Click the **Send** button.

Send

A list of your online contacts appears.

5   Click the name of the contact you want to chat with.

A conversation window opens:

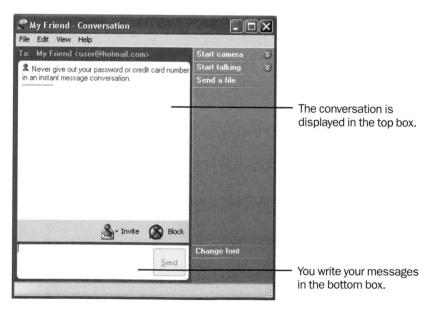

The conversation is displayed in the top box.

You write your messages in the bottom box.

At this point, your contact hasn't received any indication that you are going to send a message.

6   Type a message in the input box, and click **Send**.

The message is displayed in the conversation area. A conversation window opens on your contact's computer so that he or she can reply to you.

Tip

You can customize the color and font of your messages by clicking the **Change Font** button, making your changes, and clicking **OK**.

The status of your conversation is shown in the status bar at the bottom of the conversation window. The status bar tells you when your contact is typing a response. When your contact clicks the **Send** button, his or her response appears in the conversation area on both your screens. You can continue this conversation for as long as you like, and you don't need to receive a response to continue your side of the conversation:

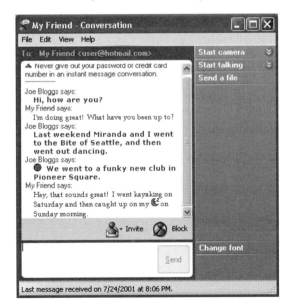

7   To add another contact to your conversation, click the **Invite** button, then click **To Join This Conversation**, and select the contact's name from the drop-down list.

A notification appears in the conversation box that a new person has been added to the conversation. The next time you send a message, a conversation box will open on the new person's computer, and he or she can join in. New participants cannot see any part of the conversation that happened before they joined.

Expressing Emotions Online

One frequent complaint about electronic communications is that emotions and intent are not always clear in typewritten messages—often leading to miscommunication between co-workers and friends. One way to clarify emotions and intent is with **emoticons.** Emoticons are graphic images that are created by typing a series of keyboard characters. These character combinations are used in electronic messages to express a sentiment.

The first emoticons represented emotions (hence the name). Recent technology has enabled the development of another series of emoticons: playful symbols representing people and things that make an amusing (if sometimes unnecessary) addition to electronic communications.

Emotions are represented by these character combinations:

Symbol	Character combination	Symbol	Character combination
●	:-) or :)	●	:-D or :D or :-d or :d or :-> or :>
●	:-O or :o	●	:-P or :p
●	;-) or ;)	●	:-(or :(or :-< or :<
●	:-S or :S or :-s or :s	●	:-| or :|
●	:'(	●	:-@ or :@

People, symbols, and things are created by typing these character combinations in a program that supports emoticons:

Symbol	Character combination	Symbol	Character combination
🐱	(@)	🎧	(^)
⭐	(*)	🎵	(8)
🕺	({)	💃	(})
🦇	:-[or :[	🍺	(B) or (b)
☕	(C) or (c)	🍸	(D) or (d)
✉	(E) or (e)	🌹	(F) or (f)
🎁	(G) or (g)	🐞	(H) or (h)
🐛	(I) or (i)	👄	(K) or (k)
❤	(L) or (l)	👤	(M) or (m)

Symbol	Character combination	Symbol	Character combination
☝	(N) or (n)	📷	(P) or (p)
💤	(S) or (s)	☎	(T) or (t)
💔	(U) or (u)	📢	(W) or (w)
⚡	(X) or (x)	✋	(Y) or (y)
🚶	(Z) or (z)		

If you don't want to type the character combination to produce the emoticons in your instant messages, do either of the following in Windows Messenger:

- On the **Tools** menu, click **Options**, and then on the **Personal** tab of the **Options** dialog box, under **My Message Text**, clear the **Show graphics (emoticons) in instant messages** check box.

- On the **Edit** menu, click **Show Emoticons** to clear the check mark.

Multiple people can chat within the conversation, and anyone can leave at any time. Comings and goings are recorded in the conversation window like this:

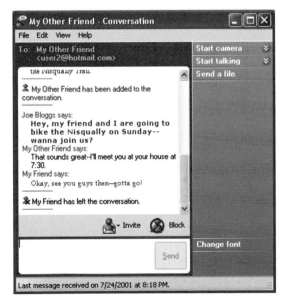

Close

8 When you no longer want to participate in the conversation, click the conversation box's **Close** button to leave the conversation.

9 Click Windows Messenger's **Close** button to close the conversation window.

The program is still running and is represented by its icon in the notification area of the taskbar.

Windows
Messenger

10 Click the **Windows Messenger** icon, and then click **Exit** on the pop-up menu to close the program.

Setting Up Outlook Express

Microsoft Outlook Express is an e-mail program that ships with Windows XP. With Outlook Express, you can quickly and easily connect to your existing e-mail server to send and receive e-mail messages and track your contacts. You can download e-mail from your server and work either **online** or **offline**. If you work offline, you can direct Outlook Express to connect to your server to send and receive e-mail messages at regular intervals. You can also block junk mail senders or other people or companies from whom you do not wish to receive e-mail messages.

Outlook Express includes an **Address Book** in which you can keep track of information about your friends, family members, co-workers, customers, and anyone else you come in contact with. You can track multiple e-mail addresses, home and work contact details, family information, NetMeeting contact information, and even digital IDs. You can also create groups of contacts so that you can send e-mail to multiple people using only one address. You can export your contact list from the Address Book as a Microsoft Exchange Personal Address Book file or as a text-delimited file that can then be imported into Microsoft Excel, Microsoft Access, and a variety of other programs.

Tip

If you have configured Windows Messenger, the Address Book also displays your Messenger contacts and their online status.

You can format your e-mail messages almost any way you like—using backgrounds, fonts, and colors—and you can create a personalized signature to automatically finish off each of your e-mails with a professional touch. You can send electronic business cards (**vCards**) to new contacts to give them all your contact information. If your contact uses Outlook or Outlook Express, he or she can drop your business card into his or her own electronic address book. If your contact information changes, you can send updated vCards to all your contacts.

An in-depth discussion about e-mail technology is beyond the scope of this book, but this topic discusses some of the basic concepts to ensure that you understand how to work with Outlook Express.

Most business people today have e-mail accounts at work. Many people also have separate e-mail accounts that they use for personal e-mail, either through their Internet service provider (ISP) or through a Web-based e-mail program such as Hotmail. With Outlook Express, you can connect to each of your e-mail accounts through the same interface. You can also connect to **newsgroups** and **Internet directory services**, including BigFoot, InfoSpace, Switchboard, VeriSign, WhoWhere, and Yahoo.

E-mail administration is managed through one or more **e-mail servers**—computers that manage your **mailbox** and send, receive, and distribute e-mail messages. E-mail servers operate under specific rules set by the server administrator. These rules govern the size of individual e-mail messages that may be sent and received, as well as the amount of space available for your individual mailbox. Incoming messages are handled by a server running one of three **protocols**: **Hypertext Transfer Protocol (HTTP)**, **Internet Message Access Protocol (IMAP)**, or **Post Office Protocol 3 (POP3)**. Each of these protocols has a different set of rules for handling e-mail messages; your network administrator or ISP will be able to tell you which protocol your server uses. Outgoing messages are handled by a server running **Simple Mail Transfer Protocol (SMTP)**.

Tip

E-mail servers can do their jobs because every mailbox has a unique **e-mail address**. This address has two parts—the **alias** and the **domain**—separated by an *at* symbol (@). For example, the e-mail address *someone@microsoft.com* represents a user named *someone* who has an e-mail account on the *microsoft.com* domain (in other words, they work at Microsoft). Business e-mail aliases generally consist of a person's first and last name or initials. The domain name that follows is also where you'll find that business's Web site—simply replace the alias and the *at* symbol with *www* and a period, and you have the URL. Exceptions are ISP and Web-based e-mail accounts, where the domain name leads to the service provider's home page.

Within your mailbox, your e-mail is stored in a series of folders. The folder structure varies depending on your e-mail program. Outlook Express includes these folders:

- *Inbox.* Your new messages are delivered to this folder.
- *Outbox.* Messages that you have sent, but that have not yet been delivered from your computer to the e-mail server, are held in this folder. If you are working offline, messages are held here until the next time you connect to the server.
- *Sent Items.* After you send a message to someone, a copy of it is stored in this folder. Depending on your e-mail program, you might have to stipulate that you want to save your sent messages.
- *Deleted Items.* Deleted messages are stored here until you purge the folder. This is the Outlook Express equivalent of the Windows Recycle Bin.
- *Drafts.* While you are preparing your message but before it has been sent, a copy of the message is saved periodically in the Drafts folder. If your e-mail program suddenly closes, or if you want to close the message and send it later, you can open the most recent version from this folder.

In addition to these standard folders, you can create your own folders in which you can organize your e-mail messages as you like. For example, you might create a folder for each project you're working on and then move messages to the appropriate folders as they arrive. Folders help to keep your Inbox less cluttered and make it easier to find specific messages later.

When you're using Outlook Express, you can choose whether you want to see all your e-mail folders and whether you want to **synchronize** your Outlook Express folders with the folders on your e-mail server. When you synchronize your folders, Outlook Express compares the folder on your computer to the folder on the server and updates both folders to the current status, downloading new messages to your computer and removing messages that have been deleted from either version.

In this exercise, you will configure Outlook Express to send and receive e-mail messages using your existing e-mail account.

There are no practice files for this exercise. You must have your e-mail account name and password, the name and type of your incoming e-mail server, and the name of your outgoing e-mail server. If you are connecting to your corporate account, you also need an active network connection and your network user name and password.

Follow these steps:

1   Log on to Windows, if you have not already done so.

2   On the **Start** menu, point to **All Programs**, and then click **Outlook Express**.

Outlook Express opens, and then the **Internet Connection Wizard** opens to help you set up an account:

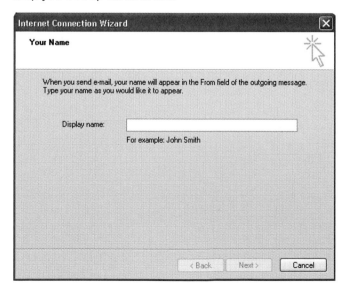

Tip

If you see a message asking whether you want Outlook Express to be your default e-mail client, click **Yes** or **No** according to your preferences.

3 Enter your name as you want it to appear to recipients of e-mail messages from you, and then click **Next** to display the wizard's second page:

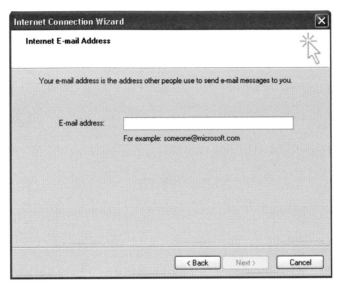

4 Enter the e-mail address you want to display to recipients of your messages, and click **Next** to move to the third page:

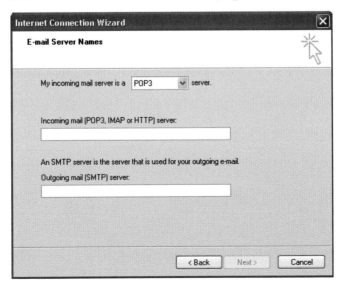

5   Type the names of your incoming and outgoing mail servers in the boxes. Then select the type of server that handles your incoming mail from the drop-down box, and click **Next.**

You move to the **Internet Mail Logon** page, where the wizard prompts you for your e-mail account name and password:

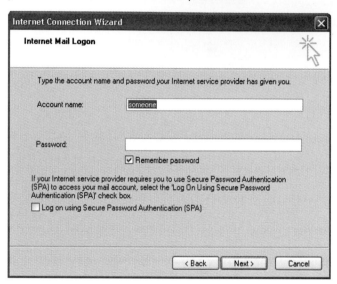

If you clear the **Remember password** check box, Outlook Express will prompt you for your password each time you start the program.

6   Click **Next**, and then click **Finish** to close the wizard.

Troubleshooting

If you are configuring Outlook Express for an IMAP server, you will also need to complete steps 7 through 12. The remaining exercises in this chapter show an IMAP account. If you have a POP3 or HTTP account and have any problems with steps 13 through 21, contact your system administrator or ISP.

7   Outlook Express prompts you to download the list of folders from your mail server. Click **Yes**.

Outlook Express downloads a list of folders and then displays the folders that are available for your account:

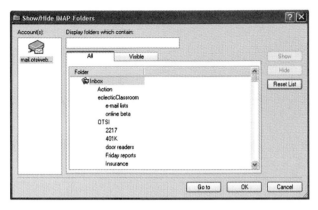

8   Double-click the folders you want to display.

An icon appears next to each folder you double-click to indicate that the contents of the folder will be downloaded.

9   Click **OK** to download the selected folders to your computer.

The account and folders are now displayed in your **Folders** list.

10   Click the account name to display the synchronization options:

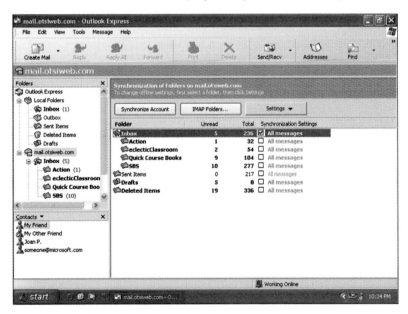

11   Select the check boxes of the folders you would like to synchronize, and then click **Synchronize Account**.

E-mail messages from the selected folders are downloaded to your computer. E-mail messages from folders that you did not select for synchronization will be downloaded the first time you select that folder for viewing.

12 In the **Folders** list, click **Outlook Express**.

Outlook Express now looks something like this:

You will see two sets of folders only if you have an IMAP account.

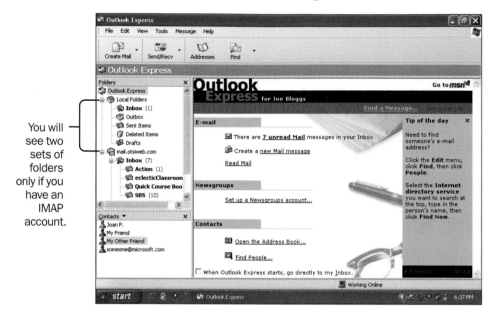

13 In the **Folders** list, click **Inbox** to open your local Inbox.

14 On the **View** menu, click **Layout**.

The **Window Layout Properties** dialog box appears:

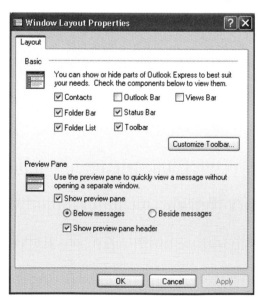

15 To maximize your working area, clear the **Contacts** and **Folder List** check boxes.

16 Make sure that the **Preview Pane** options are selected as shown, and then click **OK**.

Your Inbox now looks something like this:

17 In the preview pane, use the scroll bar to scroll through the contents of the welcome message.

18 In the Inbox, double-click the message to open it in its own window.

Initially, the message opens in a small window:

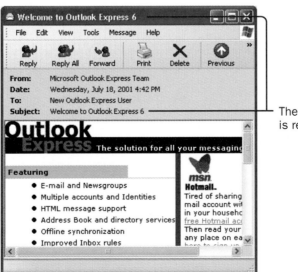

The subject of the message is repeated in the title bar.

Connecting to Newsgroups Through Outlook Express

Newsgroups are moderated or unmoderated "message boards" on which people communicate about a specific subject. You can find a newsgroup for just about any topic you can think of, from Windows XP to American Eskimo dogs and from maternity to medical treatments. If people are talking about it, there are probably people talking about it in a newsgroup.

You can add newsgroups to Outlook Express in the same way that you add e-mail accounts: Simply click the **News** tab instead of the **Mail** tab, and follow the simple instructions.

A variety of newsgroups are available for Windows XP. To see a current list of newsgroups, visit *www.microsoft.com/windowsxp/expertzone/newsgroups/*. For step-by-step instructions on configuring Outlook Express for a newsgroup, click **Windows XP Newsgroup Setup Instructions** on that site.

Maximize

19 Click the message's **Maximize** button.

The message expands to fill the screen.

Close

20 Click the message's **Close** button to close the message.

21 Click the window's **Close** button to close Outlook Express.

Sending and Receiving E-mail Messages

Although an in-depth tutorial on Outlook Express is beyond the scope of this book, it is certainly worth investigating the main capabilities of the program on your own. With Outlook Express, you can send and receive professional-looking e-mail messages with most of the features that are available in larger programs such as Microsoft Outlook. For example, you can use **stationery**, customize fonts, create personal **signatures**, request **read receipts**, and check the spelling of your messages. You can send fancy messages in **Hypertext Markup Language (HTML)** or simple messages in plain-text format. You can also send and receive files that are sent with messages as **attachments**.

Tip

With an IMAP account, until you select a message you have received, Outlook Express downloads only the message **header**. As a result, you can't see whether an e-mail message has an attachment until you select that e-mail message for viewing.

Each e-mail message that is displayed in Outlook Express is represented by an icon indicating the type of message and its priority and status. The most common icons include:

Category	Icon	Represents	Icon	Represents
Unread messages		Standard unopened message		Digitally signed
		Encrypted		Digitally signed and encrypted
Read messages		Standard opened message		Replied to
		Digitally signed		Forwarded
		Encrypted		Digitally signed and encrypted
Extra designations		Attachment		High priority
		Flagged for further action		Low priority

A complete list of icons is available in the Outlook Express Help file.

In this exercise, you will send, receive, reply to, and delete e-mail messages.

There are no practice files for this exercise. You must have an active network or Internet connection and Outlook Express must be set up on your computer as the default e-mail program.

Follow these steps:

1 Log on to Windows, if you have not already done so.

2 On the **Start** menu, click **E-mail**.

Tip

If Outlook Express is not the default e-mail program, you must click **Start**, point to **All Programs**, and click **Outlook Express**.

Outlook Express opens, looking something like this:

Folder bar

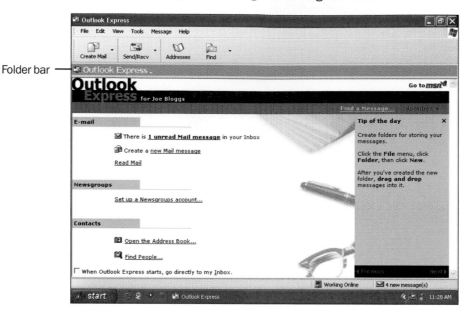

3 Click **Outlook Express** on the Folder bar to display a list of available folders:

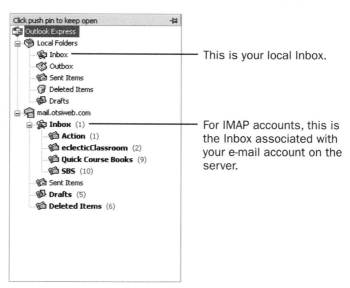

This is your local Inbox.

For IMAP accounts, this is the Inbox associated with your e-mail account on the server.

4 Click the **Inbox** folder for your e-mail account.

The **Folder List** closes.

5 On the toolbar, click **Create Mail**.

A New Message form opens with a blank background.

6 In the **To** box, type your own e-mail address (the one you used to configure this account).

7 In the **Subject** box, type **Test message**.

As you type, the text of the subject line is repeated in the title bar.

8 In the body of the message, type **This is a test of sending a new e-mail message**.

Your message is displayed in the font that is selected and shown above the body of the message, which is the default for all messages.

9 On the message form's toolbar, click **Send**.

Outlook Express sends the new message and then receives it in your Inbox:

Messages displayed in bold haven't been read yet. ⌐

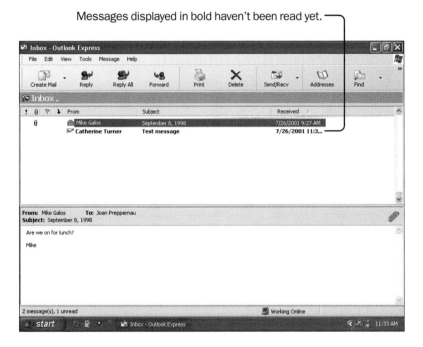

Tip

To check for new e-mail, click the **Send/Recv** button on the toolbar.

10 Double-click the message to open it.

11 On the message window's toolbar, click **Reply**.

Tip

Always check to see if anyone else appears on the **To** line or on the **Cc** line of the e-mail messages you receive. If you want your reply to be sent to everyone who received the original message, on the message window's toolbar, click **Reply All** instead of **Reply**.

A new e-mail message form opens, all set up so that you can respond to the message you received. The sender of the original message has been entered in the **To** line, and the original subject is preceded by *RE:* on the **Subject** line to indicate that this is a response.

12 In the message body, type **This is a test of replying to an e-mail message**.

13 Click **Send**.

Outlook Express sends your reply and then receives it in your Inbox.

14 Click the original e-mail message to select it, hold down [Ctrl], and click the reply e-mail message to add it to the selection.

15 On the toolbar, click **Delete**.

The e-mail messages are deleted from the Inbox. With IMAP accounts, the messages are still visible, but have been "crossed out" to indicate that they have been deleted.

16 If you have an IMAP account, click the double arrows at the right end of the toolbar to display all the options, and then click **Purge**.

The deleted e-mail messages are removed from your Inbox.

Close

17 Click the window's **Close** button to close Outlook Express.

Creating E-mail Stationery

An e-mail **stationery theme**, or template, includes background colors or pictures, fonts, and margin settings. By default, the stationery theme applied to messages is a blank background, but Outlook Express comes with 14 stationery themes from which you can choose. Many more themes are available online.

If you don't like any of the available themes, you can create your own using the **Stationery Setup Wizard**. You can create a new theme based on the current one, or you can create one of your own design.

In this exercise, you will create a simple stationery theme using the **Stationery Setup Wizard**.

There are no practice files for this exercise. Outlook Express must be installed on your computer as the default e-mail program.

Follow these steps:

1   Log on to Windows, if you have not already done so.

2   On the **Start** menu, click **E-mail**.

Outlook Express opens.

3   On the toolbar, click the down arrow to the right of the **Create Mail** button to display the stationery drop-down menu.

4   On the stationery menu, click **Select Stationery**.

The **Select Stationery** dialog box opens, showing the currently installed stationery options:

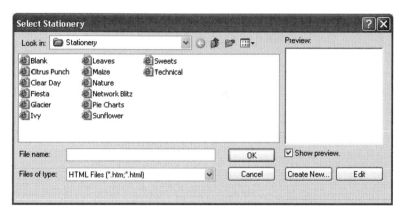

5   Click **Create New**.

The **Stationery Setup Wizard** appears.

6   Click **Next** to move to the wizard's **Background** page:

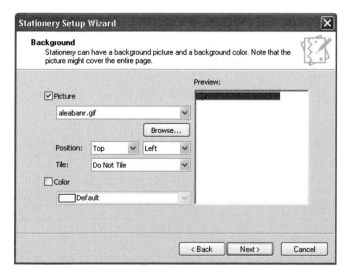

7 Clear the **Picture** check box, and select the **Color** check box.

8 Click the down arrow to the right of the **Color** box, and click **Purple** in the drop-down list.

Your color choice is displayed in the **Preview** area.

9 Click **Next** to move to the **Font** page:

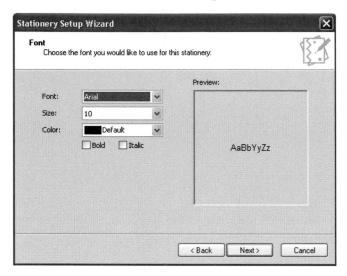

■ Click the down arrow to the right of the **Font** box, and click **Verdana** in the drop-down list.

■ Click the down arrow to the right of the **Color** box, and click **White** in the drop-down list.

■ Select the **Bold** check box.

Your choices are displayed in the **Preview** area.

10 Click **Next** to move to the **Margins** page.

The **Preview** area already displays your selected background and font selections:

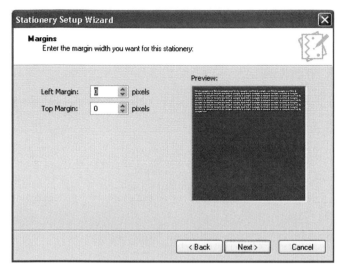

11 Make the following changes:

■ Click the up arrow to the right of the **Left Margin** spinner once to set it to 25 pixels.

■ Click the up arrow to the right of the **Top Margin** spinner once to set it to 25 pixels.

12 Click **Next** to move to the **Complete** page:

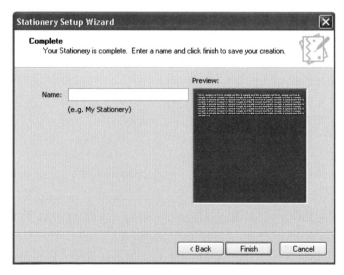

13 In the **Name** box, type **My Stationery**, and then click **Finish**.

Your new stationery is created, and the file is saved on your computer. (It is visible in the Select Stationery window.)

14 Click **OK** to open a new message form that uses your new stationery theme.

The purple background is immediately visible.

15 Click in the message body, and type **This is my custom stationery**.

Your message is displayed in bold, white, Verdana font.

Close

16 Click the message form's **Close** button to close the message without sending it.

17 When you are prompted to save the message, click **No**.

18 On the toolbar, click the down arrow to the right of the **Create Mail** button to display the stationery drop-down menu.

Your custom stationery is now available on this menu.

19 Click the window's **Close** button to close Outlook Express.

Adding Contacts to Your Address Book

Outlook Express incorporates an Address Book that enables you to very easily add contacts to your **Contact** list—and if you want, it will add contact information for you! With the **Address Book**, you can:

- Store e-mail addresses, street addresses, phone numbers, and personal information about contacts or groups of contacts that are important to you.

- Find people and businesses through **Internet directory services**, Web-based search engines that give you access to directory information from around the world.

- Create groups of contacts for mailing lists. You might want a group for each project you're working on, a group for external vendors, a group for family members, or any other type of group you want to e-mail collectively.

- Share contacts with other people who use your computer.

- Import information from and export information to other address books, including those from Microsoft Exchange, Netscape Communicator, Eudora Light, Eudora Pro, or any other program that exports comma-separated text files.

- Send and receive electronic business cards, contact information in a format that can easily be merged into other people's contact databases.

- Print your Address Book information in a variety of formats so that you can carry it with you when you don't have access to your computer or handheld electronic organizer.

By default, Outlook Express adds your Windows Messenger contacts to your Address Book, and adds e-mail contacts to the Address Book whenever you reply to them. This means that you can pretty much populate your address book without trying. It's also easy to add new contacts manually.

In this exercise, you will add three new contacts to your Address Book and then create a group of contacts.

There are no practice files for this exercise. Outlook Express must be installed on your computer as the default e-mail program.

Follow these steps:

1   Log on to Windows, if you have not already done so.

2   On the **Start** menu, click **E-Mail**.

Outlook Express starts.

3   On the toolbar, click **Addresses**.

The Address Book opens:

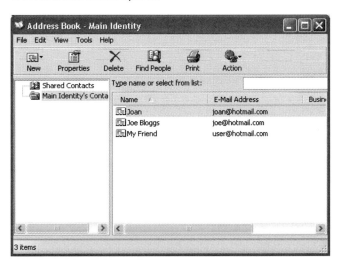

Maximize

4   Click the Address Book's **Maximize** button so you can see its contents.

5   On the Address Book's toolbar, click **New**, and click **New Contact** on the drop-down menu.

A contact form appears.

6   Create the contact by typing the following:

- ■   In the **First** box, type **Catherine**.

Tip

As you type the name, it is repeated in the title bar of the dialog box and in the **Display** box.

- ■ In the **Last** box, type **Turner**.
- ■ In the **Title** box, type **Ms**.
- ■ In the **E-Mail Addresses** box, type **catherinet@gardenco.msn.com**.
- ■ Click **Add**.

The e-mail address is added as an available e-mail address and is designated as the default address, like this:

7   Click the **Business** tab, and then do the following:

- ■ In the **Company** box, type **The Garden Company**.
- ■ In the **Street Address** box, type **1234 Oak Street**.
- ■ In the **City** box, type **Seattle**.
- ■ In the **State/Province** box, type **WA**.
- ■ In the **Zip Code** box, type **10101**.

Tip

If this were a real address, you could click **View Map** to locate the address on an Expedia Map.

- ■ In the **Web Page** box, type **http://www.gardenco.msn.com**.

Tip

If this URL were real, you could click **Go** to open the Web page in your default browser.

- ■ In the **Job Title** box, type **Owner**.
- ■ In the **Phone** box, type **(206) 555-0100**.
- ■ In the **Fax** box, type **(206) 555-0101**.

8 Click the **Home**, **Personal**, **Other**, **NetMeeting**, and **Digital IDs** tabs, and review the options available there.

9 Click **OK** to add Catherine Turner to your Address Book.

10 Position the mouse pointer over Catherine's Address Book entry.

Her contact information is displayed as a ScreenTip.

11 Repeat steps 5 through 9 to create an Address Book entry for Mr. Mike Galos. Mike's e-mail address is *mikeg@gardenco.msn.com*. Mike is the manager of The Garden Company, and he has the same business contact information as Catherine Turner.

Tip

Mike Galos, Catherine Turner, Kim Yoshida, and The Garden Company are fictional identities created for the *Step by Step* series.

12 On the Address Book's toolbar, click **New**, and then click **New Group** on the drop-down menu.

A contact form appears:

13   In the **Group Name** box, type **Work**.

14   Click **Select Members**.

The **Select Group Members** dialog box appears:

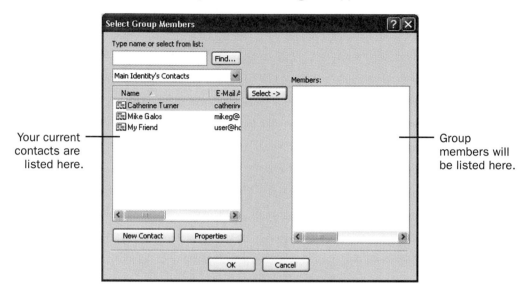

Your current contacts are listed here.

Group members will be listed here.

15   Click **Catherine Turner**, and then click **Select**.

Catherine is moved to the **Members** list.

16   Click **Mike Galos**, and then click **Select**.

Mike is moved to the **Members** list.

Tip

To locate people through an Internet directory service, click **Find** and then select a directory service from the **Look In** drop-down list.

17   Click **OK** to close the **Select Group Members** dialog box.

The **Work Properties** dialog box now lists two members.

18   Click **New Contact** to add a new group member who doesn't yet exist in the address book.

A contact form appears.

19   Repeat steps 6 through 9 to add Ms. Kim Yoshida. Kim's e-mail address is kimy@gardenco.msn.com. Kim is the purchasing manager at The Garden Company and has the same business contact information as Catherine and Mike.

Tip

To add a contact to the group, but not to your address book, enter his or her name and e-mail address at the bottom of the **Group** tab, and click **Add**.

20 After you have entered Kim's information, click **OK** to close the **Kim Yoshida Properties** dialog box.

Kim is automatically added to the Work group.

21 Click **OK** to close the **Work Properties** dialog box.

Your three contacts are listed in the right pane of the Address Book, and the Work group is shown in the left pane.

22 In the Address Book, select the **Work** group, and then click **Delete**.

23 Select and delete each of the contacts you created in this exercise.

24 Close the Address Book, and then close Outlook Express.

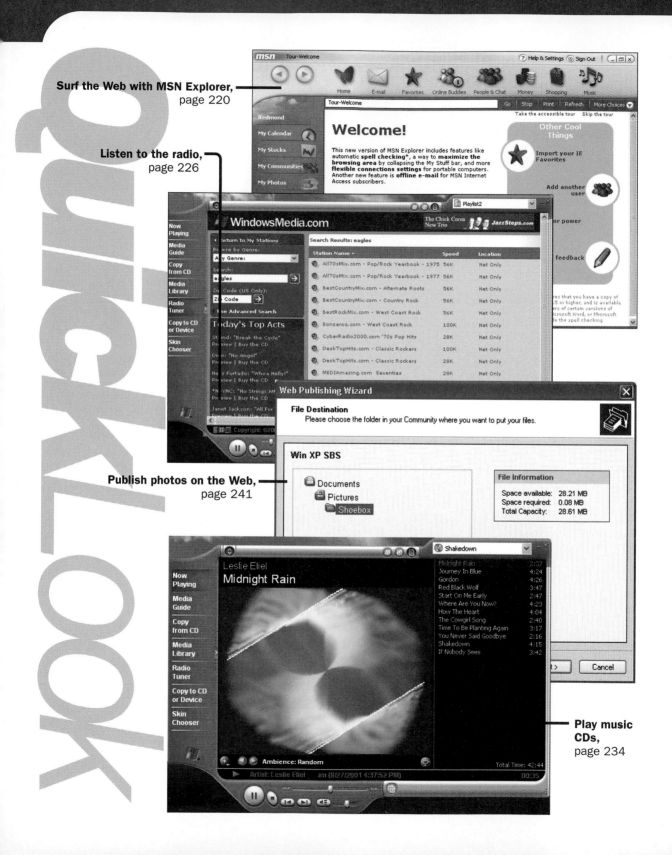

Surf the Web with MSN Explorer, page 220

Listen to the radio, page 226

Publish photos on the Web, page 241

Play music CDs, page 234

Chapter 9
Having Fun with Windows XP

After completing this chapter, you will be able to:

✔ Play games on your computer or over the Internet.

✔ Surf the Web.

✔ Use Windows Media Player to listen to music from the radio or a CD.

✔ Publish photos on the Web.

Microsoft Windows XP comes with more leisure-time options than any previous version of Windows. In addition to the traditional solitaire-style games that came with earlier versions of Windows, you now have access to multi-player games on the Internet. A number of exciting new software programs are also included with Windows XP that make it easy to surf the Web, play or create audio compact discs (CDs), play digital video discs (DVDs), create your own movies, and manage your photograph collections.

In this chapter, you explore a few of the Windows XP entertainment options. If you use Windows XP on your computer at work, playing games might not be appropriate, but other topics that fall in the entertainment category, such as working with digital photographs, might provide just the information you need to jazz up an important document or presentation.

 The practice files for this chapter are located in the *SBS\WindowsXP\Playing* folder. (For details about installing the practice files, see "Using the Book's CD-ROM" at the beginning of this book.) You can follow along with your own multimedia files if you want.

Playing Games

Computer games have been around almost as long as computers. Windows XP comes with all the standard favorites, and more. If you like card games, you can choose from FreeCell, Solitaire, Spider Solitaire, and Hearts. All are installed on your computer's hard disk, and are played alone. If cards aren't your strong suit, you can play Minesweeper or Pinball. Minesweeper is a one-person game, but Pinball can be played with up to four players on one computer.

With Windows XP and an Internet connection, you now have more gaming options than ever. Windows XP provides links to Internet Backgammon, Internet Checkers, Internet Hearts, Internet Reversi, and Internet Spades. You can play these games interactively against other players from around the world, by using the MSN Gaming Zone at *zone.msn.com*.

You access all the games that come with Windows XP from the **Games** menu. On the **Start** menu, point to **All Programs**, and then click **Games**. Instructions for playing each game are available from that game's **Help** menu.

Of course, you aren't limited to the games that come with Windows XP. You can install other gaming software or, if you have Internet access, you can play hundreds of solo and multi-player computer games through any of the many popular gaming sites, including:

- Games.com (*play.games.com*)
- Gamesville (*www.gamesville.com*)
- MSN Gaming Zone (*zone.msn.com*)
- Pogo.com (*www.pogo.com*)
- Puzzle Depot (*www.puzzledepot.com*)

Surfing the Web

A new addition to Windows XP is integration with **MSN Explorer**, an all-in-one package that gives you all the tools you need to work effectively on the Web. MSN Explorer integrates several popular MSN services, including:

- MSN Calendar, where you can keep track of appointments, tasks, and reminders. MSN Explorer can send a reminder to you via e-mail, MSN Messenger, or your cell phone.
- MSN Communities, where you can interact online with others who share common interests. You can join an existing community or start your own.
- MSN Custom Web Sites, which makes it easy to create your own Web site to share photos and files with other people around the world.
- MSN eShop, where you can research products, compare prices, and make online purchases from hundreds of retailers.
- MSN Hotmail, which you can use to send and receive e-mail messages for free.
- MSN Messenger Service, which you can use to send instant messages and files to your friends who are online, or even converse with them over the Internet, using a microphone.

- MSN MoneyCentral, where you can track your accounts and pay your bills online.

- MSN Music, which helps you find online radio stations that suit your taste, based on favorite songs, artists, albums, or just your general mood.

MSN Explorer also integrates with Windows Media Player, so you can listen to music or watch a video while you're surfing the Web or sending e-mail.

When you sign in to MSN Explorer, you are automatically signed in to the other services that are password-protected, so you don't have to retype your password when moving between them.

Important

Don't confuse *MSN Explorer* with *MSN Internet Access*. The **Microsoft Network (MSN)** spans a number of services including all of those listed above. MSN is also an ISP through which you can configure a local dial-up account from almost any location in the world. Along with your Internet access, you can also get an MSN e-mail address (*someone@msn.com*) that is part of the Passport program.

MSN Explorer is available in specialized versions for many international locations. The versions that are available at the time this book is being written, or that are under development, include:

Versions			
Australia	France	Latin America	South Africa
Austria	Germany	Malaysia	Spain
Belgium (Dutch and French versions)	Hong Kong SAR	Mexico	Sweden
Brazil	India	The Netherlands	Switzerland (French and German versions)
Canada (English and French versions)	Italy	New Zealand	Taiwan
Denmark	Japan	Norway	United Kingdom
Finland	Korea	Singapore	United States

Regional installations of MSN Explorer are available from *explorer.msn.com/intl.asp*. If you want to send the program to a friend, you can also order individual installation CDs from the MSN Explorer Web site at *explorer.msn.com*. All versions of MSN Explorer include a special automatic update feature that ensures that your software stays up to date.

Each installation of MSN Explorer supports up to nine users by maintaining a separate profile for each one. As a result, you can store your personal information, including favorite Web pages, e-mail contacts, and instant messaging contacts, without being concerned that the information will be accessed or changed by someone else. When you're away from your computer, you can have MSN Explorer deliver information to your Web-enabled cellular phone or other handheld device.

In this exercise, you will walk through the initial installation of MSN Explorer and then configure an MSN Explorer user account for yourself.

There are no practice files for this exercise. You will need to have an active Internet connection or a properly installed modem and phone line connection. If you do not have an ISP or e-mail address, you can sign up for one during this exercise.

Important

The steps illustrated in this exercise are for a computer with a full-time broadband connection. If you are using a different Internet access method, you might have to vary the steps slightly based on the on-screen instructions, but you will still be able to follow along with the exercise.

Follow these steps:

1   Log on to Windows, if you have not already done so.

2   On the **Start** menu, point to **All Programs**, and then click **MSN Explorer**.

3   If prompted to confirm that you want to open MSN Explorer, click **Yes**.

The **Welcome** page opens:

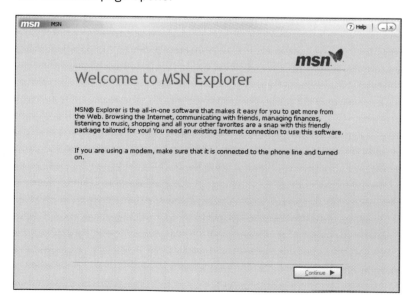

4 Click **Continue**.

The next page prompts you to enter your geographic location.

5 In the drop-down list, click your location, or the closest location within your time zone.

6 Click **Continue**.

7 If you are prompted to select a customized international version of MSN Explorer, click the most appropriate country, and then click **OK**.

Your selection governs the language in which the MSN Explorer interface is displayed, as well as the links available to you through the interface.

The next page offers you the option of signing up for MSN Internet Access:

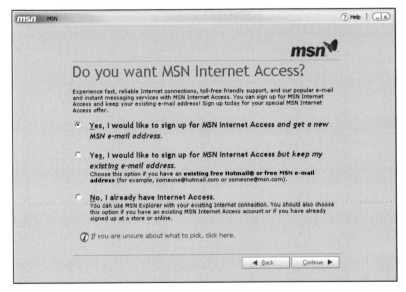

8 Select the appropriate option, and then click **Continue**:

- If you don't currently have an ISP or an e-mail address, click **Yes, I would like to sign up for MSN Internet Access and get a new MSN e-mail address**.

- If you don't have an ISP but you do have either a Hotmail or MSN e-mail address, click **Yes, I would like to sign up for MSN Internet Access but keep my existing e-mail address**.

- If you have an ISP or are using a broadband connection, click **No, I already have Internet Access**.

9 If you have chosen to sign up for MSN Internet Access, follow the prompts to complete the process, and then rejoin this exercise.

10 If you already have Internet access, the next page asks you to select the type of access you are using. Click the appropriate option, and then click **Continue** and follow the prompts.

When the sign-in process is complete, MSN Explorer opens:

11 Browse through the site to see all the great tools that are available to you.

12 When you are finished, click **Sign Out** in the window's title bar to sign out of MSN Explorer and return to the welcome screen.

Close

13 Click the **Close** button to close the MSN Explorer welcome screen.

To sign in to MSN Explorer in the future, on the **Start** menu, point to **All Programs**, and then click **MSN Explorer**. You will automatically be signed in to the entire suite of services.

Troubleshooting

MSN Explorer uses **cookies** to sign you in to the Web sites that provide its services. If you have chosen not to allow cookies to be placed on your computer, the MSN Explorer services will not be available. MSN Explorer checks the settings on your computer during the setup process and, if necessary, prompts you to change your security settings to allow cookies.

Maintaining Your Privacy

The MSN Explorer registration process requires you to supply a certain amount of personal information, including your name and address, occupation, and geographic location. This information might be supplied through your Passport, or you might be asked to enter it.

In addition to the information that you give voluntarily, MSN Explorer gathers anonymous statistical data, including how often you log on, how long it takes for your browser to display the home page, and how long you spend using the service. This data is gathered only for technical quality-control purposes and does not include any information that identifies you personally.

MSN Explorer tracks your favorite Web sites in a Favorites list that is available to you from anywhere in the world when you sign in to MSN Explorer. Your Favorites list is not shared with or available to anyone other than you (or another person to whom you have given your user account name and password).

If you experience an error while using MSN Explorer, you will be asked to send data to MSN to help them determine the cause of the error so that they can correct it in future software versions. If you choose to send this data, you can review it before sending it. Information that identifies you personally might be included in this data, but Microsoft's policy is that any such information is deleted before it gets to the person who reviews the error.

Microsoft and MSN are licensees of the TRUSTe Privacy Program, which means that every Microsoft or MSN Web site contains a link to a privacy statement that must inform you of the following:

- The types of personal, identifying information that are collected from you through the Web site.

- The name of the organization that is collecting the information.

- How the information is used.

- With whom the information might be shared.

- Your choices regarding collection, use, and distribution of the information.

- The kind of security procedures that are in place to protect against the loss, misuse, or alteration of your information.

- How you can correct inaccuracies in the information.

For more information about TRUSTe, you can visit *www.truste.org*. If you have concerns about the protection of your personal information while using MSN Explorer, you can send an e-mail message to *MSNPrivacy@msn.com*.

Using Windows Media Player

Many people enjoy playing music or videos on their computers, either while they're working or during their leisure time. With recent advances in disk drive technology, many people can now enjoy all the comforts of an entertainment center on their desktop computers or their laptops.

Tip

Many new laptops will play CDs without even being booted up. If you travel often and are in the market for a new laptop, you might consider adding this capability to your wish list.

Windows XP comes with Microsoft Windows Media Player 8, which you can use to play, copy, and catalog audio and video files from your computer, from CDs or DVDs, or from the Web. You can display Windows Media Player in either of two modes: **full mode**, which displays information about the media you're using in a television-like format, including a video display screen, taskbar, and menu bar; and **skin mode**, which is smaller and looks like a stylized remote control. It is easy to switch between modes.

Tip

Some people prefer skin mode when listening to music, because full mode's video display can be a bit distracting.

In full mode, Windows Media Player displays a taskbar, a video display area, and a list of all the audio tracks on the currently selected source. (You can choose from a drop-down list that includes the currently inserted CD and any media files stored on your computer.) You can also toggle a traditional Windows menu on and off. The taskbar, which is located on the left side of the window, includes the following options:

■ *Now Playing* includes a video display area and a playlist (which you can toggle on and off) of your currently available media files. When you are listening to music or radio programs, a visual representation, called a **visualization**, of the audio is displayed on the "screen" where videos would normally be displayed. The visualization moves in time with the music. Windows XP comes with seven visualizations—Ambience, Bars and Waves, Battery, Particle, Plenoptic, Spikes, and Musical Colors—each of which has several different versions.

- *Media Guide*, which is hosted on the WindowsMedia Web site, provides information about and links to various entertainment options on the Internet, including music download sites, video download sites, radio stations, movie discussion sites, entertainment news, and a wide variety of Webcams around the world.

- *Copy from CD* allows you to copy audio files from a CD to your computer so that you can replay the songs without having the actual CD inserted in the disk drive.

- *Media Library* is your personal catalog of audio and video files and favorite radio stations. Audio files are cataloged by album, artist, and genre; video files are cataloged by author. Your media **playlists**—individual **tracks** that you have selected and arranged—are also displayed here.

- *Radio Tuner* is an element of the WindowsMedia Web site through which you can link to a variety of radio stations worldwide. You can choose from featured stations or search for a particular station, station format, or location. You can add a station to your My Stations list, visit a station's Web site, connect to a station through its Web site, or just listen to it live.

- *Copy to CD or Device* allows you to copy audio and video files from the Media Library to a **portable device**, such as a Pocket PC or storage card, or to a CD if you have a **CD-RW** drive installed on your computer. You can also copy licensed files that you downloaded from the Internet or that you copied from CDs to your portable device.

- *Skin Chooser* lets you choose from 20 available **skins** (or more if you have an Internet connection) to tailor the appearance of Windows Media Player to your own taste. Available skins range from high-tech to goofy, with something to appeal to pretty much any gender, age group, or musical taste.

- *Play DVD* lets you watch DVD movies and download information about your DVDs onto your computer. This selection is available only if you have a DVD-ROM drive and a DVD decoder installed on your computer.

In this exercise, you will start Windows Media Player and explore the available resources. You will then locate and listen to a radio station over the Internet.

There are no practice files for this exercise. You must have speakers attached to your computer, and you will need an active Internet connection to complete the entire exercise.

Follow these steps:

1 Log on to Windows, if you have not already done so.

2 On the **Start** menu, point to **All Programs**, and then click **Windows Media Player**.

The Windows Media Player window opens:

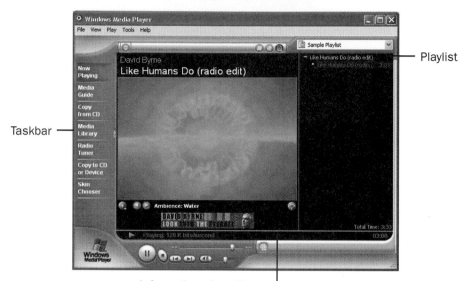

Taskbar

Playlist

Information about the current song is displayed here.

Making Movies

Windows Movie Maker

new for **Windows**XP

One of the new programs that come with Windows XP is Windows Movie Maker, a tool that helps you **capture** audio and video source material. After the source material is captured, you can use Windows Movie Maker to edit and arrange your **clips** to create movies. With Windows Movie Maker, you can download video clips from your digital video camera or import video clips from other sources, and then edit them to create your own movie. You can add music and narration to your video and even insert still photos or title slides. When your movie masterpiece is complete, you can burn it to a CD, send it via e-mail, or publish it on the Web.

To start Windows Movie Maker, on the **Start** menu, point to **All Programs**, point to **Accessories**, and then click **Windows Movie Maker**. For more information about the program, visit *www.microsoft.com/windowsxp/home/guide/movies.asp*, or start Windows Movie Maker and then consult its Help file.

When you open Windows Media Player, the sample playlist will probably open and start playing the first selection, which is *Like Humans Do* by David Byrne at the time of this writing. The display area shows the default visualization.

Auto hide menu bar

3 If you currently see a menu bar at the top of the Windows Media Player window, click the **Auto hide menu bar** button.

The window now looks like this:

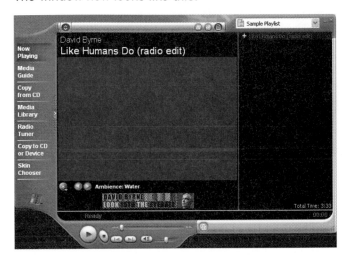

Troubleshooting

If you click the **Auto hide menu bar** button while Windows Media Player is in full mode, nothing appears to change except the look of the button. When you restore the window to a smaller size, however, the menu bar will be hidden.

4 On the taskbar, click **Now Playing** to display the current playlist.

5 If no songs are listed in the playlist, click **All Audio** on the drop-down list to display a list of available audio tracks, and start a song.

Select visualization or album art

6 Click the **Select visualization or album art** button, and then click **Musical Colors** on the drop-down list.

The visualization changes to reflect the first of the Musical Colors options, *Night Lights*:

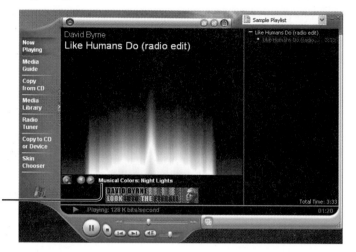

The name of the current visualization is displayed here.

Next visualization

7 Click the **Next visualization** button to move to the next of the Musical Colors options, *Colors in Motion*:

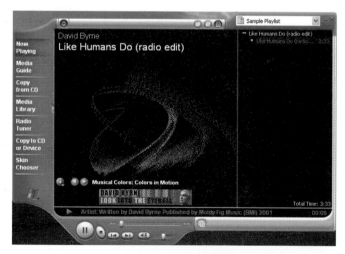

8 Use the **Select visualization or album art** and **Next visualization** buttons to look through the available options, settling on your favorite.

9 On the taskbar, click **Media Guide**.

The WindowsMedia Web site opens:

10 Browse through the Web site to see what it has to offer.

11 On the taskbar, click **Radio Tuner**.

The Radio Tuner opens:

A list of featured stations is displayed in the left pane, and links to more stations are available in the right pane.

12 In the **Featured Stations** list, click through the radio stations until you find one that has a **Play** button.

For each station, a description and its options appear.

13 Click the **Play** button to hear the station.

The radio station's Web site opens in a new window in the background, in case you want to check it out.

14 Click **Find More Stations**.

15 On the **Browse by Genre** drop-down list, click **Classic Rock**.

16 In the **Search** box, type **eagles**.

Search

17 Click the **Search** button.

A list of classic rock stations that include music by the Eagles on their play-lists is generated:

Surfing the Radio Waves

Thanks to the Internet, you are no longer limited to listening to canned music; nor do you have to miss your favorite radio programs when you're away from home. Many radio stations are now broadcasting their content via the Web, which means that you can tune in from just about anywhere, if you have an active Internet connection and speakers or headphones.

If you're looking for a specific radio station, you might be able to locate it via the Radio Tuner. To open the Radio Tuner from within Windows Media Player, click **Radio Tuner** on the taskbar. (The taskbar is displayed only in full mode.) To open the Radio Tuner from the Web, go to *www.windowsmedia.com*. You can search by genre, keyword (such as the call letters of a station or the name of a city), or zip code. If Windows Media Player can't locate the station you are looking for, you can use your favorite Internet search engine.

18 Click a radio station, and then click **Play** to hear that station.

Information about the station is displayed at the bottom of the Radio Tuner.

Close

19 Click the **Close** button to close the Windows Media Player window, and then close the window displaying the radio station's Web site.

Personalizing Windows Media Player

The default interface for Windows Media Player is a gray, black, and blue box that bears some resemblance to a space-age television or radio. This interface is called a **skin**. Twenty skins are available from within Windows, and many more can be downloaded from the Internet. The default skin is named *Windows XP*.

Tip

Don't confuse the term *skin*, which is used to refer to the look of the Windows Media Player interface, and *skin mode*, which is one of the two views in which you can display Windows Media Player. The skin you select sets the program's look whether you are in skin mode or full mode.

In this exercise, you will personalize the look and feel of Windows Media Player by changing the skin.

There are no practice files for this exercise.

Follow these steps:

1 Log on to Windows, if you have not already done so.

2 On the **Start** menu, point to **All Programs**, and then click **Windows Media Player**.

Windows Media Player opens.

3 On the taskbar, click **Skin Chooser**.

Tip

You must be in full mode to access the taskbar.

The Skin Chooser window opens, with the current skin selected on the left and the skin mode displayed on the right.

4 Click each skin option on the left until you have previewed each one.

Tip

Clicking **More Skins** takes you to the WindowsMedia Web site, where you can select from a variety of other skins.

5 Click your favorite skin, and then click **Apply Skin**.

Windows Media Player changes to reflect your selection and switches to skin mode. For example, the *Radio* skin looks like this:

Return to Full Mode

6 Click the **Return to Full Mode** button to switch the interface to that mode.

7 If you want to change back to the standard skin, click **Windows XP**, and then click **Apply Skin**.

Tip

If you don't change the skin back to the default, your screen will not match the graphics shown throughout the rest of this chapter. However, the step-by-step instructions will still apply.

Close

8 Click the **Close** button to close the Windows Media Player window.

Listening to Music from a CD or from Your Computer

Windows Media Player gives you virtually unlimited access to radio stations around the world and also enables you to listen to CDs and audio clips of various types. You can play audio clips in an order you specify or shuffle the available clips to create a random mix. You can also create a compilation of your favorite songs on your computer or, if you have a CD-RW drive installed, on a CD.

When you insert a music CD into your CD-ROM drive, Windows Media Player automatically opens and plays the CD. As the music plays, Windows Media Player displays a visualization that moves in time with the music. You can replace the visualization with a picture of the album cover, if it is available on the Windows Media Web site.

You can copy songs from a CD to your hard disk and play them from there. By default, Windows Media Player protects the files so that they can't be played on any other computer, to ensure that you don't inadvertently violate any copyrights.

In this exercise, you will use Windows Media Player to play a few songs from one of your own music CDs. You will then copy a couple of song tracks from the CD to your hard disk.

There are no practice files for this exercise, but you must have a music CD, and speakers or headphones must be installed on your computer. To complete the entire exercise, you will need access to the Internet.

Follow these steps:

1 Log on to Windows, if you have not already done so.

2 Ensure that Windows Media Player is not currently running.

3 Insert a music CD into your CD-ROM drive.

4 If the **Audio CD** dialog box prompts you to select an action, click **Play Audio CD using Windows Media Player**, and then click **OK**.

Tip

If you would like to bypass this dialog box and automatically play music CDs in the future, select the **Always do the selected action** check box.

The Windows Media Player window opens, and the first song on the CD starts playing. The artist and song title are displayed in the left pane. The album title is displayed in the drop-down list:

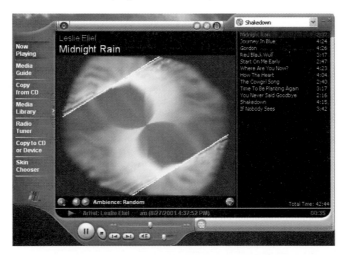

Troubleshooting

If your computer is not online when you insert the CD, the album, artist, and individual tracks are not identified by name, only by track number. If the CD is by a well-known artist, the next time you go online and open Windows Media Player, the CD's information is updated from an online database and stored on your computer, and from that point on, the information is available offline. For artists who are not in the online database, you can add track information yourself, and it will be stored on your computer.

Left unattended, the CD plays from beginning to end, and then stops.

Tip

Some audio CDs contain interactive content that is displayed while the CD is playing. This display might affect the performance of Windows Media Player, and the audio track might sound a bit jerky while your computer is working on other tasks associated with the interactive content.

5 In the CDs playlist, double-click any other track to play it.

6 On the taskbar, click **Copy from CD**.

A dialog box opens with all the audio tracks on the CD displayed and selected:

Important

The graphics in this exercise show a music CD called *Shakedown* by Leslie Eliel, who has given permission for several tracks from this CD to be used on this book's CD-ROM. Your display will reflect the music CD you are using for this exercise and will look different from the graphics shown here.

7 Clear the check box above the list of tracks to deselect them all, and then select the check boxes of two individual tracks to select them.

8 With the two check boxes selected, click **Copy Music**.

Tip

If you are connected to the Internet, you can click **Album Details** to see information from the WindowsMedia Web site about the album and artist, and you can click **Get Names** to display or update a list of the track names.

9 If the **Copy music protection** dialog box opens, giving you the option to turn off the automatic copyright protection of your copied CD files, ensure that the **Do not protect content** check box Is cleared, and then click **OK**.

As each of the selected tracks is copied to your hard disk, its status changes from *Pending* to *Copying* (with percent copied) to *Copied to Library*.

10 When both files have been copied, click **Media Library** on the taskbar.

The Media Library opens:

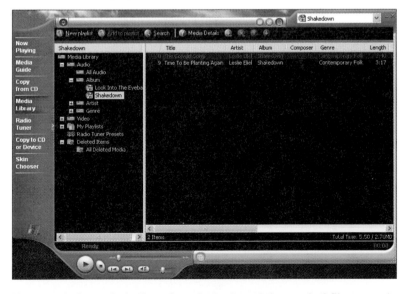

Your recently copied album is selected, and the copied files are shown in the file list on the right.

Tip

The first time you open the Media Library, you are prompted to search your computer for media files. Any files that are found are added to your library. You can repeat the search at any time to update your listings.

11 Browse through the Media Library to see how it is laid out.

12 To play one of the songs you just copied, double-click it.

Close

13 When you are finished, click the **Close** button to close the Windows Media Player window.

Creating a Music Playlist

If you often copy audio files to your hard disk, you can quickly accumulate hundreds of songs, and scrolling through folders looking for the next song you would like to listen to can be annoying. In Windows XP you can solve this problem by creating **playlists**. A playlist is a list of digital media files, such as songs, video clips, and links to a radio station. You can think of it as a virtual CD that is limited in size only by the storage capacity of your hard disk. You can treat a playlist as a collection, playing it, copying it, or burning it to a CD-ROM as a unit.

In this exercise, you will create your own playlist from audio files on your hard disk.

The practice files for this exercise are located in the *SBS\WindowsXP\Playing \Playlist* folder. (For details about installing the practice files, see "Using the Book's CD-ROM" at the beginning of this book.) To complete this exercise, you must have speakers or headphones installed on your computer.

Follow these steps:

1 Log on to Windows, if you have not already done so.

2 On the **Start** menu, point to **All Programs**, and then click **Windows Media Player**.

Windows Media Player opens.

3 Click **Media Library**, and then click **New Playlist**.

The **New Playlist** dialog box appears:

4 Type **Leslie Eliel**, which is the name of the singer/songwriter who provided the practice files, and click **OK**.

5 Without closing Windows Media Player, use Windows Explorer to browse to the *SBS\WindowsXP\Playing\Playlist* folder.

Tip

To open Windows Explorer, on the **Start** menu, point to **All Programs**, point to **Accessories**, and then click **Windows Explorer**.

6 Right-click **The Cowgirl Song**, and click **Add to Playlist** on the shortcut menu that appears.

The **Playlists** dialog box is displayed:

7 Click **Leslie Eliel**, and then click **OK** to close the dialog box.

The Windows Media Player window is now active, and you can see that *The Cowgirl Song* has been added to the Leslie Eliel playlist.

8 Return to Windows Explorer, and repeat steps 6 and 7 to add **Time To Be Planting Again** to the playlist.

9 In Windows Media Player, double-click the **Leslie Eliel** playlist to play the first song in the collection.

When the first song is finished, the second one plays.

Close

10 When you are finished, click the **Close** button to close the Windows Media Player window.

Copying Music Files to a CD or Handheld Device

If you have a CD-RW drive or removable storage device installed on your computer or if you have a handheld device, such as a Pocket PC, on which you would like to play music, you can easily copy files from your computer using Windows Media Player. To copy a file, you must first have saved it in the Media Library.

In this exercise, you will copy selected audio tracks from the Media Library to a CD-RW drive or removable storage device.

There are no practice files for this exercise, but you must have a CD-RW drive or removable storage device attached to your computer.

Follow these steps:

1 Log on to Windows, if you have not already done so.

2 On the **Start** menu, point to **All Programs**, and then click **Windows Media Player**.

Windows Media Player opens.

3 On the taskbar, click **Copy to CD or Device**.

Windows Media Player searches for appropriate storage devices. The search results are listed in the **Music on Device** pane.

4 In the **Music to Copy** drop-down list, select the album or type of music from which you want to make your selection.

The available files appear in the left pane. By default, all the listed files are selected.

5 Clear the check boxes of any files that you do not want to copy.

6 In the **Music on Device** drop-down list, select the destination drive.

If you select a removable storage device that already contains music files, the folders and audio files on the destination drive appear in the right pane.

7 Click **Copy Music**.

As each of the selected tracks is copied from your hard disk, its status changes from *Inspecting* to *Copying* to *Complete*.

The copied files are added to the list of audio files in the right pane.

Close

8 When you are finished, click the **Close** button to close the Windows Media Player window.

Sharing Digital Photos

If you have a digital camera, you can use Windows XP to easily download photographs to your computer. When you connect a Plug and Play camera to your computer, Windows XP recognizes it and starts the **Scanner and Camera Wizard** to install it. If your camera isn't Plug and Play, you can manually start the wizard. You can install as many cameras as you want. After a camera is installed, you simply connect it to your computer's input port, and the **Scanner and Camera Wizard** starts and guides you through the process of downloading files.

Tip

If your digital camera stores photos on some kind of removable memory, you can transfer those photos to your computer using an appropriate adapter.

After you have downloaded the photos, you can copy them to the My Pictures folder, or to any other folder to which you have assigned picture properties, so that all the picture-folder options are available. For example, you can view all your photos as a slide show, or you can have Windows use your photos as a personalized background for your desktop.

Tip

You can assign picture properties to a folder by right-clicking the folder, clicking the **Customize** tab, and then selecting the **Pictures** or **Photo Album** template in the drop-down list of templates.

You can also take advantage of the following new Windows XP photo-processing options:

- The **Photo Printing Wizard** walks you through the process of formatting and printing photos. After you start the wizard, you can select one or more of the photo files in the current folder for printing. The wizard then prompts you to select an appropriate printer and type of paper.

Online
Print Ordering
Wizard

new for
WindowsXP

- The **Online Print Ordering Wizard** helps you order prints of your photos over the Internet. You select a printing company, specify the size and number of prints you want, and then provide billing and shipping information. The wizard transmits your photos and information to the printing company, which then processes your order and sends you the prints. This is a great way to get prints of your digital photos without investing in a photo printer, and without even leaving your own house!

Watching DVD Movies

Most **digital video disc (DVD)** movies come complete with software that you install on your computer so that you can watch the DVD and use any included interactive content, such as Web links and video games. With Windows Media Player, you can centralize all your media files in one program and play DVDs as easily as you play CDs.

Windows Media Player has all the functionality of a regular DVD player: You can watch movies, fast forward, reverse, move between movie segments, and access all the special features included on your DVD. When you are online, you can also download information about each disc from the WindowsMedia online database.

To play a DVD, you must have a DVD-ROM drive and a Windows XP–compatible DVD decoder installed on your computer. If you don't have a DVD-ROM drive installed, or if your DVD decoder is not compatible with Windows XP, the *Play DVD* option will not be visible in Windows Media Player. After you install Windows XP, you will probably need to upgrade your DVD decoder as well. Windows XP–compatible DVD decoders are available from DVD solution providers, including the following:

- National Semiconductor Corporation (Mediamatics DVD player):
  http://www.national.com/appinfo/dvd/support/msft/

- MGI Software Corporation (Zoran SoftDVD and MGI SoftDVD Max):
  http://www.mgisoft.com/products/dvd/updates.html

- Ravisent Technologies (Software CineMaster or CinePlayer 1.0):
  http://www.ravisentdirect.com/upgrade/dvdup.html

- InterVideo, Inc. (WinDVD):
  http://www.intervideo.com/products/custom/ms/windowsxp/upgrade.jsp

- CyberLink Corporation (PowerDVD):
  http://www.intervideo.com/products/custom/ms/windowsxp/upgrade.jsp

The first time you try to access the DVD options, if you need to update your DVD decoder and you are not online, Windows Media Player creates a desktop shortcut called *Upgrade DVD Decoder*. You can double-click this shortcut to link to the update site the next time you are online.

To watch a DVD movie with Windows Media Player:

1 Insert the DVD into the DVD-ROM drive.

2 Start Windows Media Player.

   The chapters and titles on the DVD are displayed.

3 Click **Play DVD** to play the entire movie sequentially, or click a specific chapter or title and click **Play DVD** to play only that segment.

If you are working on a network, you can save your photos in a folder on your network, and if you have Internet access, you can publish your photos on the Web so that they are available for family and friends to view.

If you don't already have a Web site, you can publish your photos to an MSN Communities Web site. MSN Communities is an area of the Microsoft Network (MSN) where you can create your own "community" (interactive Web site) or participate in existing communities. You could create a community for your family, a social or work group of which you are a member, or a special-interest topic. You can share news, documents, photos, lists, appointments, and many other types of information within a community.

In this exercise, you will publish photos from your hard disk on the Web. You will need an active Internet connection to complete this exercise.

The practice files for this exercise are located in the *SBS\WindowsXP\Playing\Photos* folder. (For details about installing the practice files, see "Using the Book's CD-ROM" at the beginning of this book.)

Follow these steps:

1   Log on to Windows, if you have not already done so.

2   On the **Start** menu, click **My Computer**.

3   In the **Address** box on either the toolbar or the taskbar, type **C:\SBS \WindowsXP\Playing\Photos**, and then click **Go**.

The specified folder opens in Windows Explorer. The folder contains four photo files.

4   On the **File and Folder Tasks** menu, click **Publish this folder to the Web**.

The **Web Publishing Wizard** appears.

5   Click **Next** to continue to the wizard's **Change Your File Selection** page.

All the files contained in the folder are displayed on this page. You can select or clear each file's check box to indicate whether or not you want to publish it, or you can select or clear all the check boxes using the buttons at the bottom of the page.

6   Leave all the files selected, and click **Next**.

You are given a choice of where you want to publish the files.

7   Leave **MSN Communities** selected, and click **Next**.

You are asked whether you want other people to be able to view your files or whether they are for your private use.

8   Click **Shared**, and then click **Next**.

The first time you attempt to publish shared files, you are given the opportunity to create a new community:

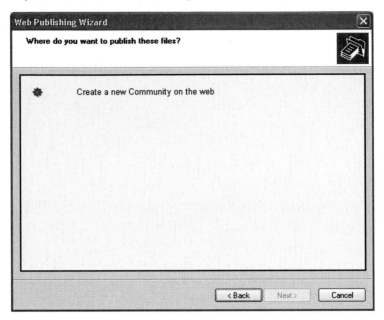

9   Click **Create a new Community on the Web**, and then click **Next**.

You use this page of the wizard to set up your community:

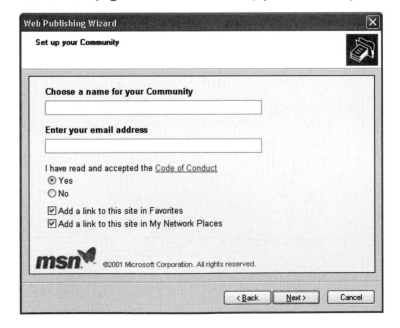

10 Type a name for your community (choose something fairly uncommon), enter your e-mail address, read and accept the Code of Conduct, and then click **Next**.

Tip

If you have a Hotmail account, your e-mail address might be entered for you.

Your MSN Community is created, with a default folder structure like this one:

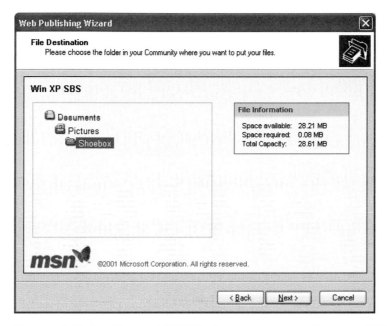

You are initially allocated 28 MB of storage space. As you add files, this page of the wizard lets you know how much space you have left.

11 Click **Shoebox** (or the equivalent name in the displayed folder structure) to specify that you want to store the photo files you are publishing there, and then click **Next**.

The next page of the wizard offers to resize your photos.

12 Leave the default options, and click **Next**.

Your photo files are copied to the MSN Web site as part of your community.

13 On the last page of the wizard, make sure that the **Open this site when I click Finish** check box is selected, and then click **Finish**.

The MSN Communities page opens in your Web browser:

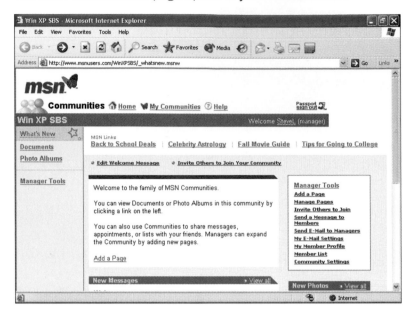

You are logged on to your new MSN community as the manager. You can view the photos you just published or try out some of the management tools provided on the right side of the page.

Tip

The next time you go to the site, you will arrive as a visitor, just like anyone else. If you would like to perform management tasks, you can click **Passport sign in** in the top right corner of the window and enter your Passport user account name and password. You will then have access to the various management tools.

14 Look through the Community page to see what it has to offer.

15 To look at the photos you uploaded, click **Photo Albums** on the menu at the left side of the screen and then click **Shoebox**.

The screen now looks like this:

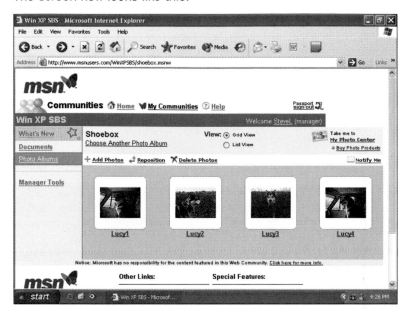

16 To make it easy to return to the page at any time, on the **Favorites** menu, click **Add to Favorites**, and then **OK**.

You can now return to your community by selecting it from the **Favorites** menu.

Close

17 When you're finished, click the **Close** button to close your browser, and then click **Close** again to close Windows Explorer.

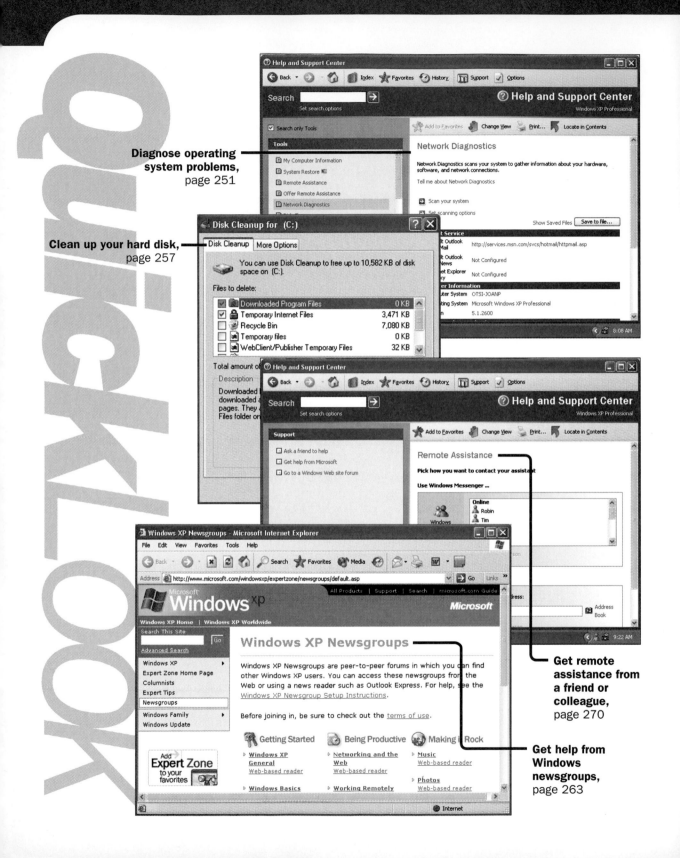

Diagnose operating system problems, page 251

Clean up your hard disk, page 257

Get remote assistance from a friend or colleague, page 270

Get help from Windows newsgroups, page 263

quickLook

Chapter 10
Solving Problems

After completing this chapter, you will be able to:

✔ Update your operating system manually or automatically.

✔ Diagnose operating system problems.

✔ Clean up and defragment your hard disk.

✔ Get answers and help from a variety of sources.

✔ Back up and restore files, folders, or your entire operating system.

Microsoft Windows XP is the most advanced Windows operating system to date. Its user-friendly interface, with menus that change depending on where you are or what you are doing, means that your time can be spent working or playing efficiently, rather than trying to figure out how to use your computer. However, the fact that Windows XP is easy to use doesn't mean that you won't ever experience a problem while using your Windows XP computer. One of the first things you learn in skiing is how to recover safely and gracefully from a fall; this is also a good thing to learn in computing.

As a Windows XP user, you can get help in a variety of ways. In this chapter, you will learn not only how to get help after a problem has occurred, but also how to keep your system up to date so that problems do not occur in the first place.

The practice files for this chapter are located in the *SBS\WindowsXP\Backup* folder. (For details about installing the practice files, see "Using the Book's CD-ROM" at the beginning of this book.)

Keeping Your Computer Up to Date

Microsoft Windows Update is an Internet-based service that scans your computer and recommends or installs any updates that are available for your operating system, your software programs, or your hardware. Quite apart from knowing that you have the "latest and greatest," Windows Update ensures that your computer is equipped with security "patches" as they become necessary and available. You can access the Windows Update site at *windowsupdate.microsoft.com* or through either the Control Panel window or the Help and Support Center in Windows XP.

During the update process, Windows Update collects the version numbers of your operating system, Web browser, and other installed software, as well as the Plug and Play ID numbers of the hardware devices that are connected to your computer, and then compiles a list of updates that are available for your system. Some updates are classified as critical and are selected for installation by default. (If you do not want to install an update that is marked as critical, you can remove it from your list of selections.) Other updates are optional and are not selected. Windows Update provides you with a list of the updates and their descriptions and then installs only those you select. When the update process is complete, the version and ID information that was collected from your computer is discarded.

If you don't want to bear the responsibility of remembering to manually update your system, or if you want to be sure you have updates as soon as they become available, you can instruct Windows XP to automatically update your system through the Windows Update site. You can choose to have Windows XP download updates and notify you when they are ready to be installed, or you can choose to be notified before the updates are downloaded.

If you have not selected an automatic update option, Windows XP prompts you to update your operating system from time to time by displaying a message in a bubble note near the notification area. Clicking the message opens the **Automatic Updates Setup Wizard**, which leads you through a short process to select your update option. You can also change your update option at any time through Control Panel or the Help and Support Center.

In this exercise, you will instruct Windows Update to automatically deliver important software and hardware updates to your computer.

There are no practice files for this exercise.

Follow these steps:

1   Log on to Windows, if you have not already done so.
2   On the **Start** menu, click **Control Panel**.
3   In the Control Panel window, click **Performance and Maintenance**.

The Performance and Maintenance window opens:

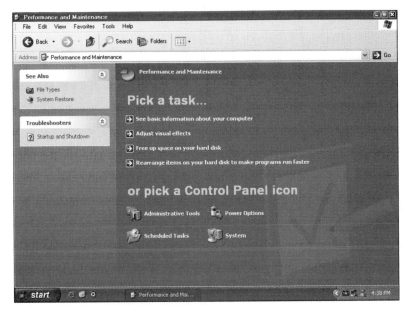

4 In the Performance and Maintenance window, click the **System** icon.

The **System Properties** dialog box opens.

5 Click the **Automatic Updates** tab.

6 Click **Download the updates automatically and notify me when they are ready to be installed**, and then click **OK** to close the dialog box and save your changes.

Close

7 Click the **Close** button to close the Performance and Maintenance window.

Diagnosing System Problems

When your computer crashes, it's a pretty obvious problem. But if it just seems to be slower than usual, it can be hard to figure out what's wrong. Windows XP comes with a variety of tools that you can use to find out what's happening with your computer, including:

■ *My Computer Information*, which you can use to find out what programs and hardware are installed on your computer and how much memory is available. You can also review diagnostic information such as the operating system and the speed of your processor.

■ *Network Diagnostics*, which you can use to gather information about your computer to help you troubleshoot network-related problems.

■ *Advanced System Information*, which links you to specialized information that a technical support person might need in order to solve a particularly difficult problem.

All these tools are available through the Help and Support Center.

In this exercise, you will gather diagnostic information about your computer.

There are no practice files for this exercise.

Follow these steps:

1 Log on to Windows, if you have not already done so.

2 On the **Start** menu, click **Help and Support**.

The Help and Support Center window opens.

3 In the Help and Support Center, click **Use Tools to view your computer information and diagnose problems**.

The Help and Support Center displays the **Tools** menu, like this:

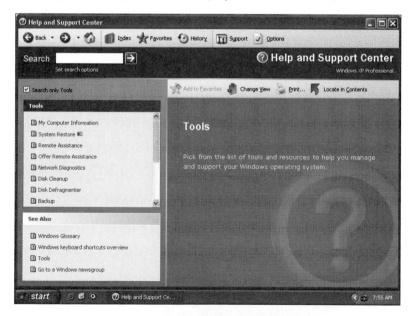

4 On the **Tools** menu, click **My Computer Information**.

The My Computer Information tool opens in the right pane of the Help and Support Center. Five options are available:

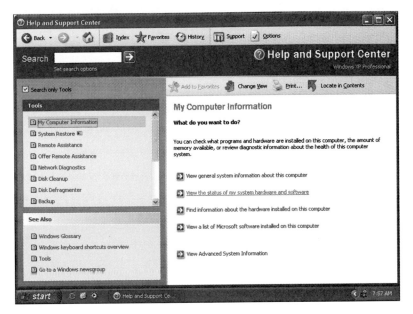

5 Click **View general system information about this computer**.

Windows XP polls your computer for general information and generates a report like this one:

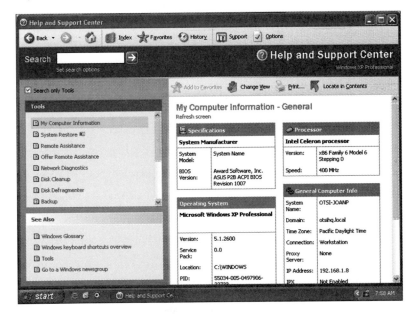

6 When you are finished looking at the report, click the **Back** button on the toolbar.

7 Click **View the status of my system hardware and software**.

Windows XP generates a report like this one:

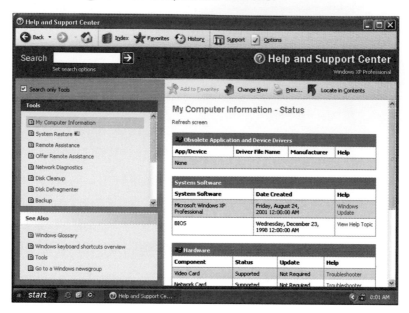

8 When you have checked out the report, click the **Back** button.

9 Click **Find information about the hardware installed on this computer**.

Again, Windows XP generates a report like this one:

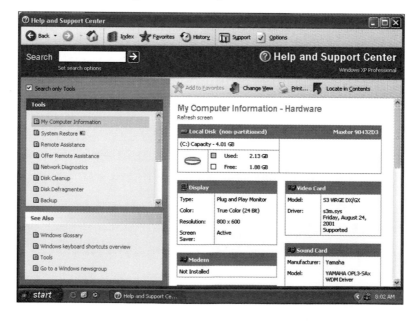

10 When you are finished looking at the report, click the **Back** button on the toolbar.

11 Click **View a list of Microsoft software installed on this computer**.

Tip

The name of this link is somewhat misleading, because the report includes all the software that runs automatically when you start your computer, and non-Microsoft software is not excluded from that list.

Windows XP polls your computer for software information and generates a report like this one:

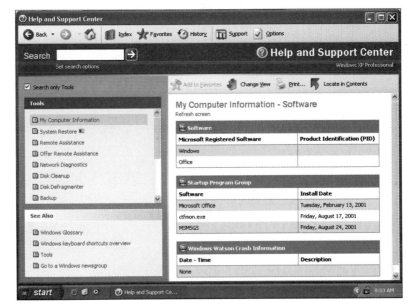

12 When you are finished looking at the report, click **Network Diagnostics** on the **Tools** menu.

The Network Diagnostics tool opens in the right pane of the Help and Support Center. These two options are available:

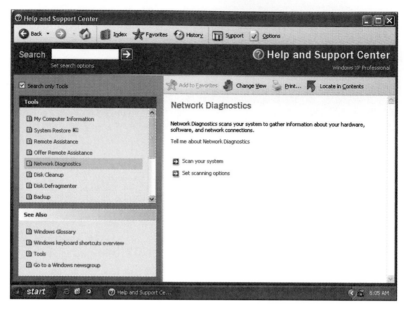

13 Click **Set scanning options**.

A list of options replaces the command.

14 Select all the check boxes, and then click **Scan your system**.

Tip

If you want to scan your entire system every time, click **Save Options**.

Command-Line Operations

Advanced (or old-fashioned) users can interact directly with their computer through the **command shell**, a non-graphical program that provides direct communication between the computer user and the operating system. Windows XP provides a complete command-line reference and a number of new **command-line tools**, which are available through the Help and Support Center.

For more information about the command-line tools, search for *command-line reference* in the Help and Support Center.

Windows XP gathers information about your hardware, software, and network connections, and then generates a report:

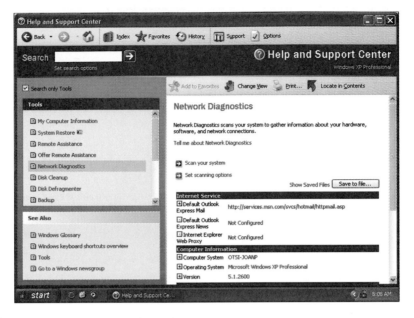

Close

15 When you are finished looking at the report, click the **Close** button to close the Help and Support Center.

Cleaning Up Your Hard Disk

Every time you open a file, access a Web page, install a program, or download a file, a temporary file is created in a specific directory on your computer. Most of these files are deleted automatically when they are no longer needed. However, poorly behaved programs sometimes don't clean up after themselves, resulting in megabytes of unnecessary files on your hard disk.

Other types of unused files can also clutter up your hard disk. A common culprit is the Recycle Bin—by default, deleted files are stored in the Recycle Bin until you empty it.

Tip

To delete a file without temporarily storing it in the Recycle Bin, press [Shift]+[Del] instead of [Del]. To always bypass the Recycle Bin, right-click the Recycle Bin, click **Properties**, select the **Do not move files to Recycle Bin** check box, and click **OK**.

You can use **Disk Cleanup** to free up space on your hard disk by removing downloaded program files, temporary files, and offline files; compressing old files; and emptying the Recycle Bin. It is a good idea to run this utility at least once a year, or as often as once a month, to keep your drive in good order. You can schedule Disk Cleanup or any other installed programs to run at regular intervals through the **Scheduled Task Wizard**. To start the **Scheduled Task Wizard**, on the **Start** menu, click **Control Panel**, and then click **Performance and Maintenance**. In the Performance and Maintenance window, click the **Scheduled Tasks** icon. In the Scheduled Tasks window, double-click **Add Scheduled Task**.

In this exercise, you will run the Disk Cleanup utility on your computer.

Tip

Depending on the number of files to be compressed and deleted, Disk Cleanup takes approximately one to three minutes to run.

There are no practice files for this exercise.

Follow these steps:

1   Log on to Windows, if you have not already done so.

2   On the **Start** menu, point to **All Programs**, point to **Accessories**, point to **System Tools**, and then click **Disk Cleanup**.

The **Disk Cleanup** dialog box appears:

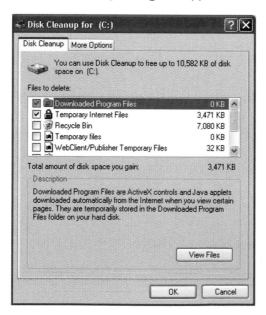

3   Select the check boxes of all the categories that currently have files available for deletion.

The total amount of disk space that will be freed up is indicated within the dialog box.

4 To view a description of the files that will be deleted, click each file type (not the check box).

The description is displayed below the check boxes. If a list of the files that will be deleted is available, a **View Files** button is also displayed.

5 Click **View Files** if it is available.

The selected files are displayed in Windows Explorer.

6 Click the **More Options** tab to display other types of files that can be deleted to free up space on your computer.

Troubleshooting

The files that you can delete through the **More Options** tab might be necessary for the running of your computer, so you might not want to make selections through this tab unless you are desperately looking for ways to free up space.

7 After you have selected all the files you want to delete, click **OK**.

8 Click **Yes** to confirm that you want to proceed with the deletion.

As Disk Cleanup completes the selected operations, a progress bar indicates how the cleanup is proceeding. You can cancel the cleanup at any point during the operation. The **Disk Cleanup** dialog box closes when the operation is complete.

Defragmenting Your Hard Disk

There can be times when, although there is nothing specifically wrong with your computer, it is not operating at its peak efficiency. You might think that your computer is simply not as fast as it used to be, and although perceived speed can be a function of your own level of patience, it might also be true that your system has slowed down since it was new. Unlike a sewing machine or a blender, a slow computer probably isn't due to the parts getting old and worn out; it might simply be that your hard disk has become cluttered and **fragmented**.

You can use **Disk Defragmenter** to analyze all the data stored on your hard disk and then consolidate fragmented files and folders into contiguous chunks to create the largest possible areas of available space. Your hard disk drive is organized into one or more **volumes** that can each be **defragmented** separately. Each volume has a drive letter assigned to it.

Troubleshooting

You must be logged on to your computer with administrative privileges to run Disk Defragmenter.

In this exercise, you will run the Disk Defragmenter utility on your computer.

Tip

Depending on the size of your hard disk, Disk Defragmenter can take up to an hour to run.

There are no practice files for this exercise.

Follow these steps:

1 Log on to Windows, if you have not already done so.

2 On the **Start** menu, point to **All Programs**, point to **Accessories**, point to **System Tools**, and then click **Disk Defragmenter**.

The **Disk Defragmenter** dialog box appears:

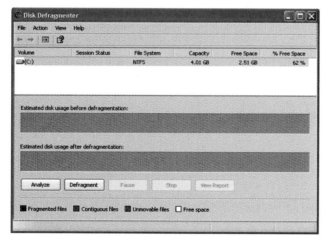

3 Click the **C:** volume to select it for defragmentation and then click **Analyze**.

Disk Defragmenter analyzes the volume and then recommends whether you need to defragment the disk.

4 Click **View Report** to see information the program collected about the volume.

5 If defragmentation is recommended and you want to do it at this time, click **Defragment**. Otherwise, click **Close** to close the report window.

6 If you choose to defragment the volume, click **Close** to close the **Disk Defragmenter** dialog box when the defragmentation process is complete.

Helping Yourself

It is fairly common for people to purchase furniture, toys, bikes, or other things that require assembly, and then neglect to read the instruction manual until they actually have a problem. Along the same lines, many people never consult the Help file in a software program, because they don't realize how much good information can be found there.

Windows XP takes the concept of the Help file to new heights with the Help and Support Center. As the name implies, the Help and Support Center is the place to go when you're having troubles—you can help yourself, or you can ask other people for help. The help offered is more than just a common Help file: It includes multimedia product tours targeted at different audiences, general and specific articles, a comprehensive glossary, tutorials and demonstrations, and links to most of the tools that you need to keep your computer running smoothly. You can choose from a list of common topics on the main page of the Help and Support Center, search the database by keyword or phrase, or look up specific topics in the index or table of contents. When you're connected to the Internet, you can easily include the **Microsoft Knowledge Base** in your searches as well.

When you search for information, your search results are divided into three areas:

- The **Suggested Topics** listing displays topics that are most likely to be of interest to you, because the search terms you entered match the keywords defined by the topic's author.
- The **Full-text Search Matches** listing displays all the topics in which the individual words of your search terms appear.
- The **Microsoft Knowledge Base** listing displays articles that pertain to your search phrase from Microsoft's online database of product support information. This listing is available only when you are online.

You can search the entire support database, and you can conduct a subsequent search within the results of a previous search, thereby narrowing down the search results to define your problem.

If you can't solve your problem on your own, you can communicate with other Windows XP users and experts via online newsgroups, consult online with Microsoft support personnel, or request remote assistance from a friend or co-worker. Using Remote Assistance, you can allow another person to connect to your computer via the Internet and take control of your computer to figure out what the trouble is.

The Help and Support Center links to Web-based information to ensure that it is always up to date. This means that you don't have access to all the features of the Help and Support Center when you are offline.

There are two ways to access the Help and Support Center:

- Click **Help and Support** on the **Start** menu.
- Press ⌗. Depending on what area of Windows you are in, this might open the Help and Support Center to a page that is specific to that area. For example, if you press ⌗ from within Control Panel, the Help and Support Center opens to the Control Panel topic.

Tip

⌗ opens the Help file for the currently active Microsoft application. Pressing ⌗ from within a Microsoft Word file opens the Word Help file; pressing ⌗ from within a Microsoft Excel file opens the Excel Help file, and so on. Many software manufacturers have made their context-sensitive help available through the ⌗ key, which is why you often hear context-sensitive help referred to as *F1 Help*.

In this exercise, you will open the Help file and search for useful information.

There are no practice files for this exercise.

Follow these steps:

1 Log on to Windows, if you have not already done so.

2 On the **Start** menu, click **Help and Support**.

The Help and Support window opens:

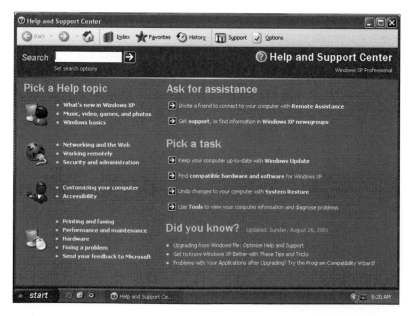

3 Click **Index**.

You see a list of available topics.

4 Click **Home**.

You return to the Help and Support Center.

Start searching

5 In the **Search** box, type **getting help**, and then click the **Start searching** button.

Tip

Search terms are not case-sensitive; typing *getting Help* produces the same results.

The results of your search are shown in the Search Results pane. The total number of "hits" is displayed at the top, and the suggested topics are shown by default.

6 In the **Search Results** title bar, click **Tips** to display a list of useful search tips.

7 When you finish reviewing the search tips, click any topic title in the left pane to display that topic in the right pane.

8 Click **Locate in Contents** to display the topic in relation to the table of contents.

You can use this feature to locate related information without going through another search.

9 Click **Back** until you return to the **Search Results** pane.

10 Click the **Full-text Search Matches** bar.

The bar slides up to display the listing.

11 Click the **Microsoft Knowledge Base** bar.

Again, the bar slides up to display the listing.

Close

12 When you finish browsing through the Help file, click the **Close** button to close the Help and Support Center.

Joining a Windows Newsgroup

Windows **newsgroups** are online forums where Windows XP users and experts from around the world interact to discuss their experiences with Windows XP. These news-groups are not officially monitored by Microsoft, and Microsoft is not responsible for any of the information available there. You can find discussion threads about many common and uncommon problems. You might find an answer to your question, or you might find an interesting topic of discussion that you want to keep up with or take part in.

Newsgroups are free of charge, and you can join or quit them at any time. You can link to the newsgroups via Microsoft Outlook Express or via a Web-based newsgroup reader. After joining the newsgroup, you can interact with a newsgroup in several different ways:

- You can visit a newsgroup to read messages.
- You can post a new message and wait for a response, either in e-mail or in the newsgroup.
- You can post a reply to a message to the newsgroup; your message then becomes part of the discussion thread and is available to anyone who visits the newsgroup.
- You can send an e-mail message to the person who posted a specific message, or forward the message to someone else via e-mail.
- You can subscribe to a newsgroup and have all its messages sent to you.
- You can subscribe to a specific discussion thread, in which case you will receive an e-mail message notifying you when a new message has been posted to the thread.

A word of warning about newsgroups: Some people see them as a forum for blowing off steam without actually communicating information that is useful or interesting to anyone else. You might find that it takes quite a while to wade through all the available messages before you find information that is pertinent to your situation. On the bright side, although Microsoft does not officially monitor the newsgroups, there do appear to be a fair number of "experts" who post useful information or respond to valid queries.

In this exercise, you will investigate the available Windows XP newsgroups using a Web-based newsgroup reader.

There are no practice files for this exercise, but you will need an active Internet connection to complete it.

Follow these steps:

1 Log on to Windows, if you have not already done so.
2 On the **Start** menu, click **Help and Support**.
3 Under **Ask for assistance** in the Help and Support Center, click **Get support, or find information in Windows XP newsgroups** to see this information:

4 In the **Support** area, click **Go to a Windows Web site forum**.

The **Windows Newsgroups** page opens.

5 Click **Go to Windows Newsgroups**.

Tip

The world icon overlaid by a red arrow indicates that you are connecting to an external Web site.

The **Windows XP Newsgroups** Web page opens:

You can read the messages of each newsgroup either in Outlook Express or in your Web browser. If you click the bold listing for a newsgroup, it opens in Outlook Express. If you click **Web-based reader** below any newsgroup name, the messages are displayed in your browser.

Tip

For step-by-step instructions on configuring Outlook Express for a newsgroup, click **Windows XP Newsgroups Setup Instructions.**

6 Select an interesting newsgroup from the list, and click the **Web-based reader** link under the title of the newsgroup.

A new Web page opens with all the messages to that newsgroup shown, something like this:

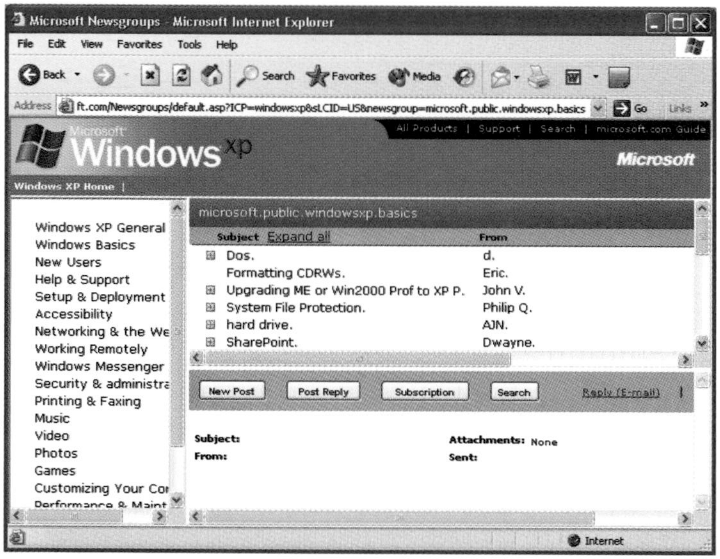

You can click any message to view it in the preview pane at the bottom of the window. You can then post a reply to the message or send an e-mail to the person who posted the message, using the buttons in the preview pane.

Close

7 When you finish looking through the newsgroup, click the **Close** button to close the Web page, and then click the **Close** button to close the Help and Support Center.

Contacting Product Support

The product support offered by software and hardware companies varies wildly depending on the type of product, the price you paid, and the company. Microsoft has traditionally offered very good product support, though getting help often involved a long telephone call, with the technician on the other end spending quite a while determining the status of your system and your actual problem.

Microsoft
Online
Assisted
Support

new for
WindowsXP

Microsoft Online Assisted Support is the relatively new face of product support at Microsoft. You can use Online Assisted Support to log specific problems with the Microsoft support staff, who then reply to your problem online. This method of handling product support is very efficient, both for you and for Microsoft.

The diagnostic tools provided with Windows XP make it easy to send all the information your product support technician needs to diagnose the problem and offer a useful solution. You can either allow your system information to be collected automatically, or you can stipulate which information may be sent to Microsoft. Your Product ID code and operating system version are the only required information. Optional information includes:

- Computer manufacturer and model
- Processor model and speed
- Amount of **random access memory (RAM)**
- General system information
- Information on your system files

If you want, you can review all of the information before it is sent. You are not required to send any information other than your Product ID and Windows XP version number, but it can be useful to the technical support people to have a more complete understanding of your computer system, because often known issues affect only certain computer models, sound cards, graphics cards, and so on. You can also send file attachments that aren't specifically requested; for example, you might send a screenshot of an error message that will help to explain the problem.

After you complete and submit an Incident Form, your data is collected, compressed, and sent to Microsoft, and an Incident Number is assigned. You can use this tracking number to follow up on your request for help at a later date. You don't usually need to keep the tracking number, but it does reassure you that your problem has become part of the product support database.

Troubleshooting

If for any reason the Incident Form is not successfully submitted, your data is saved on your computer so that you can quickly submit it later.

When you have your Incident Number, you can return to the Online Assisted Support site at a later time to view the results, or you can ask to be notified by e-mail when an answer has been posted.

In this exercise, you will walk through the process of creating an Online Assisted Support Incident report.

There are no practice files for this exercise, but you need an active Internet connection and a Passport account to complete it.

Follow these steps:

1 Log on to Windows, if you have not already done so.

2 On the **Start** menu, click **Help and Support**.

3 On the toolbar, click the **Support** button.

4 On the **Support** menu, click **Get help from Microsoft**.

Windows XP checks your Internet connection and then connects you to the Microsoft Product Support Services Web site, which opens within the Help and Support Center.

5 Enter your Passport sign-in name and password, and click **Sign In**.

Tip

If you have set up your computer to sign you in to Passport automatically, you will bypass the sign-in screen.

The first time you access Online Assisted Support, you see the information shown on this page:

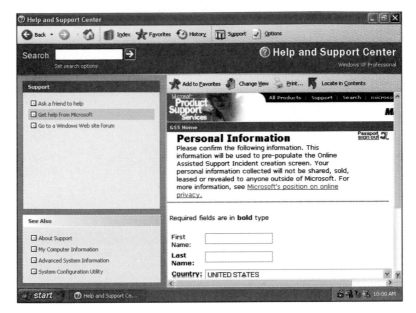

6   If prompted to do so, enter the requested information, select the **I accept the License Agreement for the use of this site** check box, and then click **Submit**.

The **Microsoft Online Assisted Support** page opens:

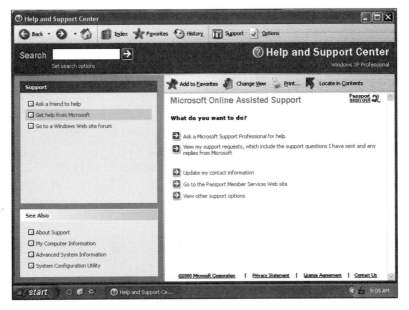

7   Click **Ask a Microsoft Support Professional for help**.

The next page prompts you to select the product for which you require support.

8 In the drop-down list, click **Microsoft Windows XP**, and then click **Next**.

9 If you are prompted to install the Web Response File Transfer Control, click **Yes**.

Tip

Your security settings might require your permission for the installation of new controls on your computer.

A new Incident Form opens.

Maximize

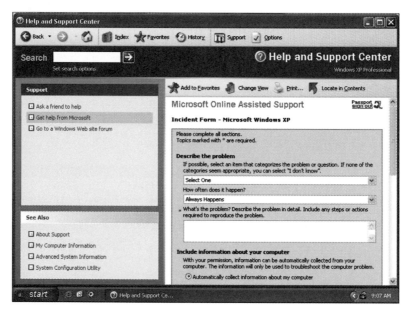

10 If the form window is not already maximized, click the **Maximize** button to expand the window so you can see as much of the form as possible.

The form looks like this:

11 Look through the input requested on the form so that you are aware of all the options. If you're actually having a problem at this time, feel free to submit an Incident Form.

Close

12 When you're finished looking at the site, click the **Close** button to close the Help and Support Center.

Asking for Help from Someone Else

If you've tried to solve a problem on your own and simply have not been successful, Windows XP makes it easy to turn to someone else for help. You have the choice of contacting Microsoft Product Support Services or asking a friend or co-worker to help you.

Remote
Assistance

new for
WindowsXP

You can use **Remote Assistance**, an exciting new feature of Windows XP, to invite another person who is running Windows XP and is connected to your intranet or the Internet to view your computer screen and use Windows Messenger to chat with you about the problem. If you want to, you can then give that person permission to work remotely on your computer, without ever leaving his or her own desk!

To initiate a Remote Assistance session, you send an invitation to the other person. You can limit the chance that someone could fraudulently gain access to your computer through the invitation by specifying the duration of the invitation, from 1 minute to 99 days. You can also require that the other person enter a password to access your computer, in which case you would supply the password to them separately from the invitation.

In this exercise, you will request and receive Remote Assistance from another person.

There are no practice files for this exercise. You must have an active Internet connection, a Passport, and an online buddy who is also running Windows XP to complete it.

Follow these steps:

1   Log on to Windows, if you have not already done so.

2   On the **Start** menu, point to **All Programs**, and then click **Remote Assistance**.

The Help and Support Center opens to the **Remote Assistance** page:

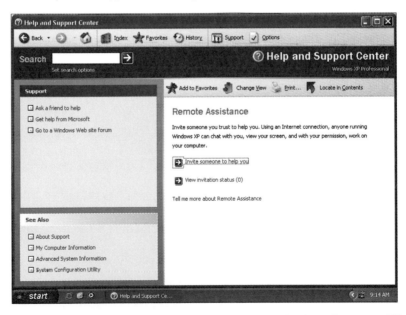

3   Click **Invite someone to help you**. If you are asked to sign on to Windows Messenger, do so.

Your **Remote Assistance** options are displayed:

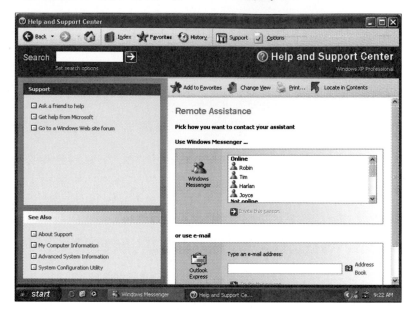

You can also send a remote assistance invitation to someone via Windows Messenger or e-mail.

4 Click the name of the person you are going to invite to help you; or type his or her e-mail address in the **Type an e-mail address** box, and then click **Invite this person**. If you used Windows Messenger, skip to step 11.

5 When the remote assistance invitation opens, type an explanatory message in the **Message** box, and then click **Continue**.

You are prompted to specify the duration of your invitation.

6 Accept the default of **01 Hours**.

7 If you want to use a password, enter the password in the **Type password** and **Confirm password** boxes, and then relay that password to your Remote Assistance buddy.

8 When you are ready to send the invitation, click **Send Invitation**.

Your invitation is sent via Windows Messenger or via your default e-mail program. You will be notified that a program is attempting to send a message in your name.

9 Click **Send**.

When your invitation has been sent, you will see a confirmation.

10 Click **View invitation status** to view your invitation, which looks something like this:

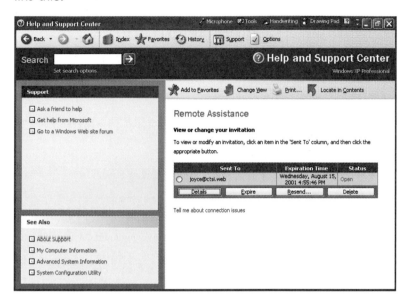

You can review, expire, resend, or delete invitations from this page at any time.

Enabling and Disabling Remote Assistance

The Remote Assistance option is turned on by default. If you are uncomfortable with the idea that other people might be able to access your computer over the Internet, you can turn off the Remote Assistance option on your Windows XP computer.

To disable Remote Assistance:

1 On the **Start** menu, click **Control Panel**.

2 In the Control Panel window, click **Performance and Maintenance**.

3 In the Performance and Maintenance window, click the **System** icon.

The **System Properties** dialog box opens.

4 Click the **Remote** tab, and then click the **Advanced** button.

The **Remote Assistance Settings** dialog box opens.

5 Clear the **Allow this computer to be controlled remotely** check box.

6 Click **OK** to close the **Remote Assistance Settings** dialog box, and then click **OK** to close the **System Properties** dialog box and save your changes.

To enable Remote Assistance, repeat the process, this time selecting the **Allow this computer to be controlled remotely** check box.

When your invitation is received and accepted by your Remote Assistance buddy, a Remote Assistance message is displayed on your computer screen.

11 Click **Yes** to allow your buddy to view your screen and chat with you.

This Remote Assistance window opens on your computer:

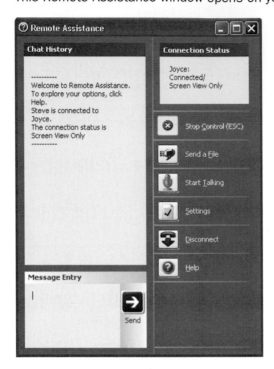

A window also opens on your buddy's computer. At this point, the two of you can chat by typing messages or, if you both have microphones and speakers, by talking. You can also send a file.

Your buddy can see everything you do on your computer, so you can open files or follow the steps that lead up to a problem and then ask for advice.

12 In the chat session, tell your buddy to take control of your computer.

He or she will need to click the **Take Control** button on the Remote Assistance toolbar. You will then receive a message asking if you would like to share control of your computer.

13 Click **Yes**.

You both now have control of the mouse on your computer. However, you should not both try to move it at the same time.

Stop Control

14 When you decide that you no longer want to share control of your computer, click the **Stop Control** button in the Remote Assistance window.

You now have exclusive control of your mouse.

Disconnect

15 When you are finished with the Remote Assistance session, click the **Disconnect** button.

Close

16 Click the **Close** button to close the Remote Assistance window.

17 Click the **Close** button to close the Help and Support Center.

Backing Up and Restoring Files

When *file* and *folder* were terms used to describe things made of paper, it was possible for your important documents to be permanently destroyed by fire, water, coffee, accidental shredding, or a variety of other natural and unnatural disasters. With the advent of electronic files and folders, your data can still be destroyed, but it doesn't have to be permanently.

The **Backup or Restore Wizard** creates a copy of the files and folders on your hard disk. If your data is lost or damaged, you can restore it from the backup file. It is advisable to regularly create a backup of any files and folders that are important to you. The frequency of the backup depends on the frequency of changes to the files, because if you lose your data, you will have to recreate anything that has occurred since the last backup. For this reason, many companies back up their important files on a daily basis.

You can select from different backup options, depending on your needs:

- *Normal* backs up all selected files and system settings for a specific folder or drive and marks each file as backed up.
- *Copy* backs up all selected files and system settings for a specific folder or drive, but does not mark the files as having been backed up.
- *Incremental* backs up only the files that have been created or modified since the last normal or incremental backup and marks each file as backed up.
- *Differential* backs up only the files that have been created or modified since the last normal or incremental backup, but does not mark the files.
- *Daily* backs up only those files that were created or modified today, but does not mark the files.

The type of backup you perform determines how complex the restoration process is. To restore after several incremental or differential backups, you must restore the last normal backup and all the incremental or differential backups since then.

When you back up your data, you designate a file name and location for the backup file. By default, backup files are saved with a .bkf extension, but you can specify any file extension. Your backup file can be saved on your hard disk, on a floppy disk, or on any other type of removable media. Considerations when choosing a backup location include the size of the backup file, the types of media you have available, and whether you want to store the file separately from the computer in case of disaster.

In this exercise, you will back up the files contained in a directory that was installed from this book's CD-ROM. You will need a formatted floppy disk for this exercise.

The practice files for this exercise are located in the *SBS\WindowsXP\Solving \Backup* folder. (For details about installing the practice files, see "Using the Book's CD-ROM" at the beginning of this book.)

Follow these steps:

1   Log on to Windows, if you have not already done so.

2   On the **Start** menu, point to **All Programs**, point to **Accessories**, point to **System Tools**, and then click **Backup**.

The **Backup or Restore Wizard** opens.

3   Click **Next** to begin the process of backing up your files.

The **Backup or Restore** page opens:

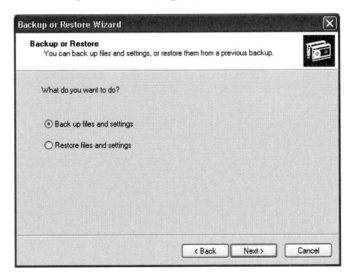

4   Click **Back up files and settings**, and then click **Next**.

The **What to Back Up** page opens:

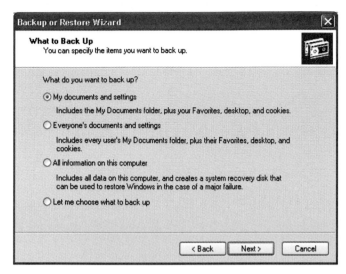

5   Click **Let me choose what to back up**, and then click **Next**.

The **Items to Back Up** page opens:

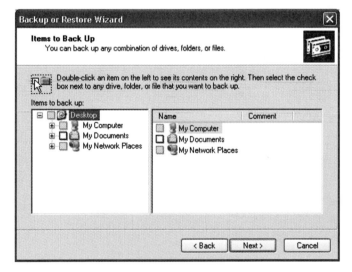

6   Browse to *My Computer\C\SBS\WindowsXP\Backup* by clicking the plus signs to the left of the folders to expand them.

7   Select the check box preceding the working folder, and then click **Next**.

Tip

If the folder structure is too wide for the pane it appears in, drag the pane's right border to the right to widen the pane.

The **Backup Type, Destination, and Name** page opens:

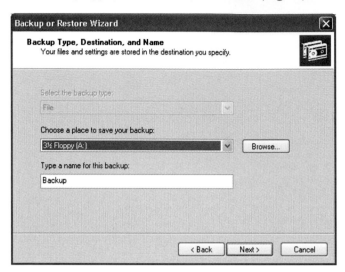

8   Accept the default destination (*3½ Floppy*) and file name (*Backup.bkf*) and then click **Save**.

Tip

You would normally want to back up to removable media with a large capacity, such as a tape drive, or a remote computer.

9   Click **Next**, and then click **Finish** to start the backup.

The **Backup Progress** dialog box displays the status of the backup process.

10   When the backup is complete, click **Close**.

11   To restore your files and folders at a later date, repeat steps 2 and 3, then select the **Restore files and settings** option, browse to and select the backup file, click **Next**, and then click **Finish**.

Tip

You can launch the **Backup or Restore Wizard** and select the backup file at the same time by double-clicking the **backup.bkf** file in Windows Explorer. To open Windows Explorer, on the **Start** menu, point to **All Programs**, point to **Accessories**, and then click **Windows Explorer**.

Restoring Your Operating System

In the beginning, you had a clean computer with a brand-new operating system. As time goes by, you install new programs, delete programs, change your system settings, and upgrade to new versions of programs. Gradually, things change.

Sometimes you might find yourself wishing you could go back to the way things were, and now you can! You can use **System Restore Wizard** to roll back your system to the condition it was in at a prior point in time. You can roll back to any of these types of checkpoints and restoration points:

- An **initial system checkpoint** is created the first time you start a new computer, or the first time you start your computer after you upgrade it to Windows XP.

- **Automatic update restore points** are created when you install updates that are downloaded through Windows Update.

- **Backup recovery restore points** are created when you use the **Backup or Restore Wizard**.

- You can manually create your own restore points (**manual checkpoints**) at any time from the **System Restore Wizard**.

- **Program name installation restore points** are created when you install a program using an installer such as InstallShield or Windows XP Installer.

- **Restore operation restore points** are created each time you perform a restoration; if you are not satisfied with the results of the restoration, you can roll back to this point.

- **System checkpoints** are scheduled restoration points that your computer creates regularly, even if you have not made any changes to the system.

- **Unsigned device driver restore points** are created when you install a device driver that has not been signed or certified.

System Restore generally saves one to three weeks' worth of restoration checkpoints. The number of restoration checkpoints available at any given time is limited by the amount of space you allocate to the System Restore function. The maximum space you can allocate is approximately 12 percent.

Restoring your computer restores Windows XP and the programs that are installed on your computer to the state they were in at the time of the selected restore checkpoint. Your personal files (including your saved documents, e-mail messages, Address Book, Internet Explorer Favorites, and History list) are not affected. All the changes made by System Restore are completely reversible, so if you don't like the results, you can restore the previous settings and try again.

In this exercise, you will see how to restore your computer to a previous state.

Troubleshooting

System Restore restarts your computer, so be sure to close any open programs before running it.

There are no practice files for this exercise.

Follow these steps:

1 Log on to Windows, if you have not already done so.

2 Close any open programs.

3 On the **Start** menu, point to **All Programs**, point to **Accessories**, point to **System Tools**, and then click **System Restore**.

Tip

You can also access System Restore by clicking **Undo changes to your computer with System Restore** in the Help and Support Center, or by opening Control Panel from the **Start** menu, clicking **Performance and Maintenance**, and then clicking **System Restore** in the **See Also** area.

The **System Restore Wizard** starts:

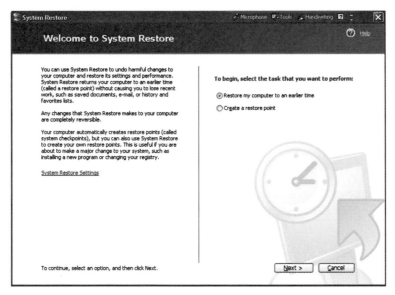

4 Click **Restore my computer to an earlier time**, and then click **Next**.

The **Select a Restore Point** page opens, displaying a calendar. The days on which restoration checkpoints were created are indicated on the calendar by a bold date.

Troubleshooting

You can move to different months by clicking the arrows on either side of the month name. These arrows are active only when restoration checkpoints exist in the previous or next months.

5   Click each of the bold dates to see the checkpoints that were created on that day:

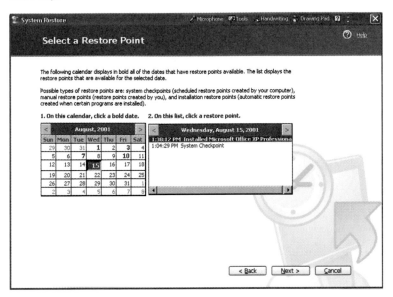

6   On the calendar, click a bold date that has a restoration checkpoint shown for that day,

7   In the description panel, click a specific restoration checkpoint.

8   Click **Next**.

System Restore displays information about your selected checkpoint.

Important

Do not continue this exercise unless you want to restore your computer to an earlier state. Although it is possible to undo the restoration, there is always a possibility of loss of data in any action such as this.

9   Click **Next**.

System Restore logs off of Windows XP, restores your files to their condition at the time of the selected checkpoint, and then restarts your computer.

10   If you normally log on to your computer with a user account name and password, you will need to enter them.

Depending on the types of changes that were made since the chosen restoration checkpoint, you might or might not notice a visible difference when the computer restarts.

Quick Reference

20   **To maximize an open window**

Maximize

- Click the **Maximize** button on the title bar.

20   **To restore an open window to its normal size**

Restore Down

- Click the **Restore Down** button on the title bar.

20   **To close an open window**

Close

- Click the **Close** button on the title bar.

21   **To display a window**

- Click the window's taskbar button.

22   **To open the Start menu**

start

- Click the **Start** button.

26   **To pin a program to the Start menu**

1. Browse to the selected program on the **Start** menu.
2. Right-click the program name, and click **Pin to Start menu** on the shortcut menu.

27   **To remove a program from the pinned programs area**

- Right-click the program link, and click **Unpin from Start menu** on the short-cut menu.

30   **To display the Quick Launch toolbar**

- Right-click an empty area of the taskbar, point to **Toolbars** on the shortcut menu, and then click **Quick Launch**.

32   **To create a desktop shortcut to a file or folder**

1. Right-click an open area of the desktop.
2. On the shortcut menu, point to **New**, and then click **Shortcut**.
3. Click **Browse** to open the **Browse For Folder** dialog box.
4. Browse to the file or folder, and then click **OK**.
5. Click **Next**.
6. Enter the name of the shortcut, and then click **Finish** to close the wizard.

34   To create a shortcut for a Web site

1   Right-click an open area of the desktop, point to **New** on the shortcut menu, and click **Shortcut**.

2   Type the URL of the Web site in the **Type the location of the item** box, and click **Next**.

3   Enter a name for the shortcut, and click **Finish** to close the dialog box.

35   To copy or move a shortcut from the desktop to the Quick Launch toolbar

1   Using the right mouse button, drag the desktop shortcut to the Quick Launch toolbar.

2   Click **Copy Here** or **Move Here** on the shortcut menu.

35   To lock or unlock the taskbar

●   Right-click the taskbar, and click **Lock the Taskbar** on the shortcut menu.

35   To delete a shortcut from the Quick Launch toolbar

●   Right-click the shortcut, and click **Delete** on the shortcut menu.

36   To Auto Arrange your desktop shortcuts

●   Right-click an open area of the desktop, point to **Arrange Icons By** on the shortcut menu, and then click **Auto Arrange**.

37   To clean up your desktop

1   Right-click any open area of the desktop, point to **Arrange Icons By** on the shortcut menu, click **Run Desktop Cleanup Wizard**, and click **Next**.

2   Select the desktop shortcuts you want to delete, click **Next**, and Click **Finish**.

39   To delete a shortcut, program, file, or folder from the desktop

1   Right-click the item you want to delete, and click **Delete** on the shortcut menu.

2   In the confirmation box, click **Yes** to delete the item.

Chapter   3   Managing Computer Security

47   To create a user account in Windows XP Professional

1   On the **Start** menu, click **Control Panel**, and then click **User Accounts**.

2   On the **Advanced** tab, click **Advanced**.

3   In the left pane of the Local Users and Groups window, click **Users** folder.

4   On the **Action** menu, click **New User**.

5   Enter the user information, click **Create**, and then click **Close**.

Close

6   Click the **Close** button to close the Local Users and Groups window, click **OK** to close the **User Accounts** dialog box, and then click the **Close** button to close Control Panel.

50   **To change the group to which a Windows XP Professional user account is assigned**

1   On the **Start** menu, click **Control Panel**, and then click **User Accounts**.

2   In the **Users for this computer** list, click the user name, and click **Properties**.

3   On the **Group Membership** tab, click **Other**, and click the group name in the drop-down list.

4   Click **OK** to close the **Properties** dialog box, and then click **OK** to close the **User Accounts** dialog box.

Close

5   Click the **Close** button to close Control Panel.

52   **To delete a Windows XP Professional user account**

1   On the **Start** menu, click **Control Panel**, and then click **User Accounts**.

2   In the **Users for this computer** list, click the user name, and click **Remove**.

3   When prompted to confirm the removal, click **Yes**.

4   Click **OK** to close the **User Accounts** dialog box.

Close

5   Click the **Close** button to close Control Panel.

54   **To create a Windows XP Home Edition user account**

1   On the **Start** menu, click **Control Panel**, and then click **User Accounts**.

2   Click **Create a new account**.

3   Enter a name for the new account, and then click **Next**.

4   Specify the account type, and then click **Create Account**.

Close

5   Click the **Close** button to close the User Accounts window, and then close Control Panel.

56   **To change a Windows XP Home Edition user account type**

1   On the **Start** menu, click **Control Panel**, and then click **User Accounts**.

2   Click the account that you want to change, and then click **Change the account type**.

3   On the **Pick a new account type** screen, click the new account type, and then click **Change Account Type**.

Close

4 Click the **Close** button to close the User Accounts window, and then close Control Panel.

56 **To create a Windows XP Home Edition user account password**

1 On the **Start** menu, click **Control Panel**, and then click **User Accounts**.

2 Click the account you want to change, and then click **Create a password**.

3 Enter a password in the **Type a new password** box, and re-enter the password in the **Type the new password again to confirm** box.

4 Enter a password hint in the **Type a word or phrase to use as a password hint** box, and then click **Create Password**.

Close

5 Click the **Close** button to close the User Accounts window, and then close Control Panel.

57 **To delete a Windows XP Home Edition user account**

1 On the **Start** menu, click **Control Panel**, and then click **User Accounts**.

2 Click the account that you want to change, and then click **Delete the account**.

3 Specify whether you want to keep or delete any files the user has created, and then click **Delete Account**.

Close

4 Click the **Close** button to close the User Accounts window, and then close Control Panel.

Chapter 4 Adding Hardware and Software
Page 64 **To install speakers**

1 Remove the speakers from their packaging, if you have not already done so.

2 Link the two speakers using the connector cable.

3 Position the speakers to the left and right of your monitor to provide stereo sound quality.

4 Plug the speakers into a nearby power outlet using the AC adapter cord.

5 Plug the speakers into the speaker jack on the sound card at the back of the computer using the connector cable.

64 **To install a microphone**

1 Remove the microphone from its packaging, if you have not already done so.

2 Plug the microphone connector cable into the audio input jack on the sound card on the back of your computer.

69 **To install a local Plug and Play printer**

● Connect the printer to the appropriate port.

69 **To install a local printer with an installation CD-ROM or disk**

1 Connect the printer to the appropriate port.

2 On the **Start** menu, click **Printers and Faxes.**

3 On the **Printer Tasks** menu, click **Add a printer** to open the **Add Printer Wizard**, and then click **Next**.

4 On the **Local or Network Printer** page, click **Local printer attached to this computer**.

5 Clear the **Automatically detect and install my Plug and Play printer** check box, and then click **Next**.

6 On the **Select a Printer Port** page, confirm that your printer is connected to the recommended printer port, or click the correct port in the drop-down list, and click **Next**.

7 On the **Install Printer Software** page, insert the installation CD-ROM or floppy disk, click **Have Disk**, and follow the instructions on the screen.

Close

8 When the installation is complete, click the **Close** button to close the Printers and Faxes window.

69 **To install a local printer without an installation CD-ROM or disk**

1 Connect the printer to the appropriate port.

2 On the **Start** menu, click **Printers and Faxes.**

3 On the **Printer Tasks** menu, click **Add a printer** to open the **Add Printer Wizard**, and then click **Next**.

4 On the **Local or Network Printer** page, click **Local printer attached to this computer**.

5 Clear the **Automatically detect and install my Plug and Play printer** check box, and then click **Next**.

6 On the **Select a Printer Port** page, confirm that your printer is connected to the recommended printer port, or click the correct port in the drop-down list, and click **Next**.

7 In the **Manufacturer** list on the **Install Printer Software** page, click the name of the manufacturer of your printer.

8 In the **Printers** list, select the model of your printer, and then click **Next**.

9 On the **Name Your Printer** page, type a name for your printer in the **Printer name** box, or accept the default name, and then click **Next**.

10 On the **Print Test Page** page, click **Yes**, and then click **Next**.

11 Click **Finish** to print the test page, and then click **OK** to close the confirmation dialog box and the **Add Printer Wizard**.

Close

12 Click the **Close** button to close the Printers and Faxes window.

75 To connect to a network printer

1 On the **Start** menu, click **Printers and Faxes**.

2 On the **Printer Tasks** menu, click **Add a printer**.

3 In the **Add Printer Wizard**, click **Next**.

4 On the **Local or Network Printer** page, select **A network printer, or a printer attached to another computer**, and then click **Next**.

5 On the **Specify a Printer** page, select **Connect to this printer**, type the computer name and printer name in the **Name** box and click **Next**.

6 If prompted, enter a user account name and password, and then click **OK**.

7 If prompted, specify a default printer, and then click **Next**.

Close

8 Click **Finish** to close the dialog box, and then click the **Close** button to close the Printers and Faxes window.

79 To install a Plug and Play scanner or camera

● Plug your scanner or camera into the appropriate port on your computer.

79 To access a Plug and Play scanner or camera

1 On the **Start** menu, click **Control Panel**, and then click **Printers and Other Hardware**.

2 In the Printers and Other Hardware window, click **Scanners and Cameras**.

3 Double-click the icon for your scanner or camera to open the **Scanner and Camera Wizard**.

80 To install an external storage device

● Plug the storage device into the appropriate port and into a power source, if necessary.

81 To install an internal CD-RW drive

1 Turn off your computer, and disconnect the power cord.

2 Remove the computer's cover, and install the internal device according to the manufacturer's instructions.

3 Replace the cover, and reconnect the power cord.

4   Turn on the computer, and log on to Windows XP.

85   **To install a software program from a folder on your hard drive**

1   In Windows Explorer, browse to the folder from which you want to install the program.

2   Double-click the **Setup** file, and walk through the installation process.

85   **To uninstall a software program from your computer**

1   On the **Start** menu, click **Control Panel**, and click **Add or Remove Programs**.

2   In the Add or Remove Programs window, click the program you want to remove, and then click the **Change/Remove** button.

3   Accept the default uninstall options to remove the program from your computer.

88   **To start a program automatically**

1   On the **Start** menu, point to **All Programs**, right-click **Startup**, and then click **Explore** on the shortcut menu.

2   Drag the program you want to start automatically into the Startup folder.

Chapter   5   **Working with Files and Folders**
Page   **94**   **To start Window Explorer in Folders view**

●   On the **Start** menu, point to **All Programs**, point to **Accessories**, and then click **Windows Explorer**.

101   **To start Window Explorer in Tasks view**

●   On the **Start** menu, click **My Computer**.

101   **To change the way you view files and folders in Windows Explorer**

Views

●   On the toolbar, click the **Views** button, and then click the desired view.

108   **To display or hide the Address toolbar**

1   Right-click the taskbar, and click **Lock the taskbar** to deselect it.

2   On the taskbar shortcut menu, click **Toolbars**, and then click **Address**.

110   **To view the properties of a file or folder**

●   Right-click the file or folder, and click **Properties** on the shortcut menu.

113   To create a new folder

1   On the **File and Folder Tasks** menu, click **Make a new folder**.

2   With the default folder name selected, type the name of the folder, and then press `Enter`.

115   To create a new text document

1   Right-click in the right pane of Windows Explorer, and on the shortcut menu, point to **New**, and then click **Text Document**.

2   With the default file name selected, type the name of the folder, and then press `Enter`.

115   To create a new bitmap image

1   Right-click an empty area of the right pane, and on the shortcut menu, point to **New**, and then click **Bitmap Image**.

2   With the default file name selected, type the name of the folder, and then press `Enter`.

117   To create a compressed folder

1   Select the file(s) you want to include in the folder.

2   Right-click the selection, and on the shortcut menu, point to **Send To**, and then click **Compressed (zipped) Folder**.

119   To make a copy of a folder

1   Select the folder. On the **File and Folder Tasks** menu, click **Copy this folder**.

2   In the **Copy Items** dialog box, browse to the folder where you want to insert the copy, and then click **Copy**.

120   To rename a folder

1   Right-click the folder, and click **Rename** on the shortcut menu.

2   With the name selected, type the new name of the folder, and press `Enter`.

120   To make a copy of a file

●   Right-click the file, and click **Copy** on the shortcut menu. Right-click an empty area of the right pane, and click **Paste** on the shortcut menu; or

●   Select the original file, and on the **Edit** menu, click **Copy**. On the **Edit** menu, click **Paste**; or

●   Select the original file, press `Ctrl`+`C`, and then press `Ctrl`+`V`.

121 **To move a file**

- Drag the file from the right pane and drop it into the new folder in the left pane; or

1 Select the file. On the **File and Folder Tasks** menu, click **Move this file**.

2 In the **Move Items** dialog box, browse to the folder where you want to move the file, and then click **Move**.

122 **To start the Search Companion**

- On the **Start** menu, click **Search**.

Chapter 6 **Personalizing Windows XP**

Page **128** **To switch between the Windows XP and Windows Classic themes**

1 On the **Start** menu, click **Control Panel**, and then click **Appearance and Themes**.

2 Click the **Change the computer's theme** task.

3 On the **Themes** tab of the **Display Properties** dialog box, click the down arrow to the right of the **Themes** box, and click **Windows Classic** in the drop-down list.

4 Click **OK** to close the dialog box and apply your settings.

Close

☒ **5** Click the window's **Close** button to return to the desktop.

131 **To apply a plain, colored desktop background**

1 On the **Start** menu, click **Control Panel**, and click **Appearance and Themes**.

2 Click the **Change the desktop background** task.

3 On the **Desktop** tab of the **Display Properties** dialog box, click **None** in the **Background** box.

4 Click the down arrow to the right of the **Color** box, and click a colored square in the drop-down list.

5 Click **OK** to apply your background selection and close the **Display Properties** dialog box.

Close

☒ **6** Click the **Close** button to close the Appearance and Themes window.

132 **To apply a desktop background photograph**

1 On the **Start** menu, click **Control Panel**, and click **Appearance and Themes**.

2 Click the **Change the desktop background** task.

3 On the **Desktop** tab of the **Display Properties** dialog box, click the background you want to apply in the **Background** box.

4 Click **OK** to apply your background selection and close the **Display Properties** dialog box.

Close

5 Click the **Close** button to close the Appearance and Themes window.

133 To create a custom photograph slideshow screen saver

1 On the **Start** menu, click **Control Panel**, and click **Appearance and Themes**.

2 Click the **Choose a screen saver** task.

3 On the **Screen Saver** tab of the **Display Properties** dialog box, click the down arrow to the right of the **Screen saver** box.

4 In the drop-down list, click **My Pictures Slideshow**.

5 Click the **Settings** button.

6 In the **My Pictures Screen Saver Options** dialog box, click **Browse**, and browse to the folder containing the pictures you want to display, and click **OK**.

7 Click **OK** to close the **My Pictures Screen Saver Options** dialog box, and click **OK** to close the **Display Properties** dialog box and apply your settings.

Close

8 Click the **Close** button to close the Appearance and Themes window.

137 To change your screen area to the maximum or minimum size supported by your computer

1 On the **Start** menu, click **Control Panel**.

2 Click **Appearance and Themes**.

3 Click the **Change the screen resolution** task.

4 On the **Settings** tab of the **Display Properties** dialog box, drag the **Screen resolution** slider all the way to the right to maximize, or to the left to minimize, the screen area.

5 Click **OK**, and then click **Yes** if prompted to confirm your change.

140 To manually reset your system time

1 Double-click the clock on the taskbar.

2 In the **Date and Time Properties** dialog box, drag the mouse pointer over the setting you want to change in the digital clock, and then use the spinner to the right of the clock to change the setting.

3 Click **OK** to close the dialog box and update your settings.

146 **To access the accessibility options**

● On the **Start** menu, click **Control Panel**, and click **Accessibility Options**.

149 **To configure the Windows XP speech recognition software**

1 On the **Start** menu, click **Control Panel**, and then click **Sounds, Speech, and Audio Devices**.

2 In the Sounds, Speech, and Audio Devices window, click the **Speech** icon.

3 In the **Recognition Profiles** area, click **New**.

4 Walk through the steps indicated by the **Profile Wizard**, the **Microphone Wizard**, and the **Voice Training Wizard**.

Chapter 7 **Making Connections**

Page 159 **To connect to the Internet via a broadband or dial-up connection**

1 On the **Start** menu, click **Control Panel**, and then click **Network and Internet Connections**.

2 In the Network and Internet Connections window, click the **Set up or change your Internet connection** task.

3 On the **Connections** tab of the **Internet Properties** dialog box, click **Setup** to open the **New Connection Wizard**, and then click **Next**.

4 On the **Network Connection Type** page, click **Connect to the Internet**, and then click **Next**.

5 On the **Getting Ready** page, click **Set up my connection manually**, and then click **Next** to display the connection options.

6 If you are connecting using a modem and phone line, select the first option, and click **Next**. When prompted, provide the name and phone number of your ISP, your user account name, and your password. Specify whether to turn on the Internet Connection Firewall for this connection and the name(s) of anyone else who has permission to use the connection.

7 If you are connecting using a password-protected broadband connection, select the second option, and click **Next**. When prompted, provide the name of your ISP, your user account name, and your password. Specify whether to turn on the Internet Connection Firewall for this connection and the name(s) of anyone else who has permission to use the connection.

8 If you are connecting using a dedicated or constant broadband connection, select the third option, and click **Next**.

Close

9 Click **Finish**, and then click the **Close** button to close the Network and Internet Connections window.

162 To set up your computer so that it can be accessed using Remote Desktop

1 On the **Start** menu, click **Control Panel**.

2 Click **Performance and Maintenance**, and then click the **System** icon.

3 In the **System Properties** dialog box, click the **Remote** tab.

4 In the **Remote Desktop** area, select the **Allow users to connect remotely to this computer** check box.

5 When the **Remote Sessions** message box appears, read the message, and then click **OK** to close it.

6 You are automatically authorized as a remote user of your own computer. If you wish to authorize additional remote users, click **Select Remote Users**, add users in the **Remote Desktop Users** dialog box, and then click **OK**.

7 Click **OK** to close the **System Properties** dialog box, and then close the Performance and Maintenance window.

162 To turn off Remote Desktop access on your computer

1 On the **Start** menu, click **Control Panel**.

2 Click **Performance and Maintenance**, and then click the **System** icon.

3 On the **Remote** tab, clear the **Allow users to connect remotely to this computer** check box.

4 Click **OK** to close the **System Properties** dialog box, and then close the Performance and Maintenance window.

162 To access your computer from another Windows XP computer via Remote Desktop

1 On the **Start** menu, point to **All Programs**, point to **Accessories**, point to **Communications**, and then click **Remote Desktop Connection**.

2 Click **Options** to expand the dialog box if necessary.

3 Enter the connection information on the **General** tab.

4 Specify the display information on the **Display** tab.

5 Specify any other pertinent information, and then click **Connect**.

165 To share a folder on your computer

1 On the **Start** menu, click **My Computer**.

2 In the My Computer folder, click the down arrow to the right of the **Address** box to display the folder hierarchy in the drop-down list.

3 Browse to the folder you want to share.

4 On the **File and Folder Tasks** menu, click **Share this folder**.

5 In the **Sharing Properties** dialog box, click **Share this folder**, and click **OK**.

Close

6   Click the **Close** button to close the window.

169   **To share a local printer**

1   On the **Start** menu, click **Printers and Faxes**.

2   In the right pane of the Printers and Faxes window, click the printer you want to share.

3   On the **Printer Tasks** menu, click **Share this printer**.

4   On the **Sharing** tab of the printer's **Properties** dialog box, click **Share this printer**.

5   In the **Share name** box, type a simple name for the printer.

Close

6   Click **OK** to close the dialog box, and then click the **Close** button to close the Printers and Faxes window.

Chapter 8   **Communicating with Other People**

Page   **179**   **To create a Passport account for a computer that is part of a network**

1   On the **Start** menu, click **Control Panel**, and then click **User Accounts**.

2   On the **Advanced** tab of the **User Accounts** dialog box, click **.NET Passport Wizard**.

3   Follow the instructions in the **.NET Passport Wizard**.

Close

4   When you are finished, click **OK** to close the **User Accounts** dialog box, and then click the Control Panel window's **Close** button to close it.

187   **To exit Windows Messenger**

Windows Messenger

●   In the notification area, click the **Windows Messenger** icon, and then click **Exit** on the shortcut menu.

188   **To add people to your Windows Messenger Contact list**

1   Sign in to Windows Messenger.

2   Click the **Add** button.

Add

3   Follow the instructions of the **Add a Contact Wizard**.

191   **To send an instant message**

1   Sign in to Windows Messenger.

2   Click the **Send** button, and click the name of the contact you want to chat with.

Send

3   Type your message in the input box, and click **Send**.

3 On the **Automatic Updates** tab of the **System Properties** dialog box, click **Download the updates automatically and notify me when they are ready to be installed**.

Close

4 Click **OK** to close the dialog box and save your changes, and then click the **Close** button to close the Performance and Maintenance window.

252 **To gather general, status, hardware, or software diagnostic information about your computer**

1 On the **Start** menu, click **Help and Support**.

2 In the Help and Support Center, click **Use Tools to view your computer information and diagnose problems**.

3 On the **Tools** menu, click **My Computer Information**.

4 In the My Computer Information tool, click the report in which you are interested.

Close

5 When you are finished looking at the report, click the **Close** button to close the Help and Support Center.

255 **To gather network diagnostic information about your computer**

1 On the **Start** menu, click **Help and Support**.

2 In the Help and Support Center, click **Use tools to view your computer information and diagnose problems**.

3 On the **Tools** menu, click **Network Diagnostics**.

4 Click **Set scanning options**, select the options that interest you, and then click **Scan your system**.

Close

5 When you are finished looking at the report, click the **Close** button to close the Help and Support Center.

258 **To run the Disk Cleanup utility on your computer**

1 On the **Start** menu, point to **All Programs**, point to **Accessories**, point to **System Tools**, and then click **Disk Cleanup**.

2 Select the check boxes of all the types of temporary files you want to delete, and then click **OK**.

3 Click **Yes** to confirm that you want to proceed with the deletion.

260 **To run the Disk Defragmenter utility on your computer**

1 On the **Start** menu, point to **All Programs**, point to **Accessories**, point to **System Tools**, and then click **Disk Defragmenter**.

2 In the **Disk Defragmenter** dialog box, click the volume you want to defragment, and then click **Analyze**.

3 Click **View Report** to see information the program collected about the volume.

4 If defragmentation is recommended and you want to do it at this time, click **Defragment**. Otherwise, click **Close** to close the report window.

5 If you choose to defragment the volume, click **Close** to close the **Disk Defragmenter** dialog box when the defragmentation process is complete.

262 **To open the Help and Support Center**

● Click **Help and Support** on the **Start** menu; or

● Press F1. Depending on what area of Windows you are in, this might open the Help and Support Center to a page that is specific to that area. For example, if you press F1 from within Control Panel, the Help and Support Center opens to the Control Panel topic.

268 **To open a new Online Assisted Support Incident report for Windows XP**

1 On the **Start** menu, click **Help and Support**.

2 On the toolbar, click the **Support** button.

3 On the **Support** menu, click **Get help from Microsoft**.

4 Enter your Passport sign-in name and password, and click **Sign In**.

5 If prompted to do so, enter the requested information, select the **I accept the License Agreement for the use of this site** check box, and click **Submit**.

6 On the Microsoft Online Assisted Support page, click **Ask a Microsoft Support Professional for help**.

7 In the drop-down list, click **Microsoft Windows XP**, and then click **Next**.

271 **To request Remote Assistance from another person**

1 On the **Start** menu, point to **All Programs**, and click **Remote Assistance**.

2 On the **Remote Assistance** page of the Help and Support Center, click **Invite someone to help you**.

3 Click the name of the person you are going to invite to help you; or type his or her e-mail address in the **Type an e-mail address** box, and then click **Invite this person**.

4 When the remote assistance invitation opens, type an explanatory message in the **Message** box, and then click **Continue**.

5 Specify the duration of your invitation.

6   If you want to use a password, enter the password in the **Type password** and **Confirm password** boxes, and then call or otherwise communicate that password to your Remote Assistance buddy.

7   When you are ready to send the invitation, click **Send Invitation**.

273   **To enable or disable Remote Assistance**

1   On the **Start** menu, click **Control Panel**.

2   Click **Performance and Maintenance**, and then click the **System** icon.

3   In the **System Properties** dialog box, click the **Remote** tab, and then click the **Advanced** button.

4   In the **Remote Assistance Settings** dialog box, click the **Allow this computer to be controlled remotely** check box to enable Remote Assistance, or clear the check box to disable Remote Assistance.

5   Click **OK** to close the **Remote Assistance Settings** dialog box, and then click **OK** to close the **System Properties** dialog box and save your changes.

276   **To back up files from your computer**

1   On the **Start** menu, point to **All Programs**, point to **Accessories**, point to **System Tools**, and then click **Backup**.

2   In the **Backup and Restore Wizard**, click **Next**.

3   On the **Backup or Restore** page, click **Back up files and settings**, and click **Next**.

4   On the **What to Back Up** page, click **Let me choose what to back up**, and then click **Next**.

5   On the **Items to Back Up** page, browse to the folder you want to back up. Select the check box preceding the folder, and then click **Next**.

6   On the **Backup Type, Destination, and Name** page, specify the backup destination and file name, and then click **Save**.

7   Click **Next**, and then click **Finish** to start the backup.

8   When the backup is complete, click **Close**.

278   **To restore a backup file**

1   On the **Start** menu, point to **All Programs**, point to **Accessories**, point to **System Tools**, and then click **Backup**.

2   In the **Backup and Restore Wizard**, click **Next** to begin the process of backing up your files.

3 On the **Backup or Restore** page, click **Restore files and settings**, browse to and select the backup file, click **Next**, and then click **Finish**.

280 **To start the System Restore Wizard**

● On the **Start** menu, point to **All Programs**, point to **Accessories**, point to **System Tools**, and then click **System Restore**; or

● On the **Start** menu, click **Help and Support**, and then click **Undo changes to your computer with System Restore**; or

● On the **Start** menu, click **Control Panel**, click **Performance and Maintenance**, and then click **System Restore** on the **See Also** menu.

280 **To restore your computer system to a previous time**

1 Close any open programs.

2 Start the **System Restore Wizard**.

3 Click **Restore my computer to an earlier time**, and then click **Next**.

4 On the **Select a Restore Point** page calendar, click a specific restoration checkpoint, click **Next**, and then click **Next** again.

Glossary

Address Book   The Address Book provides a convenient place to store contact information for easy retrieval by programs such as Microsoft Outlook Express. It also features access to Internet directory services, which you can use to look up people and businesses on the Internet.

administrative permissions   See *administrative privileges*.

administrative privileges   The highest level of permissions that can be granted to a user account. An administrator can set permissions for other users and create groups and accounts within a domain. Administrative privileges are required to install certain programs.

alias   A name used to identify the recipient of an e-mail message in an e-mail address or on a network. The alias is the portion of the e-mail address that appears before the @ symbol.

attachment   A file, picture, or other external data source sent in conjunction with an e-mail message.

automatic update restore point   A restoration checkpoint that is automatically created when you install a downloaded update, for use with the System Restore feature.

backup recovery restore point   A restoration checkpoint that is automatically created when you use the Backup utility, for use with the System Restore feature.

bandwidth   The data transfer capacity of a digital communications system, such as the Internet or a local area network. Bandwidth is usually expressed in the number of bits that a system is capable of transferring in a second: bits per second (bps). High bandwidth or broadband refers to a network capable of a fast data transfer rate.

bitmap (BMP)   Representation of characters or graphics by individual pixels arranged in rows and columns. For black and white pixels, each pixel is represented by 1 bit of data, whereas for high-definition color pixels, each pixel is represented by 32 bits.

boot   The process of starting or resetting a computer. When first turned on (cold boot) or reset (warm boot), the computer runs the software that loads and starts the computer's operating system, which prepares it for use.

Briefcase   See *Microsoft Briefcase*.

broadband connection   A high-speed connection. Broadband connections typically transfer information at a rate of 256 kilobytes per second (KBps) or faster. Broadband includes DSL and cable modem service.

burn   To copy data to a CD.

button   A graphic element on a toolbar or in a dialog box that performs a particular function when you click it. The part of a mouse that you press to click something is also called a button.

byte   A unit of data, usually the equivalent of a single character such as a letter or a digit.

cable modem   A device that creates a broadband connection to the Internet by using cable television lines. Access speeds vary greatly, with a maximum speed of 10 megabits per second (Mbps).

capture   To convert analog video or audio to digital data, which can be stored as a file on a computer.

CD Key   A unique combination of letters and numbers, usually located on a CD-ROM jewel case, that identifies the product license for the CD version of a product.

CD-RW   See *compact disc–rewritable*.

chatting   Communicating via an instant messaging program such as Windows Messenger.

Classic   The term used to describe the appearance of the user interface in versions of Windows prior to Windows XP.

clicking   Pressing and releasing the primary mouse button.

clip   In Windows Movie Maker, audio, video, or still images. Clips are stored in collections.

command   An instruction to the computer's operating system.

command shell   A separate software program that provides direct communication between the user and the operating system. The command shell has a non-graphical user interface, and it provides the environment in which you run character-based applications and utilities.

command-line tool   Tools that are specified on an MS-DOS command line.

compact disc–recordable (CD-R) A type of compact disc on which files can be written.

compact disc–rewritable (CD-RW) A type of compact disc on which files can be written multiple times.

compression The encoding of data to reduce file size. Content that has been compressed must be decompressed for use.

Computer Management A component you can use to view and control many aspects of the computer configuration. Computer Management combines several administrative utilities into a single unit, providing easy access to a computer's administrative properties and tools.

cookie A small text file stored on your computer, containing information specific to a particular Web site, such as your user name or password.

data storage device Any device on which data is stored, including floppy disks, hard disk drives, CD-ROMs, Zip disks, and so forth.

defragmentation The process of rewriting parts of a file on a hard disk to increase the speed of access and retrieval. When files are updated, the computer tends to save the updates on the largest continuous space on the hard disk, which is often on a different sector than the other parts of the file. When files are fragmented, the computer must search the hard disk each time the file is opened to find all of the file's parts, which slows down response time.

desktop The on-screen work area on which windows, icons, menus, and dialog boxes appear.

device driver A program that allows a specific device, such as a modem, network adapter, or printer, to communicate with the operating system. Although a device might be installed on your system, Windows cannot use the device until you have installed and configured the appropriate driver. If a device is listed in the Hardware Compatibility List (HCL), a driver is usually included with Windows. Device drivers load automatically when a computer is started, and thereafter run invisibly.

DHCP server A computer running the Microsoft DHCP service, which allows IP addresses to change as needed.

dialog box A window that contains buttons and various kinds of options through which you can carry out a particular command or task.

dial-up connection   A network connection that uses the telephone network. This includes modems with a standard phone line, ISDN cards with high-speed ISDN lines, or X.25 networks. If you are a typical user, you may have one or two dial-up connections, for example, to the Internet and to your corporate network. In a more complex server situation, multiple network modem connections might be used to implement advanced routing.

Digital Subscriber Line (DSL)   See *DSL*.

digital video disc (DVD)   A type of optical disc storage technology. A digital video disc (DVD) looks like a CD-ROM disc, but it can store greater amounts of data. DVDs are often used to store full-length movies and other multimedia content that requires a large amount of storage space.

direct cable connection   A link between two computers created with a single cable, rather than with a modem or other interfacing device.

Disk Cleanup   A program that deletes temporary files from your hard disk drive in order to free up storage space.

Disk Defragmenter   A program that locates and consolidates fragmented files and folders on your computer.

dock   To connect a laptop or notebook computer to a docking station; to connect a floating toolbar to one side of your Windows desktop.

domain   A group of computers that are part of a network and share a common directory. A domain is administered as a unit with common rules and procedures. Each domain has a unique name.

domain name   The name given by an administrator to a collection of networked computers that share a common directory. In accordance with Domain Name System (DNS) naming structure, domain names consist of a sequence of name labels separated by periods.

double-clicking   Pressing and releasing the primary mouse button twice in quick succession to give the computer a command.

download   To deliver or receive information over a network by copying the information to a computer on which it can be played locally. In contrast, when information is streamed, the data is not copied to the receiving computer.

dragging   To move an item to another place on the screen by selecting the item and then pressing and holding down the mouse button while moving the mouse.

driver   See *printer driver*.

DSL   Digital Subscriber Line. A type of high-speed Internet connection using standard telephone wires; also referred to as a broadband connection.

dynamic-link library (DLL)   An operating system feature that allows executable routines (serving a specific function or set of functions) to be stored separately as files with *.dll* extensions. These routines are loaded into memory only when needed by the program that calls them.

electronic business cards   See *vCard*.

e-mail   Electronic mail. A means of sending messages and data over the Internet.

e-mail address   A series of characters, consisting of an alias and a domain name, that identifies a user so that the user can receive e-mail messages.

e-mail server   See *server*.

emoticon   A symbol created by standard keyboard characters and used to represent an emotion or item in electronic communications.

End User License Agreement (EULA)   An agreement governing the use of a software product by the user. The EULA can be found in several different locations, depending on the product. The three most common locations are: (1) printed on a separate piece of paper that accompanies the product; (2) printed in the User's Manual, usually inside the front cover or on the first page of the manual; or (3) located online within the software product.

Ethernet   A method of connecting to a computer network that uses cables to transfer information between computers. Ethernet networks standard can transmit at 10 megabits (10 million bits) per second.

executable file   A program file that can be run. Files that have *.exe* extensions are executable.

expansion slot   A socket inside a computer's case, designed to hold new hardware the user installs to enhance the computer's capabilities.

extension   See *file name extension*.

external   Outside of your network or organization; not contained inside your computer's case.

file   A discrete, named unit of data or information that can be created, accessed, and modified by a program or a user. Spreadsheets, graphics, and sounds are examples of files. Files are kept in folders.

file name extension   A set of characters added to the end of a file name that identifies the format of a file, the type of content it contains, and the type of program or device it can be used with, for example, *.doc*.

FilterKeys   A keyboard feature that instructs your keyboard to ignore brief or repeated keystrokes. You can also adjust the keyboard repeat rate, which is the rate at which a key is repeated when you hold it down.

firewall   A combination of hardware and software that provides a security system, usually to prevent unauthorized access to an internal network or intranet. A firewall prevents direct communication between network and external computers by routing communication through a proxy server outside the network. The proxy server determines whether it is safe to let a file pass through to the network. A firewall is also called a *security-edge gateway*.

folder   A container for programs and files in graphical user interfaces, symbolized on the screen by an icon of a file folder. A folder is a means of organizing programs and documents on a disk and can hold both files and additional folders.

fragmentation   The scattering of parts of the same file over different areas of the disk. Fragmentation occurs as files on a disk are deleted and new files are added. It slows disk access and degrades the overall performance of disk operations, although usually not severely.

full mode   The default operational state of Windows Media Player in which all of its features are displayed. The Player can also appear in skin mode.

gigabyte (GB)   1,024 megabytes, though often interpreted as approximately one billion bytes.

Graphic Interchange Format (GIF)   An image compression method limited to a palette of 256 colors or less.

group   In networking, an account that contains other accounts, called members. Permissions and rights granted to a group are also granted to its members.

hacker   A person who attempts to gain access to computers or software programs through illegal means, often with the malicious intent of damaging computer data through the introduction of a virus.

hard disk   A device, also called a *hard disk drive*, that contains one or more inflexible platters coated with a material on which data can be recorded magnetically. The hard disk is kept in a sealed case that protects it. Data can be stored and accessed much more quickly on a hard disk than on a floppy disk.

hardware   The physical components of a computer system, including any peripheral equipment such as printers, modems, and mouse devices.

header   Part of the structure of a Windows Media stream that contains information necessary for a computer to interpret how the packets of data containing the content should be decompressed and rendered.

hibernation   A state in which your computer shuts down after saving everything in memory on your hard disk. When you bring your computer out of hibernation, all programs and documents that were open are restored to your desktop.

host name   The Domain Name System (DNS) name of a device on a network. These names are used to locate computers on the network. To find another computer, its host name must either appear in the Hosts file or be known by a DNS server. For most Windows computers, the host name and the computer name are the same.

HTTP   See *Hypertext Transfer Protocol.*

Hypertext Markup Language (HTML)   A simple markup language used to create hypertext documents that can be displayed on computers running a variety of programs and operating systems. HTML files are simple ASCII text files with codes embedded (indicated by markup tags) to denote formatting and hypertext links.

Hypertext Transfer Protocol (HTTP)   The protocol used to transfer information on the World Wide Web. An HTTP address—one kind of Uniform Resource Locator (URL)—takes the form *http://www.microsoft.com.*

icon   A small image displayed on the screen to represent an object that can be manipulated by the user. Icons serve as visual mnemonics and allow the user to control certain computer actions without having to remember commands or enter them through the keyboard.

Internet Message Access Protocol (IMAP)   A method by which e-mail programs can access e-mail messages on a mail server. IMAP allows a user to retrieve e-mail messages from more than one computer.

Indexing Service   A Search Companion feature that maintains an index of all the files on your computer to enable faster searching.

initial system checkpoint   A restoration checkpoint that is automatically created the first time you start a new Windows XP computer, or the first time you start your computer after you install Windows XP, for use with the System Restore feature.

installation checkpoint   A restoration checkpoint that is automatically created when you install a software program, for use with the System Restore feature.

Integrated Services Digital Network (ISDN)   See *ISDN*.

internal   Within your network or organization; physically contained within your computer's case.

Internet Connection Firewall   See *Microsoft Internet Connection Firewall*.

Internet Connection Sharing (ICS)   A feature that enables you to connect computers on your home or small office network to the Internet using just one connection; intended for use in a network where the ICS host computer directs network communication between computers and the Internet.

Internet directory service   An independently operated search engine used to locate people and businesses around the world over the Internet.

Internet protocol (IP) address   A 32-bit address used to identify a node on an IP network. Each node on the IP network must be assigned a unique IP address, which is made up of the network ID and a unique host ID. This address is typically represented with the decimal value of each 8 bits separated by a period (for example, 192.168.7.27). In Windows XP, you can configure the IP address statically or dynamically through Dynamic Host Configuration Protocol. See *DHCP server*.

Internet service provider (ISP)   A company that provides individuals or companies access to the Internet and the World Wide Web. An ISP provides a telephone number, a user name, a password, and other connection information so users can connect their computers to the ISP's computers. An ISP typically charges a monthly or hourly connection fee.

ISDN   Integrated Services Digital Network. A digital phone line used to provide high-bandwidth Internet connection. An ISDN line must be installed by the telephone company at both the calling site and the called site.

Jaz disk drive   An external drive that connects to your computer and uses removable Jaz disks to store data.

Joint Photographic Experts Group (JPEG)   An image compression mechanism designed for compressing either full-color or gray-scale still images. It works well on photographs, naturalistic artwork, and similar material.

keyboard shortcut   A method of invoking a command by pressing a combination of keys, instead of selecting the command from a menu with the mouse.

Kids Passport   An online service that enables children under 12 to sign in to a variety of Microsoft and commercial Web sites using a single user account name and password; Kids Passports protect the distribution of the user's personal information by specifying what information can be shared with the Web sites and what can be done with that information.

kilobytes (KB)   1,000 bytes.

local area network (LAN)   A group of computers and other devices dispersed over a relatively limited area and connected by a communications link that enables any device to interact with any other device on the network.

local computer   The computer that you are currently logged on to as a user. More generally, a local computer is a computer that you can access directly without using a communications line or a communications device, such as a network adapter or a modem.

local printer   A printer that is directly connected to one of the ports on your computer.

local/locally   On your own computer.

logging off   Disconnecting your computer from a network domain.

logging on   Connecting your computer to a network by providing a user name and password that identifies a user to the network.

mailbox   In Outlook Express, the location in which your e-mail folders are stored.

manual checkpoint   A restoration checkpoint that you create yourself, for use with the System Restore feature.

map   To assign a local drive letter to a network drive or resource so that you can easily browse to it.

megabyte (MB)   1,000 kilobytes.

menu   A grouping of related commands.

menu bar   The toolbar from which you can access the menus of commands.

Microsoft Briefcase   A program you can use to store working copies of files and synchronize them with the originals.

Microsoft Internet Connection Firewall   Firewall software that is used to set restrictions on what information is communicated between your home or small office network and the Internet.

Microsoft Knowledge Base   A searchable online database of technical support information and help tools for Microsoft products.

Microsoft Magnifier A display utility that makes the screen more readable for users who have impaired vision.

Microsoft Narrator A text-to-speech utility for users who are blind or have impaired vision.

Microsoft Network (MSN) Microsoft's online service, which includes e-mail, games, software downloads, and many other features.

Microsoft Outlook Express A program for sending and receiving e-mail messages and participating in newsgroups.

Microsoft Paint A drawing tool you can use to create simple or elaborate drawings. These drawings can be either black-and-white or color, and can be saved as bit-map files. You can also use Paint to work with *.jpg* and *.gif* files. You can paste a Paint picture into another document you've created, or use it as your desktop background.

Microsoft Speech Recognition An internal engine that recognizes spoken words and converts them to written text.

Microsoft Windows Update A program that regularly scans your computer and communicates with an online Web site to check for available updates for your computer's operating system, software programs, and hardware.

modem A device that allows computer information to be transmitted and received over a telephone line. The transmitting modem translates digital computer data into analog signals that can be carried over a phone line. The receiving modem translates the analog signals back to digital form.

MouseKeys A keyboard feature that enables you to use the numeric keypad to move the mouse pointer and to click, double-click, and drag.

MSN Explorer An integrated suite of Internet programs dedicated exclusively to MSN services and properties. MSN Explorer helps users with varying levels of computer expertise work on the Internet.

MSN Gaming Zone A Web site through which you can play a wide variety of solitaire or multiple-player games.

network A group of computers and other devices, such as printers and scanners, connected by a communications link that enables all the devices to interact with each other. Networks can be small or large, permanently connected through wires or cables, or temporarily connected through phone lines or wireless transmissions. The largest network is the Internet, which is a worldwide group of networks.

network adapter   A device that connects your computer to a network. This device is sometimes called an *adapter card* or *network interface card*.

network administrator   A person responsible for planning, configuring, and managing the day-to-day operation of the network. A network administrator is also called a *system administrator*.

Network Bridge   A tool that automates the processes required to forward information from one type of media to another.

Network Diagnostics   A tool that gathers and displays information about your computer hardware and operating system, your Internet connection, and your modem and network adapter.

network domain   A group of computers that are part of a network and share a common database of files and folders. A domain is administered as a unit with common rules and procedures. Each domain has a unique name.

network printer   A printer that is not directly connected to your machine, but rather is available to you through a network.

network time protocol (NTP)   A protocol, used by personal firewalls, that prevents time-synchronization.

newsgroup   A collection of messages posted by individuals to a news server (a computer that can host thousands of newsgroups).

Notepad   A basic text editor you can use for simple documents or for creating Web pages.

notification area   The area on the taskbar to the right of the taskbar buttons. The notification area displays the date and time and can also contain shortcuts that provide quick access to other programs. Other shortcuts can appear temporarily, providing information about the status of activities.

offline   Not connected to a network.

online   Connected to the Internet.

On-Screen Keyboard   A utility that displays a virtual keyboard on the screen and allows users with mobility impairments to type data using a pointing device or joystick. On-Screen Keyboard is intended to provide a minimum level of functionality for users with mobility impairments.

optical character recognition (OCR)   A technology that enables devices such as scanners to convert hard-copy or photographic images to data.

original equipment manufacturer (OEM)   Used to refer to computer systems manufacturers.

Paint   See *Microsoft Paint*.

parallel port   The input/output connector for a parallel interface device. Printers are generally plugged into a parallel port.

Passport   An online service that enables you to sign in to a variety of Microsoft and other commercial Web sites using a single user account name and password.

Passport Wallet   An online database in which you can store credit card and other account information, as well as online gift certificates. You can then transmit that information securely to online vendors.

password   A security measure used to restrict access to user accounts, computer systems, and resources. A password is a unique string of characters that must be provided before access is authorized. Windows XP passwords are case-sensitive and can be up to 14 characters in length.

path   A route through a structured collection of stored information, showing where on the storage medium that information is located.

peripheral device   Any external device that connects to your computer.

permission   A rule associated with an object to regulate which users can gain access to the object and in what manner. Permissions are granted or denied by the object's owner.

pixel   Short for picture element. One pixel is the smallest element that display or print hardware and software can manipulate to create letters, numbers, or graphics.

playlist   In Windows Media Player, a list of links to various digital media files on a computer, a network, or the Internet.

Plug and Play   A design philosophy and set of specifications that allow hardware and software to be automatically identified by the computer.

POP3   See *Post Office Protocol 3*.

port   A connection or socket used to connect a device—such as a printer, monitor, or modem—to the computer. Information is sent from the computer to the device through a cable.

portable device   A computing device or storage card that is not a desktop computer. Examples of portable devices include computing devices such as Pocket PCs, and storage cards such as CompactFlash cards.

Portable Network Graphics (PNG)   A file format for portable, well-compressed storage of images.

Post Office Protocol 3 (POP3)   A popular protocol used for receiving e-mail messages. This protocol is often used by ISPs. In contrast to IMAP servers, which provide access to multiple server-side folders, POP3 servers allow access to a single Inbox.

printer driver   A printer driver is software used by computer programs to communicate with printers and plotters. Printer drivers translate the information you send from the computer into commands that the printer understands.

Product Key   A unique combination of letters and numbers that identifies a program's product license.

program icon   See *icon*.

program name installation restore point   A restoration checkpoint that is created when you install a program, for use with the System Restore feature.

program shortcut   See *shortcut*.

protocol   A set of rules and conventions for sending information over a network. These rules govern the content, format, timing, sequencing, and error control of messages exchanged among network devices.

Public Profile   In Passport, a page of information about yourself that you create. You can choose how much of your Profile will be available for other people to see.

Quick Launch toolbar   A customizable toolbar that lets you display the Windows desktop or start a program (for example, Internet Explorer) with a single click. You can add buttons to start your favorite programs from the Quick Launch location on the taskbar.

random access memory (RAM)   Memory that can be read from or written to by a computer or other devices. Information stored in RAM is lost when the computer is turned off.

read receipt   In Outlook Express, an electronic receipt that is sent to you when the message recipient has displayed your message. This is useful when you are sending time-critical information, or any time you want confirmation that your message has been received.

Recycle Bin   The place in which Windows stores deleted files. You can retrieve files you deleted in error, or you can empty the Recycle Bin to create more disk space.

remote access server   A Windows-based computer running the Routing and Remote Access service and designed to provide remote access to computers on a network.

Remote Assistance   A convenient way for a friend in another location to connect to your computer from another computer and help you troubleshoot a problem.

Remote Desktop   A means of accessing a Windows session that is running on your computer from another computer.

restart   The process of ending a user session, shutting down Windows, and then starting Windows again without turning the computer off.

restore operation restore point   A restoration checkpoint that is automatically created when you restore your system, for use with the System Restore feature.

right-clicking   Pressing and releasing the secondary mouse button.

root   The highest or uppermost level in a hierarchically organized set of information. The root is the point from which subsets branch in a logical sequence that moves from a broad or general focus to narrower perspectives.

root directory   The top point of a directory tree in a hierarchical disk-based file structure. In the path C:\WINDOWS\explorer.exe, C:\ is the root directory.

screen area   The width and height of your screen, measured in pixels.

screen saver   A moving picture or pattern that appears on your screen when you have not used the mouse or keyboard for a specified period of time.

ScreenTip   The small text box that appears when the mouse pointer passes over a button, telling you the name of the command.

scroll bar   A vertical or horizontal bar that you move to change your vertical or horizontal position within a window.

Search Companion   A program that guides you through the process of searching for a file, folder, or resource on your computer, on your network, or on the Internet.

search criteria   The specific information on which a search is based.

server   A computer that provides shared resources to network users.

share   To make resources, such as folders and printers, available to others.

shared drive   A drive that has been made available for other people on a network to access.

shared folder   A folder that has been made available for other people on a network to access.

shortcut   A link to any item accessible from your computer or on a network, such as a program, file, folder, disk drive, Web page, printer, or another computer. You can put shortcuts in various areas, such as on the desktop, on the Start menu, or in folders.

shortcut menu   A context-sensitive menu of commands that appears when you right-click an item.

ShowSounds   A feature that instructs programs that usually convey information only by sound to also provide all information visually, such as by displaying text captions or informative icons.

shut down   The process of ending a user session and closing Windows so that a computer can safely be turned off.

signature   Text included at the end of an e-mail message to identify the sender.

Simple Mail Transfer Protocol (SMTP)   A member of a suite of protocols that governs the exchange of electronic mail between message transfer agents.

skin   A file that customizes the appearance and functionality of Windows Media Player in skin mode.

skin mode   An operational state of Windows Media Player in which its user interface is customized and displayed as a skin. Some features of the Player are not accessible in skin mode. By default, the Player appears in full mode.

SMTP   See *Simple Mail Transfer Protocol*.

software   See *software programs*.

software applications   See *software programs*.

software piracy   The theft of software through illegal copying of genuine programs or through counterfeiting and distributing imitation software products or unauthorized versions of software products. Piracy can include casual copying of genuine software by individuals or businesses, or widespread illegal duplication of software programs for profit.

software programs   Programs that enable you to do things on your computer.

SoundSentry   A Windows feature that produces a visual cue, such as a screen flash or a blinking title bar, whenever the computer plays a system sound.

Speech Recognition   See *Microsoft Speech Recognition*.

stand by   The process of maintaining a user session and keeping the computer running on low power with the user's data still in the memory.

Start menu   A central menu linking you to important commands, folders, and programs on your computer.

stationery   In Outlook Express, a template that can include a background image, unique text font colors, and custom margins.

stationery theme   See *stationery*.

StickyKeys   A keyboard feature that enables you to press a modifier key (Ctrl, Alt, or Shift), or the ⊞ key, and have it remain active until a non-modifier key is pressed. This is useful for people who have difficulty pressing two keys simultaneously.

synchronization   See *synchronize*.

synchronize   To reconcile the differences between files stored on one computer and versions of the same files on another computer. Once the differences are determined, both sets of files are updated.

system checkpoint   A restoration checkpoint that is automatically created by Windows XP at regular intervals, for use with the System Restore feature. System checkpoints are created every 24 hours of calendar time, or every 24 hours your computer is turned on. If your computer is turned off for more than 24 hours, a system checkpoint is created the next time it is turned on.

system date   The current date according to your operating system.

system folder   A folder containing files that are specific to your operating system. The contents of a system folder are hidden by default and should not be modified.

system time   The current time according to your operating system.

tape drive   An internal or external drive that uses tapes to transfer and store data.

taskbar   The bar that contains the Start button and appears by default at the bottom of the desktop. You can click the taskbar buttons to switch between programs. You can also hide the taskbar, move it to the sides or top of the desktop, and customize it in other ways.

text-to-speech (TTS) software   Text-to-speech (TTS) is the ability of the operating system to play back printed text as spoken words. An internal driver, called a TTS engine, recognizes the text and, using a synthesized voice chosen from several pre-generated voices, speaks the written text.

theme A set of visual elements that provide a unified look for your computer desktop. A theme determines the look of the graphic elements of your desktop, such as the windows, icons, fonts, colors, and the background and screen saver pictures. It can also define sounds associated with events such as opening or closing a program.

thumbnail A small version of a graphic that is hyperlinked to a larger version.

time server A computer that periodically synchronizes the time on all computers within a network. This ensures that the time used by network services and local functions remains accurate.

title bar The horizontal bar at the top of a window that contains the name of the window. On many windows, the title bar also contains the program icon, the Maximize, Minimize, and Close buttons, and the optional question mark button for context-sensitive Help. To display a menu with commands such as Restore and Move, right-click the title bar.

ToggleKeys A feature that sets your keyboard to beep when one of the locking keys ([Caps Lock], [Num Lock], or [Scroll Lock]) is turned on or off.

toolbar In a program in a graphical user interface, a row, column, or block of on-screen buttons or icons. When clicked, these buttons or icons activate certain functions, or tasks, of the program. Users can often customize toolbars and move them around on the screen.

track An individual song or other discrete piece of content from a CD.

Trojan horse A program that masquerades as another common program in an attempt to receive information. An example of a Trojan horse is a program that behaves like a system logon to retrieve user names and password information that the writers of the Trojan horse can later use to break into the system.

turn off The process of shutting down Windows so you can safely turn off the computer power. Many computers turn the power off automatically.

Universal Serial Bus (USB) Computer connection port, or interface, for plugging in devices such as a keyboard, mouse, printer, scanner, and telephone equipment. USBs allow devices to be plugged in and unplugged without turning the system off.

unsigned device driver restore point A restoration checkpoint that is automatically created when you install an unsigned device driver, for use with the System Restore feature.

USB ports See *Universal Serial Bus (USB)*.

user account   A record that consists of all the information that defines a user to Windows. This includes the user name and password required for the user to log on, the groups in which the user account has membership, and the rights and permissions the user has for using the computer and network, and accessing their resources.

user account name   See *user name.*

user account picture   An individual graphic representing a specific computer user account. User account pictures are only available on computers that are members of a workgroup or are stand-alone, and are not available on computers that are members of a network domain.

user interface (UI)   The portion of a software program which allows you to interact with the program.

user name   A unique name identifying a user's account to Windows. An account's user name must be unique among the other group names and user names within its own domain or workgroup.

user profile   A file that contains configuration information for a specific user, such as desktop settings, persistent network connections, and application settings. Each user's preferences are saved to a user profile that Windows uses to configure the desktop each time a user logs on.

Utility Manager   A program that enables users to check an accessibility program's status and start or stop an accessibility program.

vCard   In Outlook Express, an electronic business card format for contact information. The vCard format can be used with a variety of digital devices and operating systems.

virus   A program that infects computer files or other programs by inserting copies of itself into the files, and may execute some harmful or inconvenient action. A program that inserts itself into your e-mail program and sends copies of itself to everyone in your address book is an example of a virus.

Virtual Private Network (VPN)   The extension of a private network. VPN connections provide remote access and routed connections to private networks over the Internet.

visualization   In Windows Media Player, a feature that displays audio as moving splashes of color and geometric shapes.

volume   An area of storage on a hard disk. A volume is formatted by using a file system, such as FAT or NTFS, and has a drive letter assigned to it. You can view the contents of a volume by clicking its icon in Windows Explorer or in My Computer. A single hard disk can have multiple volumes, and volumes can also span multiple disks.

wildcard   A keyboard character that can be used to represent one or many characters when conducting a query. The question mark (?) represents a single character, and the asterisk (*) represents any number of characters.

window   A portion of the screen where programs and processes can be run. You can open several windows at the same time. Windows can be closed, resized, moved, minimized to a button on the taskbar, or maximized to take up the whole screen.

Windows Messenger   An instant messaging program that enables you to communicate with individual or multiple online contacts.

Windows Update   See *Microsoft Windows Update*.

wizard   A program that guides you through a process using a series of pages on which you select the options you want to use.

WordPad   A program used to create or edit text files that contain formatting or graphics.

work offline/online   See *offline* and *online*.

zip   See *compression*.

Zip disk drive   An external drive that connects to your computer and uses removable Zip disks to store data.

Index

S

Online Training Solutions, Inc. (OTSI)

OTSI is a traditional and electronic publishing company specializing in the creation, production, and delivery of computer software training. OTSI publishes the Quick Course® and Practical Business Skills™ series of computer and business training products. The principals of OTSI and authors of this book are:

Joyce Cox has 20 years' experience in writing about and editing technical subjects for non-technical audiences. For 12 of those years she was the principal author for Online Press. She was also the first managing editor of Microsoft Press, an editor for Sybex, and an editor for the University of California.

Steve Lambert started playing with computers in the mid-seventies. As computers evolved from wire-wrap and solder to consumer products, he evolved from hardware geek to programmer and writer. He has written 14 books and a wide variety of technical documentation and has produced training tools and help systems.

Gale Nelson honed her communication skills as a technical writer for a SQL Server training company. Her attention to detail soon led her into software testing and quality assurance management. She now divides her work time between writing and data conversion projects.

Joan Preppernau started working with computers as a PowerPoint slideshow production assistant. As a CD-ROM data-prep manager, she participated in the creation of training products for computer professionals. She now wears a variety of hats including operations manager, Webmaster, writer, and technical editor.

The OTSI team consists of the following outstanding publishing professionals:

Susie Bayers	**Marlene Lambert**
Jan Bednarczuk	**Aaron L'Hereux**
RJ Cadranell	**Robin Ludwig**
Liz Clark	**Gabrielle Nonast**
Nancy Depper	**Lisa Van Every**
Leslie Eliel	**Nealy White**
Joseph Ford	**Michelle Ziegwied**
Jon Kenoyer	

For more information about Online Training Solutions, Inc., visit *www.otsiweb.com.*

Get a **Free**
e-mail newsletter, updates,
special offers, links to related books,
and more when you

register on line!

Register your Microsoft Press® title on our Web site and you'll get a FREE subscription to our e-mail newsletter, *Microsoft Press Book Connections.* You'll find out about newly released and upcoming books and learning tools, online events, software downloads, special offers and coupons for Microsoft Press customers, and information about major Microsoft® product releases. You can also read useful additional information about all the titles we publish, such as detailed book descriptions, tables of contents and indexes, sample chapters, links to related books and book series, author biographies, and reviews by other customers.

Registration is easy. Just visit this Web page and fill in your information:

http://www.microsoft.com/mspress/register

Microsoft®

- -

MICROSOFT LICENSE AGREEMENT
Book Companion CD

IMPORTANT—READ CAREFULLY: This Microsoft End-User License Agreement ("EULA") is a legal agreement between you (either an individual or an entity) and Microsoft Corporation for the Microsoft product identified above, which includes computer software and may include associated media, printed materials, and "online" or electronic documentation ("SOFTWARE PRODUCT"). Any component included within the SOFTWARE PRODUCT that is accompanied by a separate End-User License Agreement shall be governed by such agreement and not the terms set forth below. By installing, copying, or otherwise using the SOFTWARE PRODUCT, you agree to be bound by the terms of this EULA. If you do not agree to the terms of this EULA, you are not authorized to install, copy, or otherwise use the SOFTWARE PRODUCT; you may, however, return the SOFTWARE PRODUCT, along with all printed materials and other items that form a part of the Microsoft product that includes the SOFTWARE PRODUCT, to the place you obtained them for a full refund.

SOFTWARE PRODUCT LICENSE

The SOFTWARE PRODUCT is protected by United States copyright laws and international copyright treaties, as well as other intellectual property laws and treaties. The SOFTWARE PRODUCT is licensed, not sold.

1. **GRANT OF LICENSE.** This EULA grants you the following rights:

    a. **Software Product.** You may install and use one copy of the SOFTWARE PRODUCT on a single computer. The primary user of the computer on which the SOFTWARE PRODUCT is installed may make a second copy for his or her exclusive use on a portable computer.

    b. **Storage/Network Use.** You may also store or install a copy of the SOFTWARE PRODUCT on a storage device, such as a network server, used only to install or run the SOFTWARE PRODUCT on your other computers over an internal network; however, you must acquire and dedicate a license for each separate computer on which the SOFTWARE PRODUCT is installed or run from the storage device. A license for the SOFTWARE PRODUCT may not be shared or used concurrently on different computers.

    c. **License Pak.** If you have acquired this EULA in a Microsoft License Pak, you may make the number of additional copies of the computer software portion of the SOFTWARE PRODUCT authorized on the printed copy of this EULA, and you may use each copy in the manner specified above. You are also entitled to make a corresponding number of secondary copies for portable computer use as specified above.

    d. **Sample Code.** Solely with respect to portions, if any, of the SOFTWARE PRODUCT that are identified within the SOFTWARE PRODUCT as sample code (the "SAMPLE CODE"):

    i. **Use and Modification.** Microsoft grants you the right to use and modify the source code version of the SAMPLE CODE, *provided* you comply with subsection (d)(iii) below. You may not distribute the SAMPLE CODE, or any modified version of the SAMPLE CODE, in source code form.

    ii. **Redistributable Files.** Provided you comply with subsection (d)(iii) below, Microsoft grants you a nonexclusive, royalty-free right to reproduce and distribute the object code version of the SAMPLE CODE and of any modified SAMPLE CODE, other than SAMPLE CODE, or any modified version thereof, designated as not redistributable in the Readme file that forms a part of the SOFTWARE PRODUCT (the "Non-Redistributable Sample Code"). All SAMPLE CODE other than the Non-Redistributable Sample Code is collectively referred to as the "REDISTRIBUTABLES."

    iii. **Redistribution Requirements.** If you redistribute the REDISTRIBUTABLES, you agree to: (i) distribute the REDISTRIBUTABLES in object code form only in conjunction with and as a part of your software application product; (ii) not use Microsoft's name, logo, or trademarks to market your software application product; (iii) include a valid copyright notice on your software application product; (iv) indemnify, hold harmless, and defend Microsoft from and against any claims or lawsuits, including attorney's fees, that arise or result from the use or distribution of your software application product; and (v) not permit further distribution of the REDISTRIBUTABLES by your end user. Contact Microsoft for the applicable royalties due and other licensing terms for all other uses and/or distribution of the REDISTRIBUTABLES.

2. **DESCRIPTION OF OTHER RIGHTS AND LIMITATIONS.**

    - **Limitations on Reverse Engineering, Decompilation, and Disassembly.** You may not reverse engineer, decompile, or disassemble the SOFTWARE PRODUCT, except and only to the extent that such activity is expressly permitted by applicable law notwithstanding this limitation.

    - **Separation of Components.** The SOFTWARE PRODUCT is licensed as a single product. Its component parts may not be separated for use on more than one computer.

    - **Rental.** You may not rent, lease, or lend the SOFTWARE PRODUCT.

    - **Support Services.** Microsoft may, but is not obligated to, provide you with support services related to the SOFTWARE PRODUCT ("Support Services"). Use of Support Services is governed by the Microsoft policies and programs described in the user manual, in "online" documentation, and/or in other Microsoft-provided materials. Any supplemental software code provided to you as part of the Support Services shall be considered part of the SOFTWARE PRODUCT and subject to the terms and conditions of this EULA. With respect to technical information you provide to Microsoft as part of the Support Services, Microsoft may use such information for its business purposes, including for product support and development. Microsoft will not utilize such technical information in a form that personally identifies you.

- **Software Transfer.** You may permanently transfer all of your rights under this EULA, provided you retain no copies, you transfer all of the SOFTWARE PRODUCT (including all component parts, the media and printed materials, any upgrades, this EULA, and, if applicable, the Certificate of Authenticity), **and** the recipient agrees to the terms of this EULA.

- **Termination.** Without prejudice to any other rights, Microsoft may terminate this EULA if you fail to comply with the terms and conditions of this EULA. In such event, you must destroy all copies of the SOFTWARE PRODUCT and all of its component parts.

3. **COPYRIGHT.** All title and copyrights in and to the SOFTWARE PRODUCT (including but not limited to any images, photographs, animations, video, audio, music, text, SAMPLE CODE, REDISTRIBUTABLES, and "applets" incorporated into the SOFTWARE PRODUCT) and any copies of the SOFTWARE PRODUCT are owned by Microsoft or its suppliers. The SOFTWARE PRODUCT is protected by copyright laws and international treaty provisions. Therefore, you must treat the SOFTWARE PRODUCT like any other copyrighted material **except** that you may install the SOFTWARE PRODUCT on a single computer provided you keep the original solely for backup or archival purposes. You may not copy the printed materials accompanying the SOFTWARE PRODUCT.

4. **U.S. GOVERNMENT RESTRICTED RIGHTS.** The SOFTWARE PRODUCT and documentation are provided with RESTRICTED RIGHTS. Use, duplication, or disclosure by the Government is subject to restrictions as set forth in subparagraph (c)(1)(ii) of the Rights in Technical Data and Computer Software clause at DFARS 252.227-7013 or subparagraphs (c)(1) and (2) of the Commercial Computer Software—Restricted Rights at 48 CFR 52.227-19, as applicable. Manufacturer is Microsoft Corporation/One Microsoft Way/Redmond, WA 98052-6399.

5. **EXPORT RESTRICTIONS.** You agree that you will not export or re-export the SOFTWARE PRODUCT, any part thereof, or any process or service that is the direct product of the SOFTWARE PRODUCT (the foregoing collectively referred to as the "Restricted Components"), to any country, person, entity, or end user subject to U.S. export restrictions. You specifically agree not to export or re-export any of the Restricted Components (i) to any country to which the U.S. has embargoed or restricted the export of goods or services, which currently include, but are not necessarily limited to, Cuba, Iran, Iraq, Libya, North Korea, Sudan, and Syria, or to any national of any such country, wherever located, who intends to transmit or transport the Restricted Components back to such country; (ii) to any end user who you know or have reason to know will utilize the Restricted Components in the design, development, or production of nuclear, chemical, or biological weapons; or (iii) to any end user who has been prohibited from participating in U.S. export transactions by any federal agency of the U.S. government. You warrant and represent that neither the BXA nor any other U.S. federal agency has suspended, revoked, or denied your export privileges.

DISCLAIMER OF WARRANTY

NO WARRANTIES OR CONDITIONS. MICROSOFT EXPRESSLY DISCLAIMS ANY WARRANTY OR CONDITION FOR THE SOFTWARE PRODUCT. THE SOFTWARE PRODUCT AND ANY RELATED DOCUMENTATION ARE PROVIDED "AS IS" WITHOUT WARRANTY OR CONDITION OF ANY KIND, EITHER EXPRESS OR IMPLIED, INCLUDING, WITHOUT LIMITATION, THE IMPLIED WARRANTIES OF MERCHANTABILITY, FITNESS FOR A PARTICULAR PURPOSE, OR NONINFRINGEMENT. THE ENTIRE RISK ARISING OUT OF USE OR PERFORMANCE OF THE SOFTWARE PRODUCT REMAINS WITH YOU.

LIMITATION OF LIABILITY. TO THE MAXIMUM EXTENT PERMITTED BY APPLICABLE LAW, IN NO EVENT SHALL MICROSOFT OR ITS SUPPLIERS BE LIABLE FOR ANY SPECIAL, INCIDENTAL, INDIRECT, OR CONSEQUENTIAL DAMAGES WHATSOEVER (INCLUDING, WITHOUT LIMITATION, DAMAGES FOR LOSS OF BUSINESS PROFITS, BUSINESS INTERRUPTION, LOSS OF BUSINESS INFORMATION, OR ANY OTHER PECUNIARY LOSS) ARISING OUT OF THE USE OF OR INABILITY TO USE THE SOFTWARE PRODUCT OR THE PROVISION OF OR FAILURE TO PROVIDE SUPPORT SERVICES, EVEN IF MICROSOFT HAS BEEN ADVISED OF THE POSSIBILITY OF SUCH DAMAGES. IN ANY CASE, MICROSOFT'S ENTIRE LIABILITY UNDER ANY PROVISION OF THIS EULA SHALL BE LIMITED TO THE GREATER OF THE AMOUNT ACTUALLY PAID BY YOU FOR THE SOFTWARE PRODUCT OR US$5.00; PROVIDED, HOWEVER, IF YOU HAVE ENTERED INTO A MICROSOFT SUPPORT SERVICES AGREEMENT, MICROSOFT'S ENTIRE LIABILITY REGARDING SUPPORT SERVICES SHALL BE GOVERNED BY THE TERMS OF THAT AGREEMENT. BECAUSE SOME STATES AND JURISDICTIONS DO NOT ALLOW THE EXCLUSION OR LIMITATION OF LIABILITY, THE ABOVE LIMITATION MAY NOT APPLY TO YOU.

MISCELLANEOUS

This EULA is governed by the laws of the State of Washington USA, except and only to the extent that applicable law mandates governing law of a different jurisdiction.

Should you have any questions concerning this EULA, or if you desire to contact Microsoft for any reason, please contact the Microsoft subsidiary serving your country, or write: Microsoft Sales Information Center/One Microsoft Way/Redmond, WA 98052-6399.